THE BABY AS SUBJECT

THE BABY AS SUBJECT
Clinical Studies in Infant–Parent Therapy

Edited by
Campbell Paul and Frances Thomson-Salo

KARNAC

First published in 2014 by
Karnac Books Ltd
118 Finchley Road
London NW3 5HT

British Library Cataloguing in Publication Data

A C.I.P. for this book is available from the British Library

ISBN-13: 978-1-78049-116-5

Typeset by V Publishing Solutions Pvt Ltd., Chennai, India

Printed in Great Britain

www.karnacbooks.com

CONTENTS

ACKNOWLEDGEMENTS

We are grateful to all the publishers for permission to make these papers available.

Chapter One is an abridged version of Thomson-Salo, F. (2012). Engaging with the baby as a person in their own right: early intervention with parents and infants. *Psychoanalysis*, 23: 3–9, with kind permission of the editor.

Chapter Nine was originally published in *Community Paediatric Review*, April 2001, Vol 10, with kind permission of the author.

Chapter Ten was first published in *The Signal*, 2003, Vol 11, No. 2, WAIMH and is reprinted with kind permission of *The Signal*.

Chapter Eleven. In this chapter, Part II is an abridged version of Child's Play—An assessment parameter, *Community Paediatric Review* 2003, Vol 12, with kind permission of the author; Part III was first published in *The Signal*, 2003, Vol 11, WAIMH and Part IV published in 1999, is an abridged version of Nursing Roles, advice counselling or therapy. *Paediatric Nursing, 11*: 30–32, with kind permission of the publishers.

Chapter Sixteen was originally published in *Innovations in Parent–Infant Psychotherapy*, edited by Maria Pozzi and Beverley Tydeman (published by Karnac Books in 2007), with kind permission of Karnac Books.

Chapter Twenty-One is an abridged version of the paper, "Infancy and domestic violence", published in *Children Australia*, 2002, 27: 22–23, with kind permission of the author who holds the copyright.

Chapter Twenty-Two is reprinted in modified form from The Signal, 2008, Vol 16, No. 1, WAIMH and is reprinted with kind permission of *The Signal*.

Chapter Twenty-Four was originally published in *The Signal*, 2001, Vol 9, Nos. 1–2, WAIMH and is reprinted with kind permission of *The Signal*.

Chapter Twenty-Five was subsequently published in modified form as Le bébé qui voit mais ne regarde pas, in *Devenir* (1991), 3: 62–78.

Notes

Other aspects of the work with the infant "Frank" presented in Chapter Five were previously published in Shoemark, H. (2006). Infant-directed singing as a vehicle for regulation rehearsal in the medically fragile full-term infant. *Australian Journal of Music Therapy*, 17: 54–63.

The epilogue must not be performed without permission from the author.

ABOUT THE EDITORS AND CONTRIBUTORS

Dimitra Bekos is a child and adult psychotherapist practising in Melbourne, Australia. She has worked as a therapist in some of Melbourne's major hospitals and in particular, The Royal Children's Hospital for ten years, primarily in the area of trauma with children who had been exposed to physical and sexual abuse. She has also taught on the Master of Child Psychoanalytic Psychotherapy. She is currently working in private practice and dedicates some of her time to supervising child therapists.

Mary Brown is a paediatrician who worked for many years in a community-based practice in country Victoria. There, she became increasingly interested in the relationship between physical and emotional health and the impact of family dynamics on children's wellbeing. Following retirement from active practice, she obtained a Doctorate in Medicine based on research into the health and wellbeing in early school age of a cohort of babies who cried excessively in infancy. Currently, she is studying spirituality in ageing and finds that relationships and attachment are just as vital at the end of life as they are in the early years.

Megan Chapman is a senior clinical psychologist who has coordinated the Infant Mental Health Program at the Royal Children's Hospital since 2008. Prior to this role, she has worked in a variety of child and adolescent mental health, and forensic mental health settings. She has a particular interest in developing parent–infant relationships in the neonatal intensive care environment, and utilising mentalisation techniques to promote parental reflective functioning.

Libby Ferguson is a speech pathologist with a major interest in infant mental health. Her clinical work in recent years has been predominantly with infants and young children with feeding problems and early communication difficulty. She is currently undertaking a PhD on the topic of feeding disorder in infants with oesophageal atresia.

Robyn Hayles has been employed as the executive director of Community Health and Rehabilitation Services at Barwon Health since 2009, commencing at Barwon Health in 2007 as strategic planner following eleven years employment in a variety of roles at The Royal Children's Hospital. She has a nursing background, graduating in 1991 with a Diploma of Advanced Science. Her area of focus and expertise has been in the interface between acute based and community care with a focus on hospital avoidance and service development. Robyn completed a Master of Public Health Degree in 2001, and gained a scholarship in 2003 to look at the care of patients with respiratory conditions at home in France and England.

Sarah Jones is a psychotherapist/mental health social worker in private practice, working predominantly with couples and as an infant–parent psychotherapist. Her hospital work began at the Royal Free Hospital, London, while training at the Tavistock Clinic. She worked at The Royal Children's Hospital, Melbourne, for fifteen years and is a consultant to several specialist departments, including Palliative Care and Children's Cancer Centre. She is a consultant to a number of maternal and child health services teams. She has a special interest in working with palliative care practitioners, and in the fields of perinatal and infant mental health and works in these areas clinically and as a consultant and trainer.

Brigid Jordan is an Associate Professor of Paediatric Social Work (infant and family), at The Royal Children's Hospital and is on the teaching faculty of the Graduate Diploma/Masters of Infant Mental

Health of The University of Melbourne. She has over twenty years' clinical experience in social work and infant mental health at The Royal Children's Hospital. Her research interests and experience include persistent infant crying, the impact of complex illness on infants and their families, maternal depression and infants growing up in vulnerable families. Brigid is a past President of the Australian Association for Infant Mental Health and has served on the board of directors of the World Association for Infant Mental Health. She is the lead author of the Specialist Practice Resource: Infants and their Families written for the Victorian Department of Human Services and has published policy, research and clinical papers on infant crying and feeding problems and infants at risk of abuse and neglect.

Michele Meehan has been the clinical nurse consultant, Maternal and Child Health, at The Royal Children's Hospital Melbourne since 1984. She offers specialist consultation to families in the areas of infant feeding, eating, sleeping, attachment, and emotional development. She was recently honoured to receive The Royal Children's Hospital Annual Mary Patten Nursing Award, and in 2009 completed her Master's in Health Science: Parent & Infant Mental; her thesis was entitled "They won't eat! Development of a model for treatment of infant feeding refusal". She also has a private practice called, Parenting Matters.

Ann Morgan was born in Wales and graduated in medicine at the University of London in 1951. She trained in paediatrics, worked in Boston and after arriving in Australia in 1960 she was appointed to The Royal Children's Hospital as a paediatrician. She joined the department of Psychiatry in 1961 where she worked as an infant mental health clinician for thirty years. She was the first co-ordinator of the Infant Mental Health group in the Hospital and strongly influenced this developing field. She currently works as an infant observation seminar leader on the University of Melbourne Graduate Diploma in Infant and Parent Mental Health.

Sue Morse is a senior neuroscience speech pathologist and mental health clinician. She has worked for thirty years in public health in the areas of acute and rehabilitative neurosciences, developmental medicine, chronic illness, and infant and paediatric mental health. Currently she works part time at The Royal Children's Hospital, Melbourne, with children and families with complex needs, and in private practice.

Joanna Murray Smith is an Australian playwright and novelist. Her plays have been performed all over the world, including on Broadway, the West End and at the Royal National Theatre in London.

Campbell Paul is a consultant infant and child psychiatrist at The Royal Children's Hospital, Melbourne and Honorary Principal Fellow in the department of psychiatry at the University of Melbourne. At the University he and his colleagues established a Graduate Diploma and a Masters Course in Infant and Parent Mental Health. This course developed out of his longstanding experience in paediatric consultation liaison psychiatry and work in infant–parent psychotherapy. He has a special interest in the understanding of the inner world of the baby, particularly as it informs therapeutic work with infants and their parents. With colleagues he has developed models of working in therapeutic groups with troubled parents and infants. He has been a consultant psychiatrist at the Victorian Aboriginal Health Service and has also been involved in the establishment of the Koori Kids Mental Health Network. He has worked with NT child mental health services in Central Australia. He is a member of the board of directors of the World Association for Infant Mental Health and has been a participant in, and organiser of, a number of local and international conferences and activities in the field of infant mental health.

Nicky Robson is the speech pathology manager at Barwon Health regional health service in Australia. She has worked for twenty years in paediatric speech pathology, and for the past twelve years her work has been enriched by formal training in infant and parent mental health. Nicky works clinically with preschool children in a paediatric outpatient setting, with a particular interest in infant feeding disorders.

Teresa Russo has worked for over twenty-five years in general medical practice based in community health working largely with families from diverse cultural and linguistic backgrounds, communities including refugees and asylum seekers. Over the past ten years she has also worked as an infant–parent psychotherapist and infant mental health clinician in both public and private settings having obtained her Masters of Mental Health Science (Infant and Parent Mental Health) from the University of Melbourne and currently is a seminar leader for Infant Observation in that course. She is also a member of the Balint Society of Australia and New Zealand (BSANZ) and has a particular interest in Balint group work both with GPs and medical students.

Helen Shoemark is the senior music therapist for Neonatology at The Royal Children's Hospital Melbourne, career development fellow at Murdoch Childrens Research Institute, and Adjunct Professor at the University of Queensland.

Julie Stone is an infant, child and family psychiatrist who led the development of Western Australia's first specialist mental health service for children under five. She now lives in Melbourne and travels to rural Victoria several days a week to support the development of perinatal and infant mental health services. As well as running a small private practice in the city, Julie enjoys a variety of roles combining her love of clinical teaching and supervision, writing, and consulting to non-government agencies in the hope of promoting a deeper understanding of the emotional world of very young children.

Frances Thomson-Salo is a psychoanalyst; Honorary Principal Fellow of the department of psychiatry, University of Melbourne and on the teaching faculty of the Graduate Diploma/Master of Infant and Parent Mental Health, an associate researcher for the Murdoch Children's Research Institute, senior child psychotherapist at The Royal Children's Hospital and consultant infant mental health clinician at The Royal Women's Hospital.

Robin Wilson worked for many years as a general practitioner where she developed an interest in mothers and babies with emotional difficulties. She subsequently worked for eleven years as an infant–parent therapist at the mother baby clinic (for women and babies with emotional difficulties) at a large public maternity hospital in Melbourne. She completed a Masters of Infant and Parent Mental Health and is now an infant observation seminar leader in the same programme. She currently has a private practice in parent and infant mental health.

INTRODUCTION

Campbell Paul and Frances Thomson-Salo

There is an exciting collaboration amongst many disciplines to try to understand the world of the baby and the family and what professionals, volunteers, and families can do to give the baby the best chance. In The Royal Children's Hospital Infant Mental Health Program (IMHP) there is a long history of close collaboration between mental health, paediatrics, and nursing. There is also a strong emphasis on taking the baby's point of view and trying to respect the baby's perspective. The Program is multidisciplinary and draws on developmental psychology and child health, as well as psychodynamic theory and this book aims to make available some of the papers that have come out of the thinking and work of this group of clinicians.

It may help to give an illustration of the approach to clinical work with infants and families that is at the foundation of the work of the IMHP. We believe that playful engagement and psychotherapy directly with the infant, in the context of work with the family and the broader system, is critical for the best outcome for the child. Despite the apparent success of a liver transplant, eighteen-month-old Jacob appeared withdrawn, avoidant, wasted, and he was refusing to eat. The medical and nursing staff responsible for his care were extremely concerned. There was no medical cause for his persisting lassitude and they referred him to the IMHP. In his short life, he had experienced a lot of pain and had been near to death many times as a result of the complications of his congenital liver disease. It seemed too cruel to contemplate that a person could inhabit so wretched a body and be so seemingly empty of soul as this young boy.

However, clearly he was there, inhabiting his body. There was a need for some lively interaction for him to come out and to meet his world again. His mother was surprised that the IMHP might have something to offer her son. She had been immersed in so many medical crises that she said it had never crossed her mind that he might be depressed. When staff from the IMHP were able to engage Jacob in playful behaviour his mother caught a glimpse of a child very different to the one she had so far experienced. She was startled by observing a moment of lively play that Jacob demonstrated in a simple ball game with one of the clinicians and she was then able to pursue her own more lively play with him. After his mood had improved, she was able to say that it was as if she had earlier thought that he had already died, as if in her mind, he had been psychologically dead.

Holding the child in therapy—holding him in our own minds and speaking directly with him—was of critical importance in his recovery. Our engaging him even in a brief moment of enlivened play, when witnessed by his mother, led to a transformation in the way that she experienced him in her mind. She could see her son as alive and there was a point in hope for his survival. It could also be demonstrated that her pain, her grief, her tragic sense of loss, could be contained for her sake and for her son's sake. Jacob went on to thrive and now visits the hospital for infrequent reviews as a very healthy and talkative boy.

The infant mental health programme in context

In Melbourne there is a network of services which address the infant mental health needs of babies, toddlers, and their families. There are several infant mental health programmes integrated into child and adolescent mental health services in both the public and private health setting. Increasingly the maternal and child health nurses have an additional training in Australia's university courses in infant and parent mental health so that in brief work with infants and their families they can use insightful psychodynamic concepts and effect rapid interactional change. There remain nonetheless areas of unmet need for the families within the vast rural and outback places. Families will travel long distances to access such help, but increasingly teleconferencing and the telephone are used to reach such families.

Australia is a land of migrants who have to come to terms with the traumas resulting from the Western occupation and dispossession of Australia from its indigenous peoples. While there is an improving relationship with Australia's original inhabitants the disruption of families' attachments caused by generations of dispossession has had a profound impact. Families may experience a crisis of confidence in parenting since many have lost contact with traditional baby-care practices and supports. Our work tries to reflect the multicultural nature of this country. Being drawn from such a diverse range of peoples and cultures, we hope that we have the capacity to be imaginative and playful in our work as well as our play.

To set the scene in the book, two introductory chapters convey the approach of Ann Morgan, the first infancy group co-ordinator, distilling briefly, yet poetically, how she works, and an overview of engaging with infants and their families. This is followed by a collection of papers covering an eighteen year period, which focus on clinical interventions with infants and their families, with considerable detail about what the clinicians do and say as there is considerable interest in, and wish for, this sharing of clinical practice. The distinctive voice of each clinician from within their professional backgrounds emerges to create many strands in an approach rather than a single voice. The chapters are grouped to cover topics and illustrate the work of infant mental health clinicians in Melbourne and Australia, including chapters by colleagues in the community who have been awarded the University of Melbourne Graduate Diploma and Masters in Parent and Infant Mental Health for which many members of the IMHP have lectured. This broad range of chapters indicates the influence of the thinking of The Royal Children's Hospital (RCH) clinicians.

The first section is on intervention in acute health settings, including a chapter in which the role of the infant mental health clinician in a hospital in the home programme is discussed. This is followed by a section describing different interventions with the more common infant problems of crying, feeding, and settling difficulties. The section on infant–parent therapy begins with a chapter with two vignettes showing how little is sometimes needed to bring about a response in the infant—meeting them with a wish to understand their experience.

There follows a section on interventions with infants with problems of relating and a section when there has been family violence and how in trying to reach this troubled population, some of the group's thinking about the nature of the therapeutic action is discussed. There has been a move by RCH clinicians from describing clinical interventions work as "direct work" to emphasising that it is the infant's experience that they try to understand and from that position to intervene with the parent and infant in whatever way seems best.

It also seemed relevant to include two earlier chapters, as they represent landmarks in the work of the IMHP, one describing some evolving principles of infant–parent psychotherapy and one about the effect and use of gaze.

Lastly, we are pleased to include the monologue about fatherhood specially written by Joanna Murray Smith for the 2004 World Association of Infant Mental Health congress held in Melbourne.

Every effort has been taken to protect the privacy of the patients or gain their consent. To safeguard confidentiality all names of infants and their family members and other identifying details have been changed or they are composite accounts of families with whom clinicians have worked.

Many of the papers reference the work of Donald Winnicott, the British paediatrician and psychoanalyst. His ideas infuse the work. It was his way of grasping the essence of the experience of the infant and his parents which continue to speak across the generations and we acknowledge our debt to him. The text that is probably drawn on most frequently is *Playing and reality* (1971), which elaborates his ideas about transitional space and transitional phenomena and processes, as well as his ideas about playing. The work of the developmental researchers, Colwyn Trevarthen and Daniel Stern, complement and extend many of Winnicott's ideas.

Although we acknowledge the importance of working with hospital systems or primarily at times with the parents, we have not included such papers for reasons of space. We hope that the chapters that have been included will provide a keyhole perspective on the work of one infant mental health programme within one city within our vast continent. We believe that working from the perspective of the baby within the family and drawing on multidisciplinary teamwork and a broad range of theoretical foundations, we are able to provide something hopeful and useful for infants and their families. Our focus has been on trying to distil a way of working that privileges understanding the experience of the baby as subject in the presence of the parents. We hope that this is the message that comes through.

Reference

Winnicott, D. W. (1971). *Playing and reality*. London: Tavistock.

CHAPTER ONE

What I am trying to do when I see an infant with his or her parents

Ann Morgan

Reginald Lourie's message at the 1978 International Association for Child and Adolescent Psychiatrists and Allied Professions conference (IACAPAP) in Melbourne was that "you need to go upstream". Yet to experience the infant as subject may open up unbearable situations. What do we mean by intentional relating to the infant as a subject? What I think we are struggling to do when we are involved with babies and families is to keep the baby in mind, and if we take time and effort to get to know and relate to the baby in the presence of the parents, we are making a definitive statement. We are saying that the baby is a crucial member of what we are trying to do—that the baby participates in his or her own right in the session and that this active involvement of the baby, which really may be quite difficult not only to initiate but also to sustain, can make a difference to the way in which we all think about the problem in hand.

The baby does make a difference to all experiences and relationships within the family, the baby changes things because essentially now the family has changed from one, to two, to three. One of the things this can offer to each member is that they can be the observer, they can observe the other with the baby, and this is true not only for the mother and the father but also for the baby. It gives a time when the baby can reflect on being the observer and you can see this in working with infants as young as three to four months. When one is engaged in talking to the baby, the baby can look intently at the therapist and then look at the mother, look back at the therapist and there is some work being done by the baby. One feels that the baby is really interested in how the therapist and the mother and the father are alike, but are also different. That difference, and the capacity to be aware of that for all of them, can offer them a gap, a gap in which they can allow something to emerge, and what can emerge may be a thought, an opportunity to feel that there are other ways of being.

Wherever therapeutic work with a baby and parent is done, how do we conceptualise the work? There is a constant movement between who is in the foreground and who is in the background. I think that if one privileges the baby by seeing the baby as participating in this then we can allow others to take the foreground, so that we can allow the mother to come forward and her narrative to be heard while at the same time still acknowledging and connecting to the baby, so that there is the possibility of offering to the family a suggestion that each member is of equal significance, that each member must be heard, each member must be kept in mind while the other narrative is being spoken. Why I am emphasising that the baby is part of the narrative is because it really is extremely difficult not to listen to the spoken word and our contact with the baby is often unspoken, although that is not altogether the whole story because when one contacts the baby, although a lot may be given through the gaze and the physical contact, nevertheless we all speak to the baby so that there is some talking and the baby knows this. The baby listens, the baby looks, the baby connects to the voice, the baby connects to the expression on our faces which change with each word that we speak. That is the element of the baby's narrative and what we are suggesting is the importance of including all the narratives.

In using our professional knowledge it is constant that we come to the baby with our preconceptions of the work that we do and the knowledge that we have. We know a great deal about parents, we know a great deal about babies, yet how important it is to understand that we know nothing about this baby, we know nothing about this mother and this father, but we give them our full awareness, our thinking, our knowledge, so that somehow something new can emerge for all of us who are involved in the work, for the baby, the mother, the father and for the therapist. Furthermore, it is that I think, which makes the work the challenge that it is, but also what is so rewarding, because it can be so creative.

The three things that I think are essential are that the environment must be safe, reliable, and truthful. This is what I am trying to do when I see infants and their parents.

Safety

One of the most significant things that parents do is to protect the child. We are all very aware of protecting the child from external influences. One element of what I am trying to achieve is help the child feel that her internal world is safe, and real protection for the child is to be able to feel that. We can help defend the triangle (the father, mother, and baby) to feel in touch with what the infant is trying to do so that the mother is more able to protect the infant's emerging thinking, imagination, and sense of self. What it means that an environment is safe is that the infant can experience violent, strong feelings but there is no retaliation—the adult sees behind what that experience might mean to the infant. The infant's facing the reality of her own experience can only be done in a safe environment because if we do not understand what is happening in their mind that can make it unsafe.

> I was seeing a nine-month-old boy and his mother who had been severely depressed but the difficulty in the relationship between them had been missed by the mental health professionals looking after her. He needed to be constantly at the breast as if he was desperate to get it, which she said was extremely uncomfortable. When he crawled, he clasped a toy car in each hand as well as something in his mouth as if to feel complete and wipe out a desperate injury or absence. I had been gently exploring my relationship with him over some weeks and he had made good gains. I was sitting quietly and he came up to my chair; I smiled and talked to him and as he was trying to stand I put my arm around him without touching him. His mother said something that took my attention and at the moment I turned to her he fell like a tree with a bang. Then he was frantic, rushed to his mother, did not look at her face but went straight to the breast, pulling at her clothes and sighed with relief as his mouth went around the nipple. It was an extreme panic in him that he had fallen and "come to bits" and the only thing to

put him together was to have the nipple in his mouth. I was quite shocked, wondering if my turning away had led to an acute feeling of his being on his own. Despite having begun to lock himself into a paralysing state, he was able to use the intervention and did well socially and cognitively.

Making a safe place for a baby is very important and needs active thinking and work to make it so.

Reliability

Secondly, in protecting the child's inner world, it provides somewhere for the child to have a sense of going on being, through our relationship with the child, especially if it is over time. The sense of remembering is a continuous thread. We share the experiences, and there is the sense of continuity and going on being within the baby. Protecting the baby so that he feels that his internal world is safe is related to the sense of going on being. These are important ideas when there are problems because we can get drawn in by pressure from the parents and forget to allow the child a sense of space. We are not there for the referral problem—we are there for the space, and for helping the child feel that his internal world is safe, and for the sense of going-on-being and to help if they do not feel attached. I do tend with the baby, to do some things over and over so that the baby knows what is happening. While I am doing things with the baby, I am asking the mother to think about what is going on for the baby. Mothers are often preoccupied with how they are as mothers, and I try to help them see the baby by helping them see what goes on for the baby with me. Many professionals prescribe advice, others educate. Sometimes I do translate, for example, saying, "She doesn't understand, she wants to look at you, she's wondering who I am because I'm not you but something like you."

> I had seen Bea with her mother since she was six months old and thought that her mother had been unavailable throughout Bea's life as she was extremely fragmented psychologically, and could not give her a sense of protecting her inner world. She did not speak to her baby in case she used the wrong words, and Bea did not speak for a long time. In sessions, Bea wanted a sense of history. When I sometimes changed what I did, she indicated how we did it, saying in effect that I was to be in her internal world. When

there was a break she wanted the games we had played early on, and hide-and-seek. As Bea's mother doubted her own judgement, she felt that she had to "know" in all that she did for her baby. She only wanted help with the kind of little girl that Bea was to be. She would say, "I know she's happy", whereas I tried to go behind and allow Bea space. For example, when Bea's mother thought Bea was hungry, she persisted in trying to feed her when she would not take it. As the parents and I talked, Bea's mother forgot about feeding her, relaxed and became enlivened, and Bea ate the food. She felt that as a good mother she was there to see that her baby ate and this became a concrete task. To think about and play with her infant felt as if she was abrogating her duty as a mother. The baby was overwhelmed by a sense of uncertainty, a difficulty in letting go and a difficulty taking in—all aspects of an unheld and powerful anxiety. Bea felt tension and her eyes were huge and over-alert, she would laugh but something was not right. I had never seen Bea take in anything with pleasure. With a very ill mother, the baby is lost and has a profound experience of catastrophe. If the baby thinks that he or she will die and the mother thinks so too, the baby is in great distress, exacerbated if there is an awareness of the parent's rage or anxiety. Bea's mother was devastated, thinking that her baby would die, and I was caught by the fear of Bea failing to thrive. As long as I thought that, we did not get anywhere; once I was over my anxiety things got better.

I am concerned that we take seriously what will happen later and often we do not. In it lie the roots of future mental disturbance. We should change how we work. Instead we see the referral problem as something that happens now, which we want to relieve now, and if there is a biological aspect we get hooked in to not look at other aspects. Our aim is to protect the child from that—to get across to the child something different—and it is about the child, something we can help with about the child's own experience and not only just through the parent.

Truthfulness

The last thing I think is important is truthfulness. Truthfulness is based on respect, being aware of one's own thinking, being aware of the baby's thinking and working towards understanding it, however young the baby. A relationship has to be truthful, because truthfulness is what gets through to the baby, not the words. That is an important point, when you are telling people how to be with babies—they have got to allow themselves to feel and to be with the baby. It puts a different meaning to the words that you say if you have that truthfulness and are truthful in your response—it matters to validate the baby, and I learnt this from being with babies: it is not the verbal response but the truthfulness of it, which underpins all interpretations and countertransference.

> A three-month-old baby who came with her mother always played the same game with me each week, the same routine in our relationship, and I felt that she knew me. She would look at her mother and me and see that we were alike but also very different. After about fifteen minutes the baby would give the signal to be put to the breast to feed. On one occasion, her mother was very upset and could not wait to pour out her distress, anger, and fear. The baby gave the signal and without looking at the baby, her mother picked her up and put her on the breast and the baby bit her hard. When I said, "I wonder what she's telling you", her mother immediately understood and apologised to the baby. She settled her and the baby went back to the breast and to my amazement, turned round, looked at me and smiled and went back to the breast. The point of the work was to help the mother and the baby be in a threesome. Having the baby lit up enormous rage in the mother to the father, which she knew was irrational but could not stop. It was the importance of the third, and the baby really experienced that, and experienced her relationship to me, to the other, and there was a place and a time for all three of us.

I think the key to where work with the baby as subject is different to other ways of working, is that elsewhere the doctor can say the baby is fine because the baby does not have an illness, but the baby may be suffering which is not recognised in this culture. I think that time and time again we should reiterate that because it is often missed as there is not an awareness of what the baby and the parents are suffering, because it is not diagnosable. This is the awareness that the therapist holds about the experience that is so often missed when the doctor says, "This baby won't die, is not seriously ill", and while that is an important message, the real message is that there is something that has not been understood which is the suffering and if the baby is suffering the adult is suffering.

CHAPTER TWO

Engaging with the baby as a person: early intervention with parents and infants

Frances Thomson-Salo

This chapter outlines The Royal Children's Hospital, Melbourne (RCH) approach to therapeutic interventions with parents and their baby. After describing some capacities that an infant brings to therapy, the underlying theoretical framework is outlined. Containing powerful, often distressing feelings, which become known in the countertransference through projective identification is often extremely therapeutic in the short-term, as is engaging with the infant in the parents' presence, with psychological holding, communicating with them as a person in their own right and pleasurable playfulness in the infant-therapist interaction. With infants in vulnerable families, increasing the parents' capacity to think reflectively about their infant's mind is significantly therapeutic. Worldwide an increasing number of interventions with infants and parents, individual and group, short and long-term, psychodynamic and behavioural, are reported to be effective and the task ahead is to become clearer about the mechanisms for change. Here I shall focus on short–term infant–parent psychotherapy. Sometimes because of time pressures this may be no more than a relational encounter informed by psychoanalytic thinking (such as containment of feelings and thoughts at a time when unconscious meanings, conflictual or early implicit ones, distort a parent's' relationship with their baby), and while there are cultural differences in views about infants, ideas about the importance of sensitive parenting and attachment seem universally applicable.

The baby as "subject"

Respecting "the baby as subject" entitled to an intervention in her own right is an approach which informs the work at the hospital, where the paediatricians have for about twenty-five years referred babies with emotional and psychological difficulties to the infant mental health therapists. This follows Winnicott's (1941/1958) way of working in his paper on the spatula game. The central therapeutic mechanism is thought to lie in trying to understand the infant's experience from the infant's point of view, and conveying to parents and the infant that the infant has a mind of their own, with their own understanding of their experience. This intervention usually takes place in the presence of the parents, who generally welcome this, and it aims to increase reflectiveness in them and in their infant, that is, the capacity to be reflective in a thoughtful and open way to emotional communication from others and from oneself. Responding to the baby as a person shifts the view of the baby as an object towards seeing the baby as intentional and seeking to be in a relationship. Many infants can modify interaction and behaviour in a single session with an infant mental health therapist.

We generally do not find that parents resent therapists engaging with their infant. They usually describe it as helpful that the therapist responds to their infant as more intentional than they had done. If they indicate that they feel the therapist has taken over from them as someone who could parent or play with their infant better than they could, this can usually be verbalised and worked with. Therapists try to be aware of possible resentment and jealousy in parents and to protect the parents' dignity and self-esteem. (When this approach was previously described as direct work with the infant in the parent's presence rather than as one of engaging with the infant in the parent's presence, this may have contributed to the view that the parents were not addressed, and that there was less emphasis on verbal interpretation and more on handling the infant and providing developmental help (Dugmore, 2011)).

There are a number of capacities that we think a baby brings to therapy (Thomson-Salo & Paul, 2008), including the wish to know and be known in a truthful experience. In the presence of a therapist who is trying to understand their experience, infants sense this and it usually brings containment and relief. They may look at the therapist so attentively that they seem to have an awareness that an emotionally meaningful encounter is taking place, gazing at the therapist to find out if they are available for interaction. An infant may lock on with their eyes as a seven month old boy did for forty-five seconds the first time he met me. Babies have positive and negative emotions; they bring their potential for playfulness and humour, which has links with Stern's (1985) concept of "vitality affects", and their negative affects protect their sense of self. They wish to be enjoyed from birth—to feel understood, meaningful, and valued. Their enjoyment of interaction—of joking and teasing—is not passive; they search for it, and when they find it, they feel safe, happy, and hopeful, the world becomes more meaningful, and they have more sense of themselves. When, as Trevarthen (pers. comm.) said, playing starts, things move quickly. Infants' moral capacities may also emerge quite early, even for example by ten weeks of age, when they have felt hurt or saddened by the parents' withdrawal or sarcasm, and show a rudimentary capacity to forgive by re-engaging. Lastly, infants have a drive towards being integrated, creative and "alive", bringing a willingness to enter the therapeutic process and take a risk. This links with Winnicott's (1971) view that when things are not going well for infants, they look around for what is available. Even infants with an insecure attachment, who might not be thought to easily trust a stranger, the therapist, at the first encounter, seem very prepared to take this risk. What is often omitted is an infant's sensuality, their delight in extremely pleasurable sensations. Remembering this might aid in interventions with infants who have had so many oral trauma that their autonomy is locked up in food refusal.

The underlying framework

While the interventions are often different in individual cases, they draw on a theoretical base that is shared with other therapists, whatever their discipline-specific training (Thomson-Salo, 2007). The framework includes knowledge of developmental factors, and of interventions that are developmentally appropriate depending on whether the infant is a few weeks or fifteen months old. Infants are viewed as having a mind and an intentional self from birth, as recognising very early that their own body and feelings are different from those of others, and as having a capacity for empathy. The framework includes the therapist's experience of an infant's subjectivity and capacity for self-regulation. It includes knowledge of reality factors in an infant's life, and awareness of how trauma in an infant's or their parents' history may dysregulate their functioning. Lastly it includes an awareness of transference-countertransference and unconscious factors, including ambivalence and at times hate, to fully understand the meaning of the symptom to the infant and the parents.

Containment and relational experience as intervention

A therapist engaging with a baby and their family in a hospital setting tries to create a confidential space. As clinical work in this setting can be unpredictable, often with urgent time constraints, a relatively unstructured approach, flexible and informed by analytic thinking, offers the parents containment within a relational experience. Many of the parents feel that their own parents, internal and external, are not sensitively available. The therapist observes the baby to gather a sense of their personality and feelings, engaging and talking in the baby's language.

In the countertransference, powerful, often painful feelings become known by projective identification; containment of these often contributes to development of a parent's reflectiveness. The therapist tries to accompany a parent past their "internal saboteurs" to help them see their baby as a person, trying to convey a sense of enough time in the their mind for the parent to tell their story in their own way, while intervening, as appropriate, in the first session. Parents seeing that their baby has a capacity to respond, which is enjoyable to other people, usually helps them feel that the baby is more resilient than they had thought. They may then identify with a therapist's way-of-being, shaping their own implicit memories and internalising a less severe superego, reflectiveness, and playfulness. With a parent with borderline personality difficulties who might feel jealous if a therapist engages with an infant too early, the therapist tries to avoid stirring up feelings of deprivation and envy. With parents with serious mental illness, many of the interventions, appropriately modified, are helpful (Paul, 2008).

Links and interpretation

The therapist would usually formulate some links and interpretations, commenting on some aspects more quickly than they might in other settings. Their containment also conveys many silent interpretations. They would usually quickly interpret a negative transference to themselves but mainly intervene in a parent's transference to their baby, trying to disconnect it from the past. One mother's three-month-old baby son breastfed peacefully but she saw him as like her brother who had suffered from schizophrenia and at times been abusive and the therapist worked to try and widen the gap to see him as different from his uncle. The most relieving interventions are usually around a parent's guilt and hatred.

The infant's transference

In the RCH approach the therapist does not use modelling or coaching with parents. Nor is it an enhanced play experience. Interactive play can at times feel dangerous or sloppy (Stern, 2004) when the therapist is relying on clinical sensitivity, despite this being at times transformational and amounting to relational enhancement. This approach aims to engage infants equally as participants. We suggest that the infant makes a relationship directly with the therapist, with its positive and negative aspects, and we have always worked directly with this. Therapists "interpret" what they think the infant is feeling and thinking and when they think the transference is "hot". They try to intervene as close to the infant's own language as they can. The therapist may occasionally need to work less "with" the infant's transference but always mindfully "in" it as far as possible.

What the therapist contributes can be conceptualised as threefold (Thomson-Salo, 2007):

- Psychological holding
  Babies respond to the gaze of the therapist who tries to feel their way into their mind in the same way as a parent does in embodied parental mentalising (Shai & Belsky, 2011); this builds up secure attachment. Nonverbal ways of relating contribute to infants feeling safe in the setting. When infants feel emotionally held, they sense that the therapist's mind is available to help contain and process their feelings. Parents often report in the first interview that the infant has behaved differently, as though tentatively attaching to the therapist's mind.
- Communicating with the baby as a person in their own right
  Therapists try, above all, to understand and communicate with an infant. With younger infants, they work at making a connection with words, vocalisation, gesture and gaze. If, for example, they hold out a toy so that an infant can hold it and then teasingly pull on it, the

infant becomes aware of someone playfully recognising their agency, so that they experience that they have an effect on their world. When therapists "hear" an infant's communication they can respond in a way uniquely fitted for that infant, sometimes in ways that they could not have predicted. As Trevarthen (2011) wrote: "Each child's Self actively grows by sharing meaning in relationships." (Trevarthen, 2011, p. 1)

• Pleasurable playfulness
When infants feel enjoyed by their parents in a thoughtful way, this may be the most significant factor in developing an internal good object. Seeing enjoyment on the face of the other creates a resonant state in the self. Infants want to matter to those who look after them and above all be enthusiastically enjoyed (Trevarthen, 2001). Reflective imitative play helps develop an infant's sense of self and joy, and when infants do not have a joyful sense of self, they can feel sad and ashamed, so that when a therapist relates to them, this conveys a potential for playfulness which may ease painful or despairing feelings.

Responding authentically

Infants are able to sense authenticity when others communicate with them (Siegel, 1999), including the therapist interacting either directly or indirectly with them. Communication may become confusing when a therapist makes an interpretation to the infant that is intended for the parent but is addressed to the infant to "soften" the effect for the parent. (I acknowledge that there are difficult clinical moments which require an adaptation of technique, when a parent is very negative to infant or therapist, or has serious mental illness, or may become jealous and withdraw from therapy.)

An authentic response would be engaging and talking about the present moment, about the infant's affect and experience, about the experience of being that infant. Being authentic involves the therapist partially surrendering to the process, not knowing what will happen. The therapist would be, in the words of Ruth Paris and her colleagues (2009) open and attuned to a small, unplanned moment of interaction as a potential arena for therapeutic action. As infants begin to monitor the attention of others who at times focus on them, they then monitor this attention in a way that was not possible previously (Allen &

Fonagy, 2006). The infant's face-to-face interactions with others then become radically transformed. They now know they are interacting with another intentional agent who intends things toward them. For an infant to begin to think reflectively requires a relational context in which they can explore their mind in the mind of the other; in this way therapists help co-construct new representations. The therapist mirroring, as with a parent, provides a stimulus that organises a baby's experience and names what he is feeling so that out of this interaction develops the ability to think about the mental states of others (Fonagy, 2002).

The "core principle" of infant–parent psychotherapy could be summarised as "being with the baby" as well as with the parents, relating to the infant as subject, aiming to make a connection so that therapist and infant begin an exploration of not-knowing (Thomson-Salo & Paul, 2001). As part of therapeutic action, how is a therapist's authenticity used? Buechler (2008) wrote that as the therapist becomes important to the patient, the patient observes how the therapist functions and regains emotional balance. She asked, "What do we have to do to matter enough to be watched?" Her answer would be what a therapist aims for in being watched by the infant: "(T)o be emotionally open, transparent and readable so that patients become interested in what they learn from how we tick" (Buechler, 2008, p. 36). We suggest that responding to the infant as subject promotes reflective thinking. Nothing would be more convincing to a parent that their baby has a mind that reflects and can be reflected on than a therapist being reflective with their baby.

Promoting reflective thinking in the face of attachment difficulties

In working with vulnerable families, the aim, however difficult to achieve, is towards helping them become convinced of the importance of thinking about their infant's experience, as reflective thinking promotes secure attachment. When therapists notice what an infant is doing or wonder with parents about what they think an infant means, they are functioning as observing eyes to promote reflective thinking (Fonagy, 2002). Or in video feedback with parents, parents may feel empowered to think about what their infant might be experiencing and begin to withdraw some projections.

Interacting with the baby may help reflective thinking develop in a fourfold action (Thomson-Salo, 2007). Firstly, in changing infant representations and behaviour. When infants experience their mind as existing in the therapist's mind, and are responded to in a new way, this offers the possibility for responding differently. Being in the presence of a therapist who is interested in understanding the meaning of their experience, this is mirrored back in a way that infants feel bodily with changes in behaviour and representations. Second, changing parental representation through exploring and making links, concurrent with seeing their infant differently. This re-presents the infant to the parents who have the possibility to see their infant as more robust than they had thought, the infant whom they had at some level hated for making them feel "bad" parents. Third, changing infant–parent interaction with the infant taking the changed way-of-being into the relationship with the parents, increasing their sense of having regained their infant, with their infant effectively a therapist for them. Fourth, changing parental ways-of-being with the infant: when the therapist interacts with an infant from a position of finding the infant intentional, understandable, and potentially enjoyable, the parents are likely to have mirrored in themselves a similar experience. The therapist-infant interaction may begin shaping the parents' representations in implicit memories of relational behaviours. It seems possible that in the relational encounter with the infant these representations could be modified faster than at other times. The view that the therapeutic action may begin nonverbally, at an implicit level, is supported in some neuroscience research (Pally, 2005). Interacting with the infant in the parents' presence may do more to rework implicit relational knowing than working only with the parents.

Usually the constraints of the work do not allow unlimited time to work with patients, so that the therapist does what is achievable in the short-term and refers on if longer-term help is indicated, particularly in cases of serious mental illness, substance use or related difficulties. If a mother has postpartum depression, effective treatment for this is not sufficient to improve the developing parent–child relationship: the relationship and the infant both need help for continuing difficulties (Forman et al., 2007).

Conclusion

When the focus is on helping parents and infants who are experiencing difficulty, it is usually helpful if the infant is included in the clinical work to contribute to increased reflective thinking. Infant–parent psychotherapy offers the infant an experience of being understood and communicated within their own right. As the infant and parent experience an increasingly important relationship with the therapist, this is likely to begin to modify early ways-of-being from a predominance of insecure attachments towards more secure ones. Research finds a cascade effect of change which lasts longer after the ending of psychotherapy than with other modes of intervention, because the capacity for reflective thinking has extended (Shedler, 2010).

References

Allen, J. & Fonagy, P. (Eds.) (2006). *Handbook of Mentalization-Based Treatment.* Chichester, UK: John Wiley.

Buechler, S. (2008). *Making a difference in patients' lives: Emotional experience in the therapeutic setting.* New York: Routledge.

Dugmore, N. (2011). The development of psychoanalytic parent–infant/child psychotherapy in South Africa: A review of the history from infancy towards maturity. *Journal of Child and Adolescent Mental Health, 23:* 75–90.

Fonagy, P. (2002). Understanding of mental states, mother–infant interaction and the development of the self. In: J. M. Maldonaldo-Duran, (Ed.), *Infant and toddler mental health, models of clinical interventions with infants and their families* (pp. 57–74). Washington, DC: American Psychiatric Publishing.

Forman, D. R., O'Hara, M. W., Stuart, S., Gorman, L. L., Larsen, K. E. & Coy, K. C. (2007). Effective treatment for postpartum depression is not sufficient to improve the developing mother–child relationship. *Development and Psychopathology, 19:* 585–602.

Pally, R. (2005). A neuroscience perspective on forms of intersubjectivity in infant research and adult treatment. In: B. Beebe, S. Knoblauch, J. Rustin. & D. Sorter (Eds.), *Forms of intersubjectivity in infant research and adult treatment.* New York: Other Press.

Paris, R., Spielman, E., & Bolton, R. E. (2009). Mother-psychotherapy: examining the therapeutic process of change. *Infant Mental Health Journal, 30:* 301–319.

Paul, C. (2008). Sick babies and troubled parents: Therapeutic work with parents and infants in a paediatric hospital setting: "The baby is the subject". In: A. Sved Williams & V. Cowling (Ed.), *Infants of Parents With Mental Illness: Developmental, Clinical, Cultural and personal perspectives* (pp. 231–248). Melbourne: ACER.

Shai, D. & Belsky, J. (2011). When words just won't do: Introducing parental embodied mentalizing. *Child Development Perspectives, 5:* 173–180.

Shedler, J. (2010). The efficacy of psychodynamic psychotherapy. *American Psychologist, 65*: 98–109.

Siegel, D. J. (1999). *The developing mind. How relationships and the brain interact to shape who we are.* New York/London: Guilford Press.

Stern, D. N. (1985). *The interpersonal world of the child.* New York: Basic Books.

Stern, D. N. (2004). *The present moment in psychotherapy and everyday life.* New York, New York: W. W. Norton.

Thomson-Salo, F. (2007). Recognising the infant as subject in infant–parent psychotherapy. *International Journal of Psycho-analysis, 88*: 961–979.

Thomson-Salo, F. & Paul C. (2001). Being there: The 'something more' that the baby brings to the therapeutic process. *AAIMH (Vic) Newsletter* March; pp. 1–4.

Trevarthen, C. (2001). Intrinsic motives for companionship in understanding: their origin, development, and significance for infant mental health. *Infant Mental Health Journal, 22*: 95–131.

Trevarthen, C. (2011). What young children give to their learning, making education work to sustain a community and its culture. *Monograph Issue of the European Early Childhood Education Research Journal on "Birth to Three".*

Winnicott, D. W. (1958). The observation of infants in a set situation. In: *Collected Papers: Through Paediatrics to Psycho-analysis* (pp. 52–69). London: Tavistock Publications.

Winnicott, D. W. (1971). Mirror role of mother and family in child development. In: *Playing and reality* (pp. 111–118). London: Tavistock.

PART I

INTERVENTIONS IN ACUTE
HEALTH SETTINGS

CHAPTER THREE

The sick baby in hospital

Campbell Paul

M any babies come to hospital sick, some are very sick and stay a long time. A very small number may be so sick that they may die. In such circumstances, infant mental health workers have the responsibility to work with babies, their parents, and their carers. Extremely vulnerable babies may be cared for in a number of settings in the paediatric hospital, including a general paediatric ward, the neonatal intensive care unit (NICU) or the paediatric intensive care unit (PICU).

For mental health workers, the basic hypothesis is that we should begin by acknowledging the mind, the self of the baby and working with that concept in our own mind. This helps the baby with severe illness, prematurity, or malformation to develop a stronger sense of self, of confidence in his own "damaged" body without needing to have recourse to excessive defensive withdrawal.

This raises two questions.

1. How do ordinary parents cope with this—is there such a thing as the extraordinary devoted parent? (Winnicott (1965) wrote about the

ordinary devoted mother who was "good enough"). What factors allow for the extraordinary devotion that is needed in extreme situations?

2. What are the roles of the infant mental health (IMH) worker?

I would like to discuss these issues with some clinical cases, in which I was able to engage the baby directly in front of parents in a way that allowed for understandable ambivalence and hate.

Frank

Three-month-old Frank's parents were from interstate. They came to Melbourne for his birth when antenatal ultrasound showed a severe hypoplastic left heart condition. The pregnancy had been closely monitored, for he was a very special baby born by IVF to parents desperate for a child after years of painful infertility. He was transferred to hospital for staged open heart surgery. At three weeks of age, he had been on an artificial heart and lung support system almost continuously, his lungs were poorly developed and were never likely to improve. His father, David, was referred to our mental health service because he was sure he was "cracking up—going psycho". He had periods of frozen immobility, could not get out of the parent accommodation bed, was crying and "sobbing like a child". He had pains in his body, and overwhelming feelings of dread. He said, "I'm not coping, I can't bear it. I have a terrifying feeling of dread and a crushing feeling in my chest. I can't use my right arm."

Frank seemed to love it when his father spent time with him, but David was feeling that he could no longer bear to be with him. Eventually he was able to say that he wished, "it would just be 'over'." It was like torture, not knowing—yet knowing—that his only child was likely to die. Would the machines need to be switched off and who would decide? How could he speak of such horrific things? I think that it was our role to enable him, and later his wife, to "talk" of such things. I met Frank over another five weeks and spent time with both parents and grandparents and the distressed staff. Eventually Frank succumbed to a cardio-respiratory event. David and Helen were distraught but returned home, knowing that they had really become parents—to a very brave infant.

The crisis of a premature or sick baby

It is a crisis for the baby—one of survival. While we think of premature babies as being born before thirty-seven weeks, extremely premature babies are born before twenty-eight weeks and some babies survive from twenty-two weeks gestation. Low birth weight is defined as under 2,500 grams, extremely low birth weight as less than 1,000 grams. In The Royal Children's Hospital NICU in 2003, premature infants with a birth weight of 500 to 750 grams had a forty to sixty per cent survival rate. Babies may be born prematurely with or without major complications.

Having a premature or sick baby is a crisis for the parents, with the potential loss of the hoped-for infant. There is a period of instability where there is a potential for change. The stress upon the parents is great, and the stress may see an increased rate of separation but it also allows for the possibility of emotional growth.

With which infants should we be working in NICU/PICU?

In the intensive care units there is a cast of thousands, and as an infant mental health worker we are but one of the many. We can ask, "Who is the patient?" and, "What is our role with the parents—and infants?" Our roles include direct work with the infant, work with the parents, work with the staff and with the systems in hospital. They also include engaging with the complex ethical issues, and in research and evaluation.

An infant with whom the IMH clinician works includes the symptomatic baby who is withdrawn, avoidant, severely regressed, crying,

Table 1. Infant referrals to Mental Health, The Royal Children's Hospital in a six month period in 2005

Reason for referral	Number of infants
Liver transplant	3
Congenital heart disease	2
Ventilator dependent	4
Multiple problems (e.g., tracheo-oesophageal fistula with complications)	5

Of these, four had been on the artificial heart lung machine, "Extracorporeal Membranous Oxygenation" (ECMO).
Others infants were discussed with the unit staff without formal referral.

dysregulated, and refusing to feed. How do we prioritise our work when there is a paucity of research about this? While it is very important to respond to each referral it depends on the urgency of the referral, the severity of the child's illness, and on the ongoing need to build relationships. We are not alone in the unit. The work of many other professionals overlaps with that of ours. We must work closely with other professionals involved such as the nurses, social workers, play specialists, speech pathologists, chaplains, and music therapists. It is important to develop close linkages in order to be clear about our respective roles and responsibilities.

Our ongoing role with sick children

Even when infants have managed the transition out of the neonatal intensive care unit to the general ward and then to home, there remains a significant role for us. This need not be continuous and intensive work but may be brief and serial interventions (see Stern (1995) on the importance of brief serial psychotherapeutic intervention).

Veronica

Five-month-old Veronica had a congenital laryngeal web in which the upper airway closes and there is vocal chord palsy. A tracheostomy was inserted. She had avoidant behaviour, feeding refusal, and management problems. Her mother said, "She will not eat! Does she sense my moods?" We needed to consider the impact of repeated trauma around the mouth/pharynx which led to an aversive response. The IMH worker's role was to do an assessment and then to work with Veronica to improve her sense of self through infant–parent therapy, and to desensitise her, her parents, and staff to feeding with the nasogastric tube. It was also to work with the parents and their anger, sadness and fear, and to work with the ward staff who had much ambivalence to the parents, resulting in conflict and confusion. They wondered why the parents kept bringing their daughter back to hospital with what seemed to be trivial events, such as colds and minor urinary tract infections. At eleven months old Veronica played at feeding a doll, which her father modelled. It was a complex scenario, given that her mother and grandmother had experienced eating disorders themselves. But her father helped in that he could identify with her and put himself in her shoes.

There are increasing numbers of babies in NICU/PICU with severe life threatening or disabling conditions. What are the influences upon the parents' extraordinary devotion to their baby? In this context, as IMH workers we see very few parents who abandon their infant or who cannot manage the task of care. Why? It may be some families do not have the capacity, and carefully considered decisions are made very early on to not undertake extensive or heroic treatments. The medical and nursing staff and parents reach a consensus that a life potentially so limited and disabled is not one with which medicine should intrusively and strenuously intervene. The IMH worker can sometimes play a role in ethical decision-making.

Parents' experience in NICU/PICU

Parents often feel traumatised at the outset and isolated; they may be fearful and often keep to themselves. They may fear finding out too much about the difficulties that the baby faces and fear being a burden to the parents or being burdened by their distress. They are often distanced from their baby and from most of their usual supports and networks. This may build on pre-birth family issues (Tracey, 2000). Mothers of high risk, very low birth weight premature babies report extreme stress two years later. Depression is a significant factor but parents may be too busy to consciously acknowledge it. (With babies born at less than thirty weeks gestation the prevalence of clinical depression in mothers is about thirty per cent and in fathers about ten per cent. Over time it gradually reduces). Anxiety symptoms (which may include anger, helplessness, hopelessness, terror, and guilt) are also significant, as are traumatic and post-traumatic stress disorders, with hypervigilance, re-experiencing symptoms and avoidance of affect and, in particular, avoidance of NICU and the hospital.

What parents provide their baby may be compromised. We need to consider whether we can enable them "to be with" their baby, practically and psychologically. The nursing staff must provide some of this emotional care (holding) for the baby in the interim if the parents cannot, but it is hard for the nurses too.

The basis for self in the body

The care given by parents provides a basis for the development of a working relationship between "psyche" and "soma" for the baby. The parents can help their baby develop a sense of self in the face of serious illness. So if the baby has a disability or deformity, the ordinary (or perhaps here necessarily extraordinary) devoted parents handle the baby and her body in such a way that, as Winnicott said, there is a "satisfactory working relationship" between the psyche and soma.

What does the baby experience? Ordinary physical care leads the baby to an understanding of her damaged body such that the baby tends to assume that what is there is normal—"normal is what is there". It is only much later that the baby becomes aware she is different to other children. Distortions of the ego may come from distortions of the attitude of those who care for the child.

A mother with a baby is constantly introducing and re-introducing the baby's body and psyche to each other. This task can become difficult when the baby has an abnormality that makes the mother feel ashamed, guilty, frightened, excited, or hopeless. Under such circumstances, as Winnicott said, she can only do her best. It is our job to help "hold" the mother and father when they do feel ashamed, guilty, angry, resentful, faithless, and rejecting—for them to know such feelings can be experienced and shared without the annihilation of their child. This can be a very big problem in places such as NICU/PICU.

"Personalisation"

What do parents do to help their baby? Winnicott wrote about the ordinary devoted parent and their role in personalisation of their baby. The way the parent holds and handles her baby—the actual physical care driven by a belief-investment in the baby—allows the baby in Winnicott's apt term to "inhabit" her body. The way the parent holds, touches, bathes, picks up, talks to, and looks at his baby allows for the person to emerge connected with limbs, skin, chest, hair, lips, bottom etc.!

Winnicott gives a great account of how a mother picks up her baby— not like a sack of potatoes, but gently as part of a subtle dance, giving warning, a preparation that a gentle enfolding would occur. This leads to the acquisition of a personal body schema, the "psyche indwelling in the soma". In their handling, the parents manage the infant as if the baby's mind and body form one unit. Their holding provides the basis for what gradually becomes a self-experiencing being. Physical holding of the infant is a form of loving. (Physical and psychological are still one.) The good-enough parents allow and facilitate the process of the baby inhabiting his own body. But they allow for the baby to depersonalise, to abandon the urge to exist for a moment. They facilitate a sense of security allowing for regression and dependence, especially for the sick infant.

Bonnie

Bonnie was referred to infant mental health service at eight months of age. She was in intensive care with a drug reaction which was the probable cause of fulminant liver failure. She looked very ill with severe respiratory complications and it was thought that she was so ill that a transplant might not be possible. A decision might be needed about treatment. But Bonnie seemed "positive and lively", despite being extremely ill. Looking back over her eight months of being extremely sick and in hospital, I had to ask when she was about to go home: "How has she survived?" It must be that Bonnie is a real "fighter".

Bonnie had been conceived somewhat unexpectedly, to a very young couple who had been together only four years, and already had one child, aged three years. He was as excited as his parents with the news of Bonnie's conception, and about her birth, at which he was present. He doted on her and followed every tiny movement of her tiny fingers and toes, eyes and mouth. However at about four weeks of age, a concerned maternal and child health nurse insisted on a rapid return visit when Bonnie's weight fell a little. Both parents became anxious when the nurse sent Bonnie to a paediatrician. Bonnie had become jaundiced. After an examination it was clear that she was sick. Her jaundice and poor growth were due to a very severe rare liver disorder. Subsequently she spent seven of her next eleven months in hospital—there was an attempt at a number of heroic medical treatments which saw only a little relief of her jaundice.

She was considered for liver transplant—for her it became the only way to be able to survive, but the difficulty was that she had to become bigger to be able to withstand the trauma of the operation and accept a piece of donated liver. There was to some degree a race against time—she had to grow quickly—and be lucky enough for a matching donor liver to be found.

What did we find on meeting them? Both parents were present, Bonnie lying on a pillow across her father's lap, he gently holding her fingers and occasionally stroking her head. She was small—the size of a five-week-old baby and skin of a deep yellow hue, some jet black hair and deep open eyes. What was striking was her gaze. She looked, turned her head, and gazed straight into my eyes as I entered her room—she sought me out, fixed me with a powerful stare—it seemed neither fearful nor angry. It was as if she were saying to me, "Who are you? I am interested—and curious, but not too trusting. I am safe here on my father's lap, my mother also beside me." Can a pair of eyes say so much? She was after all only eight months old. I think so, and I think that the work of her extraordinary devoted parents played a critical role in her capacity to communicate. She could communicate fear as well—she withdrew her feet especially if anyone went to touch her.

Since her first admission to hospital one of her parents had been with her at all times, except for brief visits downstairs for lunch. They slept in the same bed. She had been physically close to at least one of them most of the time. "We could not imagine leaving her here alone", they said, although they did speak positively of the nursing staff, showing some trust in their care. Importantly they observed how well the nurses could play with Bonnie—despite her being so sick and incapacitated. It seemed to me her parents saw—and perhaps cultivated the nursing staff's acknowledgement of Bonnie's personhood while they did intrusive procedures to her: her parents (and Bonnie herself) convinced the staff that "someone was home"—Bonnie was there—alive—lively and responsive.

It is as if they all had accepted the fact of some intersubjectivity—that there was, from the beginning, communication (Trevarthen, 1974). This demonstrated intersubjective process seemed to be primarily a function of Bonnie's devoted parents responding to her reaching out for connection from birth. All that they did with her was responsive to and contingent upon her own behaviour. Some may have seen them as indulgent, but in the circumstances I think not.

Bonnie received a transplant at sixteen months but her problems continued. Just prior to her going home she had a serious drug reaction which reduced her capacity to respond to any sort of infection, but Bonnie continued to develop—in communication, differentiation, and demands. She has survived and thrived after leaving hospital … but this seemed a consequence of her parents superhuman devotion as much as her medical and nursing care.

The mirror role of the mother

What does the baby see when he looks at his mother's face? The expression on the mother's face reflects what she sees in her baby. But when the mother is depressed, her face is a mirror to be looked at, not into (Winnicott, 1971, p. 112). Father and siblings too. This role of an alive mirror is very important—but it can be perturbed by the parents' feelings. In Bonnie's case the mirror role was the father's. He gave up his business to be the primary carer in the hospital, which was shared with his wife. If the parents are very cut off, this can be very problematic. We also have to help parents (and the staff) grapple with the sometimes disabling state of ambivalence (as with Frank's father).

Ambivalence

If ambivalence is "deep", does it abuse? The mother of eighteen-month-old Jessie said, "You doctors don't know anything—who do you think you are! Just doing this to a person—you've got no idea what it is like and what we have to go through—what sort of life is it for a child like ours and for us? Maybe you should ask us before you save lives—it may be better not to, you know!" Exhausted parents can wish for a peaceful end to their child's struggle and yet at the same time desperately hope for a miracle, a reprieve.

A paradox is that while the parents may be better able to see the baby's mind than us, but Jessie's mother, having voiced her anger, her fear, her resentment that her life already difficult, was turned totally on its head, it may be that she can then more readily see her baby as an autonomous person. This would be good for Jessie, although I expect it does not easily allow for regression. We may need to provide very active containment.

The infant's responses

The withdrawn baby may not be suffering a disorder in itself. How does the baby cope? What determines whether the baby's "shut down" is adaptive or pathological? It depends on the baby's inner resources including "temperament", the intrauterine experience, the parents' role and commitment (having two parents to share the dilemma means that one can be up, while the other is down).

Dissociation can be a useful defence. We need to consider the concepts of shutdown versus survival, whether the infant and family are experiencing post-traumatic stress disorder or an acute stress response, and to consider their resilience. All this is underpinned by neurochemical changes, including the pain experienced by the baby.

Is it unkind to overcome defences that may see the self of the very sick or terminally ill baby denied? Would it not be better to allow parents (and staff) to retain a clinical distance from their baby whose chance of survival is so remote, to allow him to die with minimal perturbation to his parents and carers?

What can the IMH worker do with a baby?

The possibilities include infant–parent therapies, direct work with the baby in the presence of the parents and nurses, and work with siblings. Infants and their families may need brief serial therapies as a response in critical times (Stern, 1995). It can help that the IMH workers are not part of the core medical team; they can receive negative feelings.

The IMH worker facilitates the relationship between parent and baby and helps parents overcome some of the fear or resistance to seeing the baby there. Premature babies respond differently: it is harder to read subtle signals. There is a role for the baby as patient, who can also be a co-therapist for their mother and father.

Working with parents

In NICU/PICU parents often say how hard it is to talk to anyone (even their partner). How could they conceivably talk about their own doubt? "Why are you going on treating my baby?—such painful risky procedures! Cutting down into flesh to insert catheters!—restraining them in their humidicribs—painfully pricking their tiny heels to squeeze out tiny drops of blood." What can they say when they feel, "Enough! Why can't you stop it?" Or even, "Why can't you let my baby die?!" They fear that these words cannot be spoken to the nurses and doctors, lest they be taken at face value, consciously or unconsciously. It would be horrific if the staff acted as the parents' fought against fantasies. Just because their own courage seemed to be failing they did not really want their baby's death—but they do. So often, parents have to keep these poisonous secrets within themselves.

While every baby has a different story there is much in common, such as feeling a lack of support. It is part of the IMH worker's task to help at the appropriate time open up the feelings and phantasies especially in the confidential manner of one who is part of the baby's system of care but at the same time distant and apparently removed from decision-making processes. If ambivalence or hate can be spoken about, it loses some of its poison, especially towards the baby himself.

The effects of maternal depression

The effects of maternal depression may lead to problems in the parent–infant relationship, which may lead to later problems in infant development. Premature babies are more protected and can be close to their mother. But parents may be less "physical" with their infants who have to initiate more themselves. The mother's depression may constitute an ongoing trauma, affecting the sense of self for the child. Postnatal depression may also be thought of as a relationship disorder. Tracey (1991) showed that the depth of the trauma is often unresolvable.

Music therapy programme

One way of responding to distress in baby and parents is to facilitate music therapy. The music therapy programme (Chapter Five) is a music therapy intervention in NICU with babies with severe problems. The intervention is determined by the baby's state and response, a contingent intervention designed to facilitate her ability to calm and self regulate. A post discharge follow up found a positive sleeper effect for the baby so that there is a need to identify those who are most vulnerable (See also Malloch, 1999; Shoemark, 2004).

Other possible mental health roles in NICU/PICU

Minde (2000) has written about influencing the hospital ecology. IMH workers help parents and staff to clarify roles, explain behaviours of staff and parents to each other, help parents understand their feelings and regain control, and teach principles of child development.

The IMH worker needs patience in NICU/PICU, to "be there" to become known and credible. Credibility from service delivery is very important. The IMH worker needs to be there to respond to referrals, attend ward rounds, and psychosocial meetings (along with art, educational and play therapists, chaplains), the nurses' group meetings and the nurse-run coffee morning meeting (PICU) and to consult with care managers and social workers regularly without the need for a referral. The IMH role with staff includes support, debriefing and collaborating in decision-making. Are there ethical questions in particular that they can be involved with?

Work with staff around "ECMO"

The staff who provide for children the lifesaving intensive heart lung machine, ECMO (Extracorporeal Continuous Membranous Oxygenation), are a close knit team. The individual team members can experience severe stress, when such a grave demand falls on the shoulders of a small team of specialists. The actions they take are under very close moment to moment scrutiny: it is a very delicate and demanding task to perform for the baby, the essential functions of human life. There are concerns over ethical and clinical decision-making. Powerful emotional attachments are formed with the infant and her family. Although up to seventy per cent of babies survive, when a baby dies the staff may also experience traumatic symptoms.

What are some of the problems of working with babies?

These include competing demands placed on the staff as people and on the skills of the staff. They need to have a special approach because the baby cannot talk and they have to avoid reducing the baby simply to a technical problem to be solved. It can be hard to identify with the baby.

There are countertransference issues for the nurses and IMH workers. We need to be careful not to demonise parents or vice versa—to ignore the baby herself, saying that it is too hard to enter her world. (See Paul, in Tracey, 2000, where there is a fuller discussion of issues of stress and countertransference.) Nurses talking about one infant who had been in the unit a long time, having been very sick and through many crises, vividly described the real person that they had come to know. "We were really upset; we could see how she pulled out her central venous line. She tears at her own skin as if she is distressed and wants to get it out." Their identification with her and her experience is deep and profound, and they were themselves traumatised by her distress. A doctor described another infant, seeing him as having become sad and distressed. "You look into his eyes and he looks straight back at you. The look he gives is like he has just given up." It can be an intensely difficult task to allow an infant to die with dignity, as it is exciting and exhilarating to see those survivors go into the world; it is equally important to help those parents whose children do not go home to get to know their child as well as they can while they can.

Research

We need to show how our intervention works, and over what period of time. But any successful interventions are subject to the claim that this would have happened anyway. Large-scale clinical research is difficult, with the lack of specificity of a diagnosis and the rapidity of developmental change. Also while most studies look at acute loss of a baby, the impact of the death of a baby has been less studied.

Are premature babies prone to depression? Currently researchers are studying a matched small cohort of sick babies, carrying out an assessment of withdrawal and depression. But depression/withdrawal in such babies is hard to compare because of the diverse range of problems and severity experienced by them. Does the baby's depression persist or create ongoing difficulties? It may do so, although most premature babies can certainly do well developmentally. It depends on the degree of prematurity and whether there were major complications.

Conclusion

It seems that from the clinical experience which we have accrued working alongside very sick babies, their parents and our colleagues, there is an important role for keeping the mind of the baby as an important component of the narrative which unfolds. Although parents are severely stressed we believe that it is helpful for them to be able to relate to their baby as a person to whom they will have a lot to give. Developing this relationship, no matter how brief it might be, is critical for each baby and her devoted parents.

References

Malloch, S. (1999). Mother and infants and communicative musicality. *Musicae Scientificae*, Special Issue, 29–57.

Minde, K. (2000). Prematurity and serious medical conditions in infancy. In: C. H. Zeanah (Ed.), *Handbook of Infant Mental Health* (pp. 176–194). New York: Guilford.

Paul, C. (2000). The experience of staff who work in neonatal intensive care. In: N. Tracey (Ed.), *Parents of premature infants: their emotional world*, (pp. 229–240), London: Whurr.

Shoemark, H. (2004). Family-centred music therapy for infants with complex medical and surgical needs. In: M. Nocker-Ribaupierre (Ed.), *Music Therapy for Premature and Newborn Infants*, (pp. 141–157). Gilsum NH: Barcelona Publishers.

Stern, D. N. (1995). *The motherhood constellation: a unified view of parent–infant psychotherapy*. New York: Basic Books.

Tracey, N. (1991). The psychic space in trauma. *Journal of Child Psychotherapy, 17*: 29–44.

Tracey, N. (Ed.) (2000). *Parents of premature infants: Their emotional world*. London: Whurr.

Trevarthen, C. (1974). Psychobiology of speech development. In: E. Lenneberg (Ed.), Language and Brain: Developmental Aspects. *Neurobiology Sciences Research Program Bulletin, 12*: 570–585.

Winnicott, D. W. (1965). The Maturational Processes and the Facilitating Environment. *International Psycho-Analytical Library, 64*: 1–276. London: The Hogarth Press and the Institute of Psycho-Analysis.

Winnicott, D. W. (1971). The mirror role of the mother and family in child development, *Playing and Reality*. London: Tavistock.

Winnicott, D. W. (1972). On the basis of self in body. In: Psychoanalytic Explorations, 1989. Harvard University Press.

CHAPTER FOUR

Perceptions of parents of tube fed babies: a preliminary analysis

Libby Ferguson and Campbell Paul

Introduction

Provision of adequate nutrition to enable growth and development is one of the most important aspects of caring for a baby. The responsibility for feeding the baby usually falls on the parents, particularly on the mother. The feeding relationship between baby and parent is important and forms a crucial basis for the emotional development of the baby and contributes greatly to the parent's ability to experience the care of their baby with confidence and satisfaction. (Satter, 1999). Rosenblum (2004, p. 61) describes feeding as a "relationally embedded phenomenon". When oral feeding of the baby is compromised, or even impossible, the parent–infant interaction is made more complex and is at risk of disruption (Drotar & Robinson, 2000; Benoit, 2000).

Many infants who begin life in a neonatal intensive care unit (NICU) or in a special care nursery (SCN) receive some or all of their nutritional needs through a feeding tube, most often a nasogastric tube (NGT) or a gastrostomy tube. It is difficult to separate the issues surrounding the need for tube feeding from the complex medical and/or surgical problems that necessitate the placement of the tube in the first instance (Minde, 2000). The parent's perception of the tube may be difficult to disentangle from their experience of having a baby with a life threatening illness.

Increasingly infants are discharged from hospital while remaining dependent on the feeding tube to maintain growth. Parents must learn to manage all aspects of tube feeding to enable their baby's discharge from hospital. As well as learning the complex process of administering a tube feed many parents also undertake the responsibility for inserting the NGT through their baby's nasal passage and pharynx to the oesophagus, whenever it needs replacing.

Literature review

A growing body of literature related to parental perceptions of tube feeding, more specifically, usually gastrostomy tube feeding, in older infants and children is emerging. Literature related to psychosocial aspects of paediatric medical complexity and chronic ill health provides further insights into the experiences of parents and their children.

Family dynamics, coping mechanisms and reference to "psychological scars" have been described as relevant to discharge planning for young children with gastrostomy tubes (Huddleston & Ferraro, 1991).

Physiological gains, supplemented by some data supporting psychosocial impact of tube feeding are documented in the qualitative literature (Tawfik et al., 1997). Families report problems with family functioning and stress (Smith et al., 1999; Pederson et al., 2004; Dudeck-Shriber, 2004). Specific psychosocial problems revealed by Smith and colleagues were restricted mobility, difficulty with respite care, impact on relationship with the child and the child missing the taste of food.

Craig and colleagues (2003) used semi-structured interviews to explore the impact of tube feeding. The following themes emerged: experiences of feeding, referral, significance of oral feeding, the child's enjoyment of feeding, maintaining skills, perceived benefits and the need for evidence, complications of the procedure, the anti-reflux procedure and emotional and support needs. The authors recommended that families and clinicians might benefit from discussion of hopes, expectations, and limitations of the procedure prior to insertion of a feeding tube.

Two related articles in the nursing literature outline the experience of long-term gastrostomy in children with disability, and with insights from nursing staff (Thorne et al., 1997; Radford et al., 1997). These papers examined the perceptions of nurses and parents. Among the categories delineated were: giving up hope, ending the struggle, caregiver convenience, relinquishing normal and maternal failure. Wallander and Varni (1998) found that family adjustment to chronic physical disorder was influenced by intra-personal factors, social-ecological factors, and stress processing. In a review of literature on family coping with chronically ill children, Meleski (2002) discussed shifting responsibilities and disequilibrium during transition times, along with chronic sorrow. Mismatch of perceptions between home care nurses and parents regarding caring for technology dependent children was raised by O'Brien and Wegner (2002). The authors recommended improved communication and collaboration between parents and home care nurses.

Franklin and Rodger (2003) studied parental perspectives and psychosocial implications of feeding the children using in-depth interviews and a mealtime observation. The following themes emerged: fear for the child's survival, stress on the parent-child relationship, increased parenting responsibility and adjustment and coping with chronic stress. This shift to consideration of the parent-child relationship indicates the emergence of some focus on the child as well as the parent.

Study method

Approval for the study was obtained through the Ethics committee of the interviewer's employing hospital, The Royal Children's Hospital. Parents of six babies from the interviewer's clinical caseload were interviewed, using semi-structured interviews. Minichello's (1991) description of in-depth interviews formed the conceptual basis for the interviews. Interviews were conducted either in the hospital setting or in the interviewees' own home as preferred by the interviewees. Interviews were videotaped and the data transcribed to personal computer for analysis.

Analysis of data used the constant comparative process (Glaser & Strauss, 1967). An open coding system (Miles & Huberman, 1994) was used to code each conversational turn, or embedded unit of meaning, in the interviews. Codes were progressively refined as themes emerged. Relationships between codes were identified and themes labelled according to collections of topics and meanings (Frick, 2002). Analysis ceased when all units of relevant conversational turns were assigned to a theme.

Table 2. Participants

Interview number	Gender of baby	Age in months	Medical condition	Hospital stay	Parents available	Length of interview
1	Female	4	Hypoxic Ischemic Encephalopathy	18 days	Mother Father	47 min
2	Female	9	Short Gut Syndrome	294 days	Mother Father	36 min
3	Female	9	Hypo-pituitarism	280 days	Mother	37 min
4	Male	10	Exomphalos	53 days	Mother	49 min
5	Female	6	Cerebral palsy	19 days	Mother	41 min
6	Male	5	Obstructed labour	98 days	Mother Father	38 min

Results

Families of six infants, between the age of four and ten months were selected for interview. Three couples, comprising mother and father, and three mothers alone were interviewed. Data regarding gender, age at time of interview, main medical diagnosis, length of initial hospital stay and length of interview is presented in Table 2.

Emerging themes

A visual reminder of illness

When parents first see the feeding tube it reinforces for them that their baby is severely ill.

- "… a constant reminder that things aren't exactly right with her …"
- "It concerned me more than anything, because that meant it was something serious … you see tubes and you think that."
- "The thing up her nose was the least of our worries."

The tube as a necessity

Parents generally acknowledge that the feeding tube is essential to keep their baby well nourished.

- "But it does mean that she gets everything nutritionally".
- "But then again there may be positives to it. Because then you know what she is getting nutritionally. That she is getting everything she needs."

The hospital context

The hospital is a difficult environment but one for which parents develop coping strategies.

- "With my sister, both her and I were reprimanded for looking at the other babies and thought, 'Goodness, what have we gotten into here?' When we found out what the rules are we thought, 'Oh well. We'll fit in here.'"
- "You quite like coming in here and seeing other children with tubes. You think Yeah! They're quite normal in here."

Interaction with hospital staff

Parents were thankful for the work done in keeping their child alive but expressed a range of negative perceptions. They felt powerless, unlistened to, and, with their baby, at the mercy of the system.

- "People are generally here to make her healthier and happy."
- "I don't think a lot of people are really that experienced at putting the tube in."
- "It's because they have to do it. It's not just doing it for the sake of … 'Oh we'll practice this on Jennifer.'"
- "They don't want to take any advice from you or talk about it and realise that you know your own baby."
- "If you're not happy, learn to say no, learn to ask the nurses how they are doing it. Don't assume or trust."

The trauma of inserting the tube

Parents feel traumatised and recognise the trauma to their baby. They may "switch off" to the trauma.

- "I burst into tears. I couldn't believe I had just done that to my son. It was my way of helping him, to bring him home."

- "Oh, it's horrible. You want to tear them apart. When Frank does it at home ... the two of us nearly kill each other through the whole time it's being done."
- "If you are gentle you can actually feel it go down. And you can feel when it's stopping. If she's upset or crying you just stop it there and then she'll calm down a bit, she'll breathe in and it will go through. It just sucks itself through."
- "I know it has to go in. You sort of switch off to her cries. Usually the people who try to help me get all distraught."

Social reactions to the tube

Parents feel criticised but also acknowledge that strangers feel concerned about their child. The tube is the focus for comment rather than the baby.

- "And people think we're like, you know, bad parents or something. Friends who have got kids think we must have done something wrong that we can't feed our baby ..."
- "I had a guy in the bank one day come up to her and say, 'What's that up its nose for?' at the top of his voice .... And we've also had people who were just gorgeous. It brings out the good side in people."
- "I went out to the shops once when it was out and I really did notice a difference ... A lot of people came up and said, 'Oh look at the red hair' rather than just looking at the tube."
- "Some people think it's a bit strange. It's being cruel, you know. How can you shove something up her nose and feed her that way?"

Effect on social interaction

Complex medical conditions limit social interaction and lead to feelings of isolation. However, parents express the need to find ways to manage.

- "You can still go out sometimes and feed them out. I've done it before. It can be horrible sometimes because you do get looks."
- "I've been to playgroup committee meetings and just hung up the tube and carried on."

- "I've done them in all sorts of places. I've hung it on the tree when my cousin was getting married."
- "We've slowly started to visit our friends. At first the tube isolated him."

Need for information

Parents appreciate the teaching they received in hospital but felt a lack of written information to refer to when away from the hospital.

- "I think there needs to be a bit more … not necessarily maybe a support pack but I think definitely more information about the tube and what it's doing and how it's done, to the parents."
- "(So you learned from watching other people do it?) Yeah, and basically, when you get the um, the tube, it has instructions."

The baby's reaction to the tube

Parents perceive the baby as having a love-hate relationship with the tube. They attribute the baby with acceptance but also the wish to be rid of it.

- "I think he knows it's the only way."
- "He starts to gag or go blue. Maybe he's retaliating."
- "She's a very forgiving little person. Often after she been screaming, having the tube done she looks up as though to say, 'Well. Thank you.' She seems to know that it's necessary, that it's not a deliberate ploy on my part to torture her."
- "She loves the tube. She plays with it."

The tube as "part of the baby"

Parents perceive that the baby might think that the tube was a part of his or her body but acknowledge that the baby was aware of its intrusiveness.

- "It's part of her. If she hasn't got it in I think she looks so strange."
- "You know it's just like playing with your foot."

- "She was little at that stage, to see something like that go into her body was horrible, you know."
- "Often when she gets distressed she will try to rip it out ... but other than that that it's quite normal for her."

Responsibility

The parent who takes on most of the responsibility might express disappointment and anger towards their partner and other family members. They also feel unable to rely on the usual community support networks.

- "I panic if my partner is not here. I need someone else."
- "Try to teach someone else how to change the tube. I never did."
- "I've got a good friend who's a nurse and she said she wouldn't baby sit her."
- "You can't just rock up to a normal childcare centre and say, 'Here's my child'... They all go, 'Ooooh'".

Summary of findings

- The tube has multiple meanings, often contradictory:
  - It keeps the baby healthy, but it is unnatural and inconvenient;
  - It is part of the baby but it is an intrusion into his or her body;
  - It signifies severe illness but does not need to restrict normal life.

- Concern for their baby, and the effect of the tube on the baby, underpins many of the parents' perceptions regarding the feeding tube.
- Parents express ambivalence towards the tube and tube feeding, and about the care provided for their baby.
- Parents report anxiety about the potential for events that may threaten their baby's life and the need to be constantly vigilant.
- Responsibility for tube changes usually falls on one parent, who feels unsupported.
- The presence of the tube need not limit social interaction but uninformed members of the public cause parental frustration and anger.
- Hospital staff are generally skilled and helpful but not always consistent; some staff are inexperienced causing frustration to parents and distress to the baby.

Discussion

The aim of this study was to use a qualitative research paradigm to describe the parental experience of caring for a child who received some or all of their nutrition via a feeding tube. Only one child had undergone surgical insertion of a gastrostomy tube, and the insertion of the gastrostomy tube followed six months of NGT use. While some of the issues discussed might span the use of both types of tube feeding, most of the findings relate directly to perceptions about the use of a NGT.

As expected, separating perceptions of tube feeding from perceptions related to the baby's complex medical condition and the need for extended hospital stays was not always possible. All of the infants began life with an admission to the NICU at a major teaching hospital, some in a NICU and some in a Special Care Nursery (SCN). Experiences with hospital staff, and with the hospital environment as a whole, were clearly remembered and described by many parents. Even when a parent stated that they had difficulty remembering the first few days or weeks, when an NGT was inserted, they went on to give accounts that suggested firmly implanted memories, held close to the surface and probably influencing day to day perception of the infant and the feeding process.

In this study the experience of tube feeding for the baby can only be deduced from parental perceptions of the baby's experience. While the baby clearly responded to their parent's distress and to positive emotional expressions, specific responses to tube feeding could only be surmised.

At times, the perceptions outlined by the parents' were contradictory, perhaps reflecting a degree of ambivalence. Parents, on the one hand, were thankful towards the hospital and hospital staff for enabling their child to survive and thrive. At other times during the interviews the same parent might be critical of the hospital and staff and give clear expression of anger and frustration caused by staff behaviours and/or the hospital environment.

Ambivalence towards the tube was also expressed. The tube was hated and the source of trauma to parent and baby but was also loved by the baby and a useful means of nourishing the baby for the parent. Times without the NGT were described as a source of pleasure for the parent, a break from society's assumptions regarding the tube and enabling glimpses of the child who was more usually hidden behind the tube. The same parents had also to assure the interviewer that they loved their baby even with the tube in place.

Only one parent explicitly talked about difficulties with attachment to their baby. This mother referred to attachment by talking about the need to "make friends with" her baby because of the number of people closely involved with him in the SCN setting. The topic of parent-child interaction in the NICU and SCN environment is written about by Minde (2000) and within the field of infant mental health is a frequent focus of clinical assessment and intervention with infants with complex medical conditions. Further exploration of the attachment process in this population of tube fed, medically complex babies would be a welcome addition to the literature in this field.

This study was exploratory in nature. It revealed themes that were specific to medically complex infants, not raised in other studies involving older children from different diagnostic categories. There were also themes which were applicable across wider populations of children, similar to some of the themes outlined in the literature (Craig, Scambler & Spitz, 2003; Smith, Camfield & Camfield 1999; Thorne, 1997). The current study adds new information to the very sparse body of literature related to the needs of parents and infants when the infant has a feeding tube.

A study that focused on the experience for the baby would provide information important to the understanding of tube feeding and its impact on development of oral feeding and interaction with caregivers.

References

Benoit, D. (2000). Feeding disorders, failure to thrive, and obesity. In: C. H. Zeanah (Ed.), *Handbook of Infant Mental Health* (pp. 339–352). New York: Guilford.

Craig, G. M., Scambler, G., & Spitz, L. (2003). Why parents of children with neurodevelopmental disabilities requiring gastrostomy feeding need more support. *Developmental Medicine and Child Neurology* 45: 183–188.

Drotar, D. & Robinson, J. (2000). Developmental psychopathology of failure to thrive. In: A. J. Sameroff, M. Lewis & S. M. Miller (Eds.), *Handbook of developmental psychopathology*, 2nd edn, (pp. 351–364). New York: Plenium Press.

Dudeck-Shriber, L. (2004). Parent stress in the neonatal intensive care and the influence of parent and infant characteristics. *American Journal of Occupational Therapy, 58*: 509–520.

Flick, U. (2002). *An introduction to qualitative research.* 2nd edn. London: Sage.

Franklin, L. & Rodger, S. (2003). Parents' perspectives on feeding medically compromised children: Implications for occupational therapy. *Australian Occupational Therapy Journal 50*: 137–147.

Glaser, B. G. & Strauss, L. A. (1967). *The discovery of grounded theory: Strategies for qualitative research.* New York: Aldine de Gruyer.

Huddleston, K. C. & Ferraro, A. R. (1991). Preparing families of children with gastrostomies. *Pediatric Nursing, 17*: 153–158.

Meleski, D. (2002). Families with chronically ill children: A literature review examines approaches to helping them cope. *American Journal of Nursing 102*: 47–54.

Miles, M. B. & Huberman, A. M. (1994). *Qualitative data analysis: An expanded sourcebook* 2nd edn. London: Sage.

Minde, K. (2000). Prematurity and serious medical conditions in infancy. In: C. H. Zeanah (Ed.), *Handbook of Infant Mental Health,* (pp. 176–194). New York: Guilford.

Minichiello, V., Aroni, R., Timewell, E., & Alexander, L. (1991). *In-depth interviewing: Researching people.* Melbourne, Australia: Longman Cheshire.

O'Brien, M. & Wegner, C. B. (2002). Rearing a child who is technology dependent: Perceptions of parents and home care nurses. *Journal of the Society of Pediatric Nurses, 7*: 7–15.

Pederson, S. D., Parsons, H. G., & Dewers, D. (2004). Stress levels experienced by the parents of enterally fed children. *Child Care Health and Development, 30*: 507–513.

Radford, J., Thorne, S. & Bassingthwaighte, C. (1997). Long Term gastrostomy in children: Insights from expert nurses. *Issues in Comprehensive Pediatric Nursing, 20*: 35–50.

Rosenblum, K. (2004). Defining infant mental health. In: A. J. Sameroff, S. L. McDonough & K. L. Rosenblum (Eds.), *Treating parent–infant relationship problems—Strategies for intervention* (pp. 43–75). New York: Guilford Press.

Rouse, L., Herrington, P., Assey, J., Baker, R. & Golden, S. (2002). Feeding problems, gastrostomy and families: A qualitative pilot study. *British Journal of Learning Disabilities, 30*: 122–128.

Satter, E. (1999). The feeding relationship. In: D. B. Kessler & P. Dawson (Eds.), *Failure to thrive and pediatric nutrition: A transdisciplinary approach.* (pp. 121–145). Baltimore: Brookes.

Smith, S. W., Camfield, C. & Camfield, P. (1999). Living with cerebral palsy and tube feeding: A population-based follow-up study. *Journal of Pediatrics, 135*: 307–310.

Strauss, L. A. & Corbin, J. (1990). *Basics of qualitative research*. London: Sage.

Tawfik, R., Dickson, A., Clarke, M. & Thomas, A. G. (1997). Caregivers' perceptions following gastrostomy in severely disabled children with feeding problems. *Developmental Medicine and Child Neurology, 39*: 746–751.

Thorne, S., Radford, J., & McCormick, J. (1997). The multiple meanings of long term gastrostomy in children with severe disability. *Journal of Pediatric Nursing, 20*: 35–99.

Wallander, J. L. & Varni, J. W. (1998). Effects of pediatric physical disorders on child and family adjustment. *Journal of Child Psychology and Psychiatry, 39*: 29–46.

CHAPTER FIVE

Contingent singing as a therapeutic intervention for the hospitalised full-term neonate

Helen Shoemark

The Neonatal Music Therapy programme at The Royal Children's Hospital Melbourne (RCH) offers a family centred programme for newborn infants hospitalised at birth for major surgical or medical care. In partnership with the family, live singing is used to create opportunities for the development of neurocognitive and social capabilities. To illuminate the potential of live singing as an intersubjective experience this chapter focuses on the use of contingent singing in therapist-directed work with an infant. Such work usually occurs only when parents or family are unavailable to the infant for extended or frequent periods, but always with the permission of the parents.

The environment

The primary purpose of the Neonatal Intensive Care Unit (NICU) is the physical survival of prematurely born and full-term infants with high-risk medical conditions at birth. There are no maternity facilities at RCH, so infants are transferred from the hospital in which they were born, often on the first day. Many undergo surgery on that day and certainly within the first weeks of life, while others will remain hospitalised for extended diagnostic tests and medical care.

Traditionally, high-risk infants have been under-researched because of their unpredictable and complicated clinical pathways. However research is now emerging to characterise outcomes for neurodevelopment (Brosig et al., 2007), mother–infant interaction (Faugli et al., 2008), risk of psychopathology (Faugli et al., 2008) and early predictors of mental health issues for adolescents (Faugli et al., 2008). From a study of toddlers with major birth defects requiring surgery, Laing (2010) and colleagues recommended that preventative programmes should occur at the earliest possible opportunity. As medical and surgical care of medically fragile infants improves, such programmes can commence in the newborn period during the hospital admission.

Why use music?

Music is commonly recognised by its organising elements of pulse, rhythm, tonality, and melody. Each element forms a different key for the musical styles we love—melody for ballads, rhythm for rock and roll etc. (Shoemark, 1994). The more subtle elements such as tempo, register, timbre, and attack are often neglected in terms of their intrinsic value but have been significantly acknowledged as pivotal aspects of interaction between mother and infant (Malloch, 1999; Stern, 1982). In work with neonates and infants, the music therapist consciously employs these naturally occurring elements for therapeutic benefit (de l'Etoile, 2006a, 2006b; O'Gorman, 2006, 2005; Trevarthen & Malloch, 2000).

Neonatal music therapy

Music therapy is one of the allied health services provided to families in the NICU and Special Care nurseries at RCH. The programme is organised in two frameworks: infant-focused and family-centred work utilising live music making and recorded music for different purposes. The basis for using recorded music is articulated in the work of Standley and others whose research has focused on the safety and suitability of the stimulus for premature infants (Caine, 1991; Cassidy & Ditty, 1998; Cassidy & Standley, 1995; Schwartz & Ritchie, 1999; Shoemark, 1998; Standley, 1996). The predominant theme in neonatal music therapy research is to examine the physiological impact of the stimulus, with the intention of maintaining homeostasis. However in clinical work with full-term infants, there is an evident need to address the infant's social availability and developmental readiness within a contingent relationship. Structured intervention such as music therapy can be used to compensate for the lack of naturally occurring stimulation and interaction available in the Unit. It may serve to reassure the infant that other kinds of relationships will be available (Shoemark, 2004). It has been suggested that in addition to vital interaction with parents, the therapeutic relationship may serve as a useful opportunity for additional rehearsal of positive interaction. The well-prepared therapist brings a contained presence without the extremes of emotional presence, which accompany parents in crisis. With refined skills of attunement this is a strongly bounded relationship.

A referral for ongoing developmental work with an infant is made when a long hospital admission is evident (the hospital regards four weeks or more as a long admission). This may occur because the infant is either recovering from surgery and establishing feeding, or may be waiting to grow and put on weight prior to surgery. It is a phase of relative wellness, during which there are windows of opportunity for development. More significantly, it is a time when parents begin to recover from the initial crisis, and often need support in seeing their developing baby rather than just the "sick child" (Dun, 1999). The referral can also occur if the family is in some way compromised in their ability to be present for the infant often because of physical distance or ability to travel.

At the point of referral, the age range of infants is commonly from about two weeks to sixteen weeks of age. It is a time when infants should be learning that their vocal and gestural expressions have an effect on those around them. So, the question is—what happens when the environment is largely non-contingent? If the infant cries out during a procedure, the procedure will not be stopped. His primary carers cannot "save" him, and when procedures are repeated often, what does he learn about his ability to influence the world? This is exemplified in the care of infants who have oesophageal atresia, a condition in which the oesophagus does not connect to the stomach, but ends in a sack. While the infant awaits surgery for this condition, all secretions which pool at the bottom of the oesophagus must be removed to prevent aspiration into the lungs. This is achieved by one of two means. Continuous suctioning of the secretions is achieved via a "replogle" tube which is a fine tube inserted via the mouth down the oesophagus and held in place by a string and tape on the infant's face. It is attached to a machine which is dependent on gravity and so it is located on the floor and thus the infant is restricted to the bed. Alternatively, the nurse or parent inserts a fine tube down into the oesophagus and "vacuums" the secretions out. This occurs regularly, and for some infants as frequently as every twenty minutes. During the procedure, the infant cannot breathe, and it causes immense distress. This repeated trauma is life-preserving, and must occur.

I feel strongly that the infant needs to experience sensitively contingent relationships which may serve to balance negative experiences over which they have no control. In a world which is anything but normal, opportunity for self-regulation, non-distress expression and communication is so dramatically diminished, that the creation of a therapeutic relationship provides unique opportunities for this achievement. There is a basic assumption in this that the infant and therapist can establish a relationship in which the infant can understand the intention of the therapist through her voice and thus can make use of opportunities for self-regulation. Broadly, this application of music as therapy is strongly framed by dynamic systems theory in which any action of an individual is interpreted by the behaviour of both partners (Jaffe et al., 2001). The contingent relationship provides opportunities for dyadic achievement which represents an expanded state of consciousness (Tronick, 1998). The infant may rehearse the implicit relational procedures (Lyons-Ruth, 1998) of how to simply "be" with another person, and convey feelings and needs without words or even voice.

Therefore with infants experiencing extended admission to hospital in the neonatal phase, the aim of live music making is to:

- Encourage self and mutual-regulation through contingent interaction.
- Provide opportunities for non-distress gestural, facial and vocal expression.

Live singing is commonly applied as an interactive technique, drawing heavily on the principle of infant-directed singing in which the singer holds the infant in his mind so perceptibly that not only does the infant detect it, but so do naïve listeners (Papousek & Papousek, 1991; Trehub et al., 1993).

The music therapist consciously utilises all the features of infant-directed speech and distils them into "contingent singing" (Malloch et al., 2012) which can be brought into the relationship at any time or place. Bergeson and Trehub (2002) demonstrated that mothers' singing is more consistent in rendition than their speech, thus providing their infant with a more recognisable stimulus each time. As consistency and predictability are sorely lacking in the NICU, song becomes a potent vehicle in therapeutic interplay.

In therapy, the song may be well-known or improvised. The infant may not have an existing repertoire, so the song is reflective of the situation at hand (Shoemark, 2011). As in Ann Morgan's work (cited in Thomson-Salo & Paul, 2001), the therapist's selection of technique, and elements within it, is in direct response to the client. Song provides an intersubjective space for interaction with her client.

I maintain that the lesser-acknowledged elements of register and timbre (smoothness and breathiness) reflect the implicit elements of contingency and contribute a significant potential in the adult-infant therapeutic relationship (Shoemark, 2003). The following case vignette serves to illustrate how the conscious use of these musical elements might support the infant.

Frank

At thirty-five-weeks and two days' gestation, Frank was born with the assistance of low forceps. He needed stimulation and additional oxygen to increase his intake. He was "growth retarded" and the diagnosis of oesophageal atresia was confirmed. He had surgery on day one to create a gastrostomy so he could be fed directly to his stomach. The surgeon also determined that it was a long gap between the bottom of his oesophagus and his stomach which meant that it would be nearly twelve weeks before until Frank's oesophagus grew sufficiently for the surgery to take place.

While he waited for the operation, Frank had a replogle tube taped in place. This caused him visible discomfort, and he was often irritable. He wore mittens most of the time to prevent his opportunistic attempts to remove the tube. The connected machine was not portable and thus Frank was confined to bed. He could be lifted above the bed to have the bedding changed, and he could be raised into the vertical plane to look around, but he could not leave his bed in the corner of the ward. Here he remained for six weeks.

Initially Frank's mother remained in the maternity hospital with medical complications, but on discharge she visited him daily. Frank did not develop self-consoling behaviours such as finger sucking, self-stroking or holding. He could not make the transition from wake to sleep without external assistance and he slept poorly. His threshold for stimulation was very low, and even sensitive and nurturing interaction was not well-tolerated. He would often strain as if to pass a bowel motion, and as this can be a sign of over-stimulation, our work proceeded very gently.

I met Frank when he was nearly eight weeks old. On my first visit, I positioned myself in his field of vision; he seemed to be aware of me, and so after a moment I spoke to him in a supportive and undemanding tone (soft, breathy, high register, with descending intonation). In response, he exhibited surprise (eye wide enough to see the sclera (the white) all around, mouth open, arms presenting with jerky movement and fingers splayed), moving fairly quickly into hiccups, a stronger cue of disengagement (Lieb et al., 1980). It was clear that his tolerance for stimulation was instantly reached, and the process of interaction between us would proceed very slowly. With this primary evidence of his dysregulation, my objective was to support his return to a calm state. Aware that any stimulation could cause this response, I spoke in short soothing phrases, leaving a longer than usual silence between the phrases (but with my face bright, eye-brows raised, mouth smiling (Sullivan & Lewis, 2003). Over a few minutes, he became accustomed to the predictable pattern of the spoken phrases and regulated back into a calm state. I concluded the session shortly thereafter. Given his extreme response to infant-directed speech I did not use singing in this first session, as I felt it may be a new stimulus too far outside his realm of expectation (Beebe & Lachmann, 1994).

The second session was similar to the first: his initial surprise at the sound of my voice, and a gentle acclimation to it. The second session included a brief phrase of infant-directed singing. As he successfully strained for a bowel motion, I commented to him lightly that he was trying to "poo". He looked at me more intently and with interest (turned to look, brow slightly raised, mouth slightly open). A word spoken by the therapist that draws the infant's attention serves as turning point for a transition into singing (as does highly intonated speech or a strong gestural action from the infant). The word "poo" is often appealing to infants, perhaps because of the combination of plosive and vowel (p-oo). With this interest, I transitioned into singing, using our keyword "poo", as the basis for the improvised song:

> I sing a song for me and you, [pause]
> Helen sings, and Frank does poo. [pause]
> I sing a song for me and you, [pause]
> Helen sings and Frank does poo. [pause]
> Yes he does, yes he does.

The first two lines were repeated both lyrically and melodically, and the final phrase ("Yes he does, yes he does") concluded downward. At the end of each phrase, the pause afforded him time to respond gesturally, facially, or vocally. Initially, he responded to the song as a new stimulus—his eyes widened. This response did not escalate, and so he accommodated my offering. To keep this experience safely within his expectation, I repeated the song several times, with Frank coping well as it progressed (more relaxed tone in his body and face). When he regulated the stimulus by looking away, I concluded the song, returned to the more familiar supportive speech and concluded the session. Importantly I learnt that Frank was able to cope with singing as a medium and within that field of interplay, he regulated his state.

In the third session, my starting point was again very simple. His mother had indicated that his preference for positioning was to be held in a semi-reclined seated position. I brought him up into this position, offering a positive smiling face, and some simple verbal description of what we were doing. As before, he began with wide eyes and jittery arms movements. I sought to reassure him by using a high vocal register (reminiscent of his mother), with a light and breathy timbre, my face in a relaxed smile. I asked him, "Do you have stories for me today?" His movements stilled, and he fixed his gaze on my face. In the silence after my question, he moved his hands slightly and smoothly, and his brow lifted just perceptibly. I affirmed this response of calm interest by nodding my head gently and using a melodically descending "Yes". I repeated the question and he repeated his response. On the basis of this calm interest, I shifted my expectation towards greater interplay, and asked, "Shall we sing a song?" To minimise disruption I re-introduced the "poo" song from the preceding session (one day before). I used the same melodic line, but modified lyrics for this session:

> Yesterday we sang a song [short pause]
> A song for me, a song for you, [short pause]
> Helen sang and Frank did poo.

I reproduced the short phrases several times, and he coped well with this (body quite still and eyes fixed on me). With this increased attunement, I pursued a more active response from him. At the end of each line I asked "Yeah?", using a high-pitched, upturned melodic interval. My brow was raised and head tilted in inquiry. He responded by uttering a small open vowel sound, and his face seemed to relax. Twice more he responded vocally or with smooth gesture. Then he broke his gaze and gently looked away. It was enough.

The work continued with Frank for eleven sessions prior to his surgery. I went on leave and on my return he had been discharged.

The conscious employment of musical elements in contingent singing provided a finely attuned and sensitive interplay in which Frank was acknowledged and supported. The breathy and light timbre of my voice was strongly reminiscent of the "loving" tone used for lullabies (Rock et al., 1999) thus providing a nurturing support, while upturned melodic interval at the end of the lyric phrase gently enticed his more active participation. The replicated song offered Frank consistency and continuity. In the "space" of the song, Frank was comfortable enough to utter positive vocalisations which established his purposeful and positive engagement with another person.

Conclusion

The non-prosodic aspects of the human voice are only now being scrutinised for their impact in naturally occurring and therapeutic intervention (Norman, 2001; Trevarthen & Malloch, 2000). In the work with newborn hospitalised infants, voice is our most powerful and consistently available interpersonal tool. When the voice is consciously used in a therapeutic relationship, the potency of the interplay is enhanced by consideration of the musical elements employed. In work with hospitalised neonates and infants, the elements of pitch, melody, rhythm, timbre, and silence become vital elements in creating a meaningful and safe intersubjective space for therapeutic interplay.

While the spoken word is a transitory auditory experience, song may be easily replicated. It offers a comfortable and familiar "space" for the infant and adult which can be repeated and varied as required. Music is powerful in both its range and depth of subtlety. In music therapy, contingent singing and song can be controlled to offer hospitalised neonates and infants opportunities for reassuring companionship.

Further research into the elements of music is warranted to develop a protocol for use by those responsible for enhancing the wellbeing of the hospitalised infant.

Acknowledgement

This case vignette is drawn from the "Music Therapy for Vulnerable Infants Study" supported by an Australian Research Council Linkage Project Grant, LP0219693. The grant was administered by MARCS Auditory Laboratories, University of Western Sydney, and conducted in collaboration with The Royal Children's Hospital, Melbourne.

References

Beebe, B. & Lachmann, F. (1994). Representation and internalisation in infancy: Three principles of salience. *Psychoanalytic Psychology, 11*: 127–165.

Bergeson, T. & Trehub, S. (2002). Absolute pitch and tempo on mothers' songs to infants. *Psychological Science, 13*: 72–75.

Brosig, C., Mussatto, A., Kuhn, E., & Tweddell, J. (2007). Neurodevelopmental outcome in preschool survivors of complex congenital heart disease: Implications for clinical practice. *Journal of Pediatric Healthcare*, Jan/Feb: 3–12.

Caine, J. (1991). The effects of music on selected stress behaviors, weight, caloric and formula intake, and length of stay of premature and low birth-weight neonates in a neonatal intensive care unit. *Journal of Music Therapy, 28*: 180–192.

Cassidy, J. & Ditty, K. (1998). Presentation of aural stimuli to newborns and premature infants: an audiological perspective. *Journal of Music Therapy, 35*: 70–97.

Cassidy, J. & Standley, J. (1995). The effect of music listening on physiological responses of premature infants in the NICU. *Journal of Music Therapy, 32*: 208–227.

de l'Etoile, S. (2006a). Infant behavioral responses to infant-directed singing and other maternal interactions. *Infant Behavior & Development, 29*: 456–470.

de l'Etoile, S. (2006b). Infant-directed singing: A theory for intervention. *Music Therapy Perspectives, 24*: 22–29.

Dun, B. (1999). Creativity and communication: aspects of music therapy in a children's hospital. In: A. Aldridge, (Ed.), *Music therapy in palliative care: New voices* (pp. 59–67). London: Jessica Kingsley.

Faugli, A., Emblem, R., Veenstra, M., Bjørnland, K., & Diseth, T. (2008). Does esophageal atresia influence the mother–infant interaction? *Journal of Pediatric Surgery, 43*: 1796–1801.

Jaffe, J., Beebe, B., Feldstein, S., Crown, C., & Jasnow, M. (2001). Rhythms of dialogie in infancy: Co-ordinated timing in development. *Monographs of the Society for Research in Child Development, 66*: vi–131.

Laing, S., McMahon, C., Ungerer, J., Taylor, A., Badawi, N., & Spence, K. (2010). Mother–child interaction and child developmental capacities in toddlers with major birth defects requiring newborn surgery. *Early Human Development, 86*: 793–800.

Lieb, S., Benfield, D., & Guidubalki, J. (1980). Early effects of intervention and stimulation of the preterm infant. *Pediatrics, 66*: 83–90.

Lyons-Ruth, K. (1998). Implicit relational knowing: Its role in development and psychoanalytic treatment. *Infant Mental Health Journal, 19*: 282–289.

Malloch, S. (1999). Mother and infants and communicative musicality. *Musicae Scientificae*, Special Issue, 29–57.

Malloch, S., Shoemark, H., Newnham, C., Črnčec, R., Paul, C., Prior, M., Coward, S., & Burnham, D. (2012). Music Therapy with Hospitalised Infants—the Art and Science of Intersubjectivity. *Infant Mental Health Journal, 33*: 386–399.

Norman, J. (2001). The psychoanalyst and the baby: A new look at work with infants. *International Journal of Psychoanalysis, 82*: 83–100.

O'Gorman, S. (2005). The infant's mother: Facilitating an experience of infant-directed singing with the mother in mind. *British Journal of Music Therapy, 19*: 22–30.

O'Gorman, S. (2006). Theoretical interfaces in the acute paediatric context: A psychotherapeutic understanding of the application of infant-directed singing. *American Journal of Psychotherapy, 60*: 271–283.

Papousek, H. & Papousek, M. (1991). The meanings of melodies in motherese in tone and stress languages. *Infant Behaviour and Development, 14*: 415–440.

Rock, A., Trainor, L., & Addison, T. (1999). Distinctive message in infant-directed lullabies and play-songs. *Developmental Psychology, 35*: 527–534.

Schwartz, F. & Ritchie, R. (1999). Music listening in neonatal intensive care units. In: C. Dileo (Ed.), *Music Therapy & Medicine: Theoretical and Clinical Applications*. (pp. 13–22). Silver Springs, MD: American Music Therapy Association.

Shoemark, H. (1994). The process of music therapy as it relates to the development of children with multiple disabilities. In: A. Lem (Ed.), *Music Therapy Collection* (pp. 45–49). Canberra: Ausdance.

Shoemark, H. (1998). Indications for the inclusion of music therapy in the care of infants with Bronchopulmonary Dysplasia. In: A. Wigram &

J. DeBacker (Eds.), *Clinical applications of music therapy in developmental disability, paediatrics, and neurology* (pp. 32–46). London: Jessica Kingsley.

Shoemark, H. (2003). *Let's start at the very beginning: Early intervention for chronically ill newborn infants.* Paper presented at the twenty-ninth National Music Therapy Conference, Brisbane.

Shoemark, H. (2004). Family-centred music therapy for infants with complex medical and surgical needs. In: M. Nocker-Ribaupierre, (Ed.), *Music Therapy for Premature and Newborn Infants* (pp. 141–157). Gilsum NH: Barcelona Publishers.

Shoemark, H. (2011). Contingent singing: The musicality of companionship with the hospitalized newborn infant. In: F. Baker & S. Uhlig (Eds.), *Therapeutic Voicework in Music Therapy* (pp. 229–249). London: Jessica Kingsley.

Standley, J. (1996). Music research in medical/dental treatment: An update of a prior meta-analysis. In: C. E. Furman (Ed.), *Effectiveness of music therapy procedures: Documentation of research and clinical practice* (pp. 1–60). Silver Spring MD: National Association for Music Therapy.

Standley, J. & Moore, R. (1995). Therapeutic effects of music and mother's voice on premature infants. *Pediatric Nursing, 21*: 509–512, 574.

Stern, D., Spieker, S., & MacKain, K. (1982). Intonation contours as signals in maternal speech to prelinguistic infants. *Developmental Psychology, 18*: 727–735.

Sullivan, M. & Lewis, M. (2003). Emotional expressions of young infants and children: a practitioner's primer. *Infants and Young Children, 16*: 120–143.

Thomson-Salo, F. & Paul, C. (2001). Some principles of infant–parent psychotherapy: Ann Morgan's contribution. The Signal, Nos 1–2, WAIMH.

Trainor, L., Austin, C., & Desjardin, R. (2000). Is infant-directed speech prosody a result of the vocal expression of emotion? *Psychological Science, 11*: 188–195.

Trehub, S., Unyk, A., & Trainor, L. (1993). Adults identify infant-directed music across cultures. *Infant Behavior and Development, 16*: 913–212.

Trevarthen, C. & Malloch, S. (2000). The dance of wellbeing: defining the musical therapeutic effect. *Nordic Journal of Music Therapy, 9*: 3—17.

Tronick, E. (1998). Dyadically expanded states of consciousness and the process of therapeutic change. *Infant Mental Health Journal, 19*: 290–299.

CHAPTER SIX

Two children in acute wards

Sue Morse

I. "I see you"—Intensive Care Unit: Peter

Being admitted to a neonatal or paediatric intensive care unit is by necessity about survival. Life or death is the question. The body is the focus, the person secondary to the constituent parts—blood pressure, electroencephalograms, heart rate, temperature, and the anomalies that have brought the small person there in the first place. The focus shifts between the body and the machines that decipher and monitor the body's condition. Parents are drawn to watch the machines and listen for the alarms reassuring themselves that there is life. It is precious— more than the survival of the body is at stake.

It is a paradox that to survive the infant must, in fact, give up. In contrast to the gradual stabilisation and regulation of physiology the infant achieves for himself in the neonatal period, the infant in an Intensive Care Unit (ICU) must give up basic control of the physiology to the machines and the medical system which works on the infant's behalf, for example, a giving over of control of breathing to a ventilator, control of hunger and satiation to a schedule of nasogastric feeds. This work occurs twenty-four hours a day by dedicated teams, the lights do not go out, it is never quite silent, and someone is always monitoring, looking and listening for the machines to alarm, following the schedule of care.

What does this "giving up" control of the fundamental physiology mean for the infant's development of self-regulation and autonomy, the understanding of their body? How does this dependency and special care affect the development of the infant's attachments and relationships? How can parents see the development of their child when their view can be dominated by the medical discourse and the requirement that they require intensive nursing skills (rather than parenting skills) in order for their child to survive at home? How does the infant constitute an identity as a subject when so treated as a special and fragile object?

These questions are not easy but, with them in mind, I would like to tell you part of the story of Peter, who had been on life support from the moment of birth. It is part of a story that I have chosen to try and amplify the voice that is not often heard.

Peter at one week of age lay quietly and fraily in his humidicrib. He had a ventilator tube in one nostril, a nasogastric tube in the other. He had plastic lines into his veins on his hand and the red light of his oximeter on his finger. His dummy lay just in front of his face. The nappy folded across his neck and face acted to prevent him scratching his face. He slept.

Peter was born three weeks early by planned caesarean section. Ultrasound had identified a complex syndrome with many anomalies. It was planned that he be born early, go immediately on to a ventilator and have two essential operations; a colostomy and vesicostomy, so that he could poo and wee. It was then discovered that Peter could not breathe on his own. One diaphragm did not move because of a phrenic nerve palsy, and it was not clear that the other was sufficient.

The doctors' speculation was that Peter's quality of life was going to be poor and they advised turning off the machines that supported him. The family was constantly present—anger was split off and directed toward the medical decision-making team. His parents, in contrast to giving up, were ever seeking the next procedure in order to ensure their son's survival. They had great trust. The decision was made when Peter was eight months to perform a tracheotomy. His ventilator would be connected to his tracheostomy tube, thus allowing Peter more freedom to move and experience the world and decrease the aversive procedural care of suctioning from his nose and mouth.

Meeting Peter

I met Peter when he was nearly nine months old. I was asked to help him with his transition to oral feeding and to assist his communication—both things that he must do for himself. The plan was to get him home before he turned one year of age—hence the shift to life and developmental skills. At this stage he had never seen anyone eat, or even had the taste of food in his mouth, had not sat in a bath of water and had not been outside the room that he was in on the unit. His world and experience was not the usual.

Peter was cute and able to engage with his eyes and quick smile, both evident on our first meeting. We looked and smiled at each other and I talked to him gently, telling him who I was and showing him some toys. He looked at them but did not reach for them. When I put them in his hands he would play. He did not mind me touching his toes or hands. He made no sound but was alert to the sounds around him. A baby across the room started to cry with a procedure. A look of anxiety came across his face and he dissolved into silent tears. He looked at me with what felt like helplessness. I thought of a kind of empathy, a sharing of suffering, perhaps a fear of "Was I next?" I looked about and wondered—who else noticed Peter's pain?

Peter's eyes gripped mine. I tried to look back with empathy and understanding. Was he making the most of what he could get? An opportunist? After all, we had only just met. When I had to leave I told him that I would be back. He cried but made no effort to move or watch me go. I felt a degree of futility—it was useless to protest.

On subsequent visits I saw how he was fearful at times of procedures for example, taking blood, changing his tracheostomy tube. He would appeal with his eyes which those around him avoided. His mother would leave the room expressing her own distress as she was phobic of needles and found his distress unbearable. Peter would frequently fall asleep.

He had a small group of preferred toys, and videos were played for him. The video playing on the TV screen was a consistent, even predictable, narrative into which Peter and his mother escaped—blocking out the world around. These stories have stayed an important part of his imaginary discourse.

What did my turning up mean for Peter and indeed his mother and father? I felt that he and his mother had adapted to life, streetwise in social survival in ICU. Peter was cute, he captured people with a smile, was even perhaps promiscuous, consoling himself with sleep or videos or rapid shifts of attention. Everyone thought that he was a beautiful boy, a great kid, very brave—about this there was no doubt. However I felt that what was not seen was his sadness, his tendency to be over-whelmed and his passivity—so easily mistaken for co-operation. Why did he not reach out in charge of his body and take what he wanted, rather than wait for it to come to him when someone else obliged?

My task was to see Peter as the subject that he was, without avoiding the pain. To not be duped by his "false self" (Winnicott, 1960). Many times this meant most practically not leaving him in the lurch when procedures interrupted our sessions but to stay and not avoid his eyes, and use words that acknowledged his feelings. My task was to be real and different. To stand in a position of difference to the medical dis-course that dominated the staff and often the parents' view. By this I mean to notice but not privilege his machines and anomalies above him as a person. To offer my gaze as a mirror that might reflect his true self (Winnicott, 1967). To truly see him.

To be different in ICU meant not to come and go but to linger and take him in. To give sustained attention and to notice and respond to Peter's agenda—indeed to expect him to have one. His mother, with me, learned to wait a moment to allow space for him to look at a toy offered, to acknowledge his request before giving it to him. The look became a point, the pointing a statement of what he wanted. The want that belonged to him.

His parents discovered that it was they and not the machines that would support this psychological shift. The second year of Peter's life was substantially changed by his transition to home. His mother felt that finally she could bring her baby home. She could not wait to get up to her baby overnight because that is what mothers do.

Peter had begun to point and so, following this lead, we introduced ordinary gestural language—hand out for request and waving good-bye. We also introduced some formal sign language—"dog" since they had one and "bath" for that strange sensory experience in water about which he was so frightened. Words mean power, a triumph of symbol-ism over the experience.

Peter had begun to initiate and own his body in the movements of play and communication. Could Peter begin to find his voice? Even when he was no longer on a ventilator and was breathing for himself with sufficient space around his tracheostomy tube for air passage, he did not seem to realise that he had a voice. When his tracheostomy was removed he still cried silently. In fact Peter had never heard his own voice since being ventilated from birth. Ventilators push air into the lungs. While air goes in it displaces air up through the vocal cords. Vocal noises are made on the inspiratory phase of the ventilator's cycle. In order for Peter to make voice he had to learn to reverse the phonation pattern of the ventilator and make his voice occur on expiration—like all of us.

This he learned in a fairly deliberate way through play with microphones, animal noises and so on. His voice was first incorporated into his affective expression when he surprised himself with laughter. It took some time for him to use his voice when crying.

By the time he attended kindergarten and was preparing for school the following year Peter had come a long way in his growth and development. He spoke for himself, could learn, was physically active, did not like needles, got anxious in large groups and was hypersensitive to noise. He remained frightened of eating saying that he might choke and die, although he did have a small range of foods, which he relished. He scored in the lower average range on standardised tests of language and cognitive ability, and had friends. The drama of his health was significantly more settled and yet the dramas of his relationships stormed around him. His mother complained of his activity, his overfriendliness to strangers, his demand for attention, his repetitive questions—the answers to which he already knew.

There is no doubt that Peter is a vulnerable boy in a vulnerable system. Thousands of dollars have been spent on his physical survival and scarcely anything on his psychological survival. There are few articles in a Medline search looking at psychological or adaptive outcomes of children who have lived in our medical systems. It seems urgent that once commenced on a fight for life within our medical systems there be no giving up on the infant's and families' fight for psychological survival. Creating a different space, a psychological space in intensive care, is a priority.

II. A toddler living with cancer: Adam

Adam had taken his first steps and spoken his first words. He and Miss Pig, his transitional object, had already been through an enormous amount of growing up. But there was something wrong. Adam seemed to be giving up on walking, crying to be carried. His smiling face looked more often miserable, he became clingy and at times when crawling he would put his head to the cool floor and just lie there. Later he started vomiting. His parents had taken him to doctors but it took several weeks for his vague signs to be understood and a clear diagnosis made.

Children and brain tumours are two concepts not usually thought of in the same moment and yet childhood brain tumours are the second most frequent malignancy of childhood and the most common form of solid tumour. The US National Cancer Institute reports that tumours of the central nervous system comprise twenty-two per cent of all malignancies occurring among children up to fourteen-years of age and ten per cent of tumours occurring among fifteen to nineteen-year-olds (http://nci.nih.gov December 2004). In general five year survival figures are quoted at around fifty per cent with significant morbidity in terms of neurological, cognitive and behavioural outcomes (National Cancer Institute, 2004).

For families this diagnosis is of catastrophic proportions: an embarking on a roller coaster of "treatment" with an uncertain end. Survival becomes a major focus particularly in the crisis phase of the illness, but does not entirely go away as families must live with the anticipation of loss (Rolland, 1990). The world of the family is challenged, the ordinary assumptions that a child will outlive the parent, that life and future can be planned, that parents can control what happens are sorely tested by the illness and the adjustments necessary for treatment (Giammona & Malek, 2002). Children endure enormous stress on their body and psyche as they submit to the treatments that offer the hope of cure. Parents suffer, blaming themselves, guilty for feeling so angry or helpless.

Research recognises that children with cancer are at an increased risk of psychosocial difficulties during their adjustment to treatment that is, coping with hospitalisation, invasive procedures, effects of chemotherapy and feeling ill, however generally this is seen as a temporary phenomena which dissipates after children are well and return to school (Vannatta & Gerhardt, 2003). However longer term effects for children who survive may include physical health and appearance as well as functional capacity for example, fatigue or endurance, and may not be immediately apparent at the end of treatment but become so as the child grows and matures (Vannatta & Gerhardt, 2003).

The subgroup of children with brain tumours appears more at risk for sustained psychosocial difficulties, particularly if very young, due to their central nervous system disorder and the effects of the treatment to their developing brain (Vannatta & Gerhardt, 2003). Stargatt and Anderson (2004), in their study of the neuropsychological, behavioural, and academic outcomes of children with posterior fossa tumours in particular, found that outcomes were determined by a range of medical, psychosocial, and environmental factors. A broad developmental view suggests that children with brain tumours who survive, experience behaviour and emotional disturbance at the time of diagnosis, and for those who have posterior fossa tumours this increases over the first twelve months of treatment (Stargatt & Anderson, 2004). For their cohort, the main behavioural problems related to psychological distress such as anxiety, depression or withdrawal.

At the heart of the tragedy, there is a child: a child who, despite needing to somehow cope with the rigours of illness and treatment, has a life to be lived. It is this life that is at risk, not only by the uncertainty of prognosis for the body but by the tendency for the medical emergency to obstruct or overwhelm ordinary life relationships and experiences. The following is an account of a therapeutic intervention for Adam while living in hospital, a toddler trying to grow and meet the developmental tasks and challenges of becoming himself.

Initial recovery and establishment of a relationship

Adam's brainstem tumour was diagnosed when he was fifteen-months of age. It was in the posterior fossa region at the base of his brain resting next to and infiltrating into the delicate structures of the brainstem which are responsible for vital body functions such as respiration and swallowing. In a long procedure his surgeon removed what was possible, unable to fully resect the tumour because of its difficult position. Adam was ventilated in intensive care for two weeks before transfer to the neurosurgery ward where he would stay for the next two and a half months. He suffered significant morbidity. Following surgery Adam could not swallow his saliva or manage his own airway. He was dependent on supplementary oxygen, could not hold his body up against gravity without full support. He needed a tracheostomy tube for breathing, a gastrostomy tube for nutrition, and time to stabilise and recover, while ongoing plans for his medical treatment were made.

Adam was referred for assistance with his communication and eating. I went to meet them. I was probably not the last of a long line of others they had met since coming to the ward. The parents' look of bewilderment changed to "Oh, you're Sue, we've been waiting for you." The ward had told them that I could help, and I was aware immediately of their expectation or anxious demand. Adam looked alarmed, searching to catch his mother's gaze, worried about who I was or what I would be doing. I tried to appear reassuring and moved back and away, turning towards his mother and father and talking quietly. It was clear that his parents knew that he did not feel safe and used their gaze, voice and touch to respond to his distress and anxiety. These first exchanges in which I was both participant and witness revealed not only Adam's fearful and vulnerable state, but also his capacity to seek comfort and security within his relationships with his parents.

Adam's fearfulness of people and withdrawal and panic when encroached upon, put a limit on what type of assessment I, and others, might do to investigate his capacities to act on his own behalf that is, to swallow, poke out his own tongue etc. This behaviour also helped to prioritise a focus of intervention. Observation of his use of his own body, an account of his medical history and careful listening to the story his parents related were the initial sources for clinical decision-making around eating, talking, and feeling safe. For Adam's eating there was no immediate urgency as his nutritional needs were managed already by gastrostomy tube, and it was evident that he was requiring suction multiple times each day. Adam and his parents struggle to understand and recover in the face of their stress and sense of loss, and recapturing their sense of agency or autonomy were the compelling priorities for intervention.

Damasio (2003), in his book, *Looking for Spinoza*, reminds us that the biological nature of organisms and the complex nature of regulation of state of all body systems, are geared towards not only survival, but for humans what we consider wellness and wellbeing. This notion that the body wants to and is active in trying to recover and return itself to balance places the baby's biology in an active partnership with medical treatment rather than merely a passive recipient. Bowlby's (1982) attachment system is an example of a complex regulation of behaviours between people in the interest of survival. Adam's fear on my arrival activated him to seek proximity, that is, search for his mother, who was then able to soothe and comfort and help him feel once more secure. This was a strong point to acknowledge with his parents; that their child was trying to become well and that they had a role to play beyond endurance. An essential task is to understand the symptoms, behaviours, or defences that the child is using as their unique way of trying to manage the situation. Greenspan (2002) underlines the importance of this in helping the child feel safe and develop a sense of security. He writes of the child's need to be with their family where there is trust and a nurturing relationship, which takes precedence over the hustle and bustle of activity surrounding them. Play, behaviour, and verbal exchanges are listened to with empathy and understood as a prelude to reassurance. The wider system of care has a responsibility to promote an environment, that is, support the capacities of parents and the infant–parent relationship, so that they can be as responsive and containing as possible in the challenging culture of a hospital ward.

The medical and nursing team moved Adam to his own room. This became a safe haven where the random interruptions, noise, and activity could be better regulated, thus minimising ongoing distress (Scheeringa & Gaensbauer, 2000). As the routines of living and care became clearer, his parents felt more in control and Adam more secure. I would arrive at Adam's room and knock at the door, establishing my routine by announcing I was there to talk, first with his parents but eventually with Adam directly. I would look at and say hello to Adam and Miss Pig, but not move towards them. In this way my position was different to many of the others involved in his care, who needed to approach and act on his body in some way. At the end of the bed I talked to his mother or father, found out what was happening, listened to concerns, provided the technical information that they requested. I stayed tuned to Adam, responding to things Adam did in a general way, commenting or smiling. Each visit I would be slightly closer or respond directly and more frequently to Adam, expecting that he might relate but not demanding it. It took several days of gradual exposure for his curiosity to surpass his fear. One morning, he held out his hand for my pen, his own initiation of an act of request. I gave it to him and his gaze shifted from my pen, to my face, and to my diary. I "got the message". This new relationship to a hospital person had begun and was signed in scribble in my diary.

This moment where Adam made a request of me, was a moment where he acted as a subject on his own behalf, a moment of "treatment" where his self was taken up, rather than his body acted upon. Perhaps a moment of living his life.

Mapping a new world and remembering the one that is

Adam's recovery continued and he gradually became stronger, tolerating sitting supported on his parent's lap or in his bed. The ordinary care routines of a toddler's life for example, sleeping, dressing, having a wash, changing nappies, wiping noses, were expanded to include suction, tracheostomy tube changes, gastrostomy feeds, stomal care, medications, resuscitations. His range of toys grew to include suction catheters, syringes, medical packaging and the like. His parents became proficient with these new aspects of his care as they were incorporated into their repertoire, and Adam's tolerance grew. As well as learning the new, his parents and I engaged in a process of conversation and remembering who their son already was. Together they remembered his preferences and pleasures, his mood and reactions, the language of their own interaction with him.

We embarked on the process of developing trust, through interaction, play, and fun. Adam enjoyed small figurines of characters that he knew. We would line them up along his bed and he would point to the one that I should knock over and then tell me to put them all back. This we repeated again and again. One of the legacies of Adam's tumour was that he had impaired control of his breathing, so that he was prone to "breath holding" attacks, causing him to lose consciousness and require active assistance with breathing. In this way there was a constant lived repetition of the drama of life and death for him and his family, and his parents were required to learn the art of resuscitation as if it was an "ordinary" event. This circular routine of knock-them-over, stand-them-up again was like an enactment of his illness and recovery, over and over again. Despite this ongoing ordeal, gradually the figurines walked, chased Miss Pig, hid and surprised, and Adam's affect increased in range and he became more daring. We talked about the changes to his body, the extra body parts in effect, that is his tracheostomy tube, gastrostomy tube, oxygen mask. The childhood game of pointing to eyes, nose, and mouth was transformed to include these new body sites. His mother gave me a name, "Little Sue with the long hair" as she intuitively tried to help her son sort out and map the new world they were in.

Adam's father was a draughtsman, unfulfilled in his work, but for whom family meant everything. He used humour to both entertain and distract his son, becoming absorbed in the cartoons and play that were the creative stuff of their "nonsense" together. Adam's mother, an interior designer with enormous energy, was used to making what she wanted happen. She "created" their space in the ward befriending and making personal her attachments to staff. They had come to Australia following the death of the maternal grandmother. Adam's mother missed her own mother acutely, speaking frequently of her, and using a scarf that belonged to her mother to wrap around her son and herself in a type of "holding". She struggled with the "uncanny" repetition of the care procedures, for example suction, that she had learned as she nursed her mother during her terminal illness. She comforted herself with the notion that her mother had helped her learn what she needed to know and that if her son should die, then his grandmother would be there already to keep him safe.

The couple had moved to the "lucky country" where they had expected to create a better life, and put their grief behind them. They spoke of how their luck had changed as they mourned the loss of their perfect son. It was an intolerable idea that Adam may not eat or speak. Adam could not move his tongue, and his tracheostomy tube redirected the air from his lungs so that he was unable to make his voice. They grieved for the conversations they would miss and altered their behaviour, no longer eating in front of him as they felt this added to his burden. They would accommodate for the needs of their son, tolerate the need for the hospital, but not "give up" on their dream of family and home.

Talking without speech: putting his words into action

Adam now felt safe and secure in his pusher. From this base he was happier to take in the world and once loaded up with an oxygen cylinder, he could venture out into the surrounding corridors. Often we would "go for a walk", his mother, Adam, and myself. Adam shifted from a passive observer, to soon pointing at objects along the way. His mother patiently provided the labels; fish tank, elevator, chair, B1, and B2, interpreting his "point" as a question concerning names, that is, what's that or who's that? She asked me, "Why does he keep asking what he already knows?" My reply startled her as I suggested that maybe his point was not always a question, but maybe it could be a statement, a comment, a command, or request. His point might confirm something, or own something or try to make something happen. This was akin to a remembering for his mother of the way in which he "spoke" before he had lost his speech, and for Adam an opportunity to exert his sense of agency. Coggins and Carpenter (1981) describe a taxonomy of speech acts or intentions of preverbal infants which might be found in gesture, emotion or behaviour, facial expression etc. These linguistic and extralinguistic behaviours are the components of human communication. The task of the toddler is to progress with his acquisition of the language system in the service of extending his capacity to communicate and act in the world. Their conversation grew as Adam's mother attributed to him his broader scope of intentions. As well as Miss Pig, Adam clutched a small can of custard, a favourite; able to have it, to own it, but not able to eat it. His grasp on the tin of food made a statement, one where loss was signified in a real way, a loss of his ability to solve his own hunger, the loss of the sensory pleasure of his mouth, and also the loss of his speech.

Communication and language became a major focus of intervention, with expression for Adam in the mode of action and signing. Where he might once have toddled off when his interest had subsided, or since admission to hospital cried or withdrew, he learned to sign "finished". He took his part in "Ready, set, go" with a wave of his hand thus finding there were games and actions he could control. He pointed to his tracheostomy tube in a request for suction, knowing that he could relieve his own discomfort. This fundamental speaking through sign afforded Adam a way to act on his own behalf, make choices and regulate the actions of others within the constraints of his developmental stage.

Plans were made for Adam to be discharged from the ward and detailed arrangements for assistance at home were put in place. Our therapy included conversations about home and Adam's father agreed to illustrate a simple storybook. The narrative structure started at home and identified the important people and relationships, moved to the hospital and the key elements of illness and sadness. It then progressed to recovery and going home, back to the same people and relationships. The drawings present the idea of an ordering of events and a naming of emotions and like all children's storybooks allows for an embroidering of words as the reader responds to the pictures. In this way the event of going home was rehearsed in the reading and re-reading and once home, the event of being in hospital was talked about. Figure 1 presents

Figure 1. An abridged version of the storybook narrative about being ill and going home.

an abridged version of the actual book, which Adam read in the repetitive way of a toddler or young child.

The world of Adam's thoughts and intentions was made clearer through his gesture and affect and his family settled into a routine of work, shared care with nurses, play at home and ongoing visits to the hospital. Over some months of adjustment at home, his mother patiently taught Adam the names of the colours of the rainbow. Together he and his mother would sing and sign a rainbow song—on the one hand filling the world with colour, movement and hope, and on the other a longing. A longing for something other, a land heard of once in a lullaby.

When Adam was three years old, he drew a picture of his family, a series of circles enclosing each other, like a set of Russian dolls. The

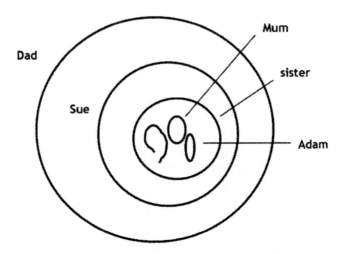

Figure 2. Family drawn when Adam was three years old.

drawing, figure 2, shows his father the outer and largest circle, next the one named for myself, then his younger infant sister at the time, and then two small circles he called himself and his mother. There is also a third which I am not sure about. For the therapist to be included in the family constellation to me is not surprising, given the frequency and intensity of our contact and his developmental age. Adam had made a relationship, just as his family did. This "family circle" seems to catch an essence of what was a holding dynamic, a protective cocoon around himself and his mother.

Afterwards: living a life

Adam is now almost ten years old. He loves karate, wants to be a vet and look after lost animals, is mad about the *Lord of the Rings* story and identifies with Aragorn, the leader who was king. He has a vivid imagination and a talent for art. He is a great talker and creator of stories. He has two younger sisters.

Our therapeutic contact has continued over this time in varying intensity and guises, a mixture of speech pathology and psychotherapy, alongside his medical treatment. By the time he was five-years-old he was able to speak in a way that was clear enough for those who did not know him to understand. He went to kindergarten and progressed to school, and with this coming of age was able to manage eating a restricted range of foods.

Adam has had over eighty hospital admissions and innumerable outpatient appointments. He no longer has his tracheostomy tube or gastrostomy but has a raft of long-term effects—chronic lung disease, short stature, ongoing eating limitations, learning difficulties, social isolation, physical weakness, and balance problems. He tends to lack confidence in physical pursuits and avoids them as much as he can. His health remains in question and two years ago his tumour recurred.

For the past two years he has come regularly to talk. This is a different phase of therapy but built on a continuity that seems important. Toddlers, even ill toddlers grow up. Adam's complaints were not simply with the issues of his health, but importantly with the vicissitudes of living his life. Over time, Adam has managed to achieve a movement from the hospital as the defining story of his life. Despite being ill, this is not all he thinks about. When he draws his family now, it is filled with cousins, uncles, and encompasses the entire world. He now can locate himself in the history and stories of his family, and I although close, am in some other place. Attwood (2005) in the ABC programme "Words" talked about the human functions of language, as being the ability to tell stories and the ability to ask questions. The development of language therefore creates the possibility of asking the universal questions of our existence, that is, who am I, and where do I come from? And speaking allows the opportunity to realise your own answer.

At one point I asked him what he remembered of his experiences. He summed them up by saying, "I don't like needles!" This sounds like an amazing understatement even despite the obvious pain associated, but it made me think about Fraiberg's (1976) discussion of the toddler's sense of wholeness as a person and the integrity of the body. She tells the anecdote of a toddler's need of bandaids, "(I)t's as if a leak in the container, the body, is sealed up and his completeness as a personality is re-established" (Fraiberg, 1976, p. 130). Perhaps with the puncturing of his skin is both the remnant, or reminder of the risk of losing body and soul.

References

Attwood, M. (2005). Interview on ABC TV programme Words. Viewed January 2005. http//abc.net.au/sundayafternoon.

Bowlby, J. (1982). *Attachment and loss.* Vol. 1: *Attachment.* New York: Basic Books.

Coggins, T. E. & Carpenter, R. L. (1981). The communicative intention inventory: A system for observing and coding children's early intentional communication. *Applied Psycholinguistics, 2*: 235–251.

Damasio, A. (2003). *Looking for Spinoza.* New York, London: Harcourt.

Fraiberg, S. H. (1976). *The Magic Years.* London: Methuen.

Giammona, A. J. & Malek, D. M. (2002). The psychological effect of childhood cancer on families. *Pediatric Clinics of North America, 49*: 1063–1081.

Greenspan, S. I. (2002). *The secure child,* (pp. 45–78). Cambridge, MA: Perseus Publishing.

National Cancer Institute Website http://nci.nih.gov accessed December 2004.

Rolland, J. S. (1990). Anticipatory loss: A family systems developmental framework. *Family Process, 29*: 229–244.

Scheeringa, M. S. & Gaensbauer, T. J. (2000). Post traumatic Stress Disorder. In: C. H. Zeanah (Ed.), *Handbook of infant mental health,* 2nd ed. (pp. 369–381). New York, London: Guilford Press.

Stargatt, R. & Anderson, V. (2004). Neuropsychological consequences of Posterior Fossa Tumours: the first twelve months. *Brain Impairment, 5*: 32.

Vannatta, K. & Gerhardt, C. (2003). Pediatric Oncology, psychosocial outcomes for children and families. In: R. Roberts (Ed.), *Handbook of Pediatric Psychology 3rd Ed,* Ch 10. New York, London: Guilford Press.

Winnicott, D. W. (1960). Ego distortions in terms of true and false self. In: *The Maturational Processes and the Facilitating Environment.* London: Hogarth Press & Institute of Psychoanalysis, 1965.

Winnicott, D. W. (1967). Mirror-role of mother and family in child-development. In: P. Lomax, (Ed.), *The Predicament of the family* (pp. 26–33). London: Hogarth & Institute of Psychoanalysis.

CHAPTER SEVEN

Working in twilight: infant mental health interventions with babies who may die

Megan P. Chapman and Campbell Paul

Infant mental health has a long tradition of work within paediatric hospital settings. Working with sick infants and their families has been a focal point of the infant mental health programme at The Royal Children's Hospital in Melbourne (RCH) since its inception, and Campbell Paul, Brigid Jordan, and Frances Thomson-Salo have previously written about this important work, specifically about cases where our interventions are useful and successful, in allowing the infant to develop as a knowable person, for themselves and for their family. There is another component to the work with sick infants, which seems to be not as easily explored. This is the work with sick babies who do not get well, with babies who die.

This chapter will explore working in twilight. Working with babies and their families when the outlook is grim. Working to try to prevent these babies becoming disturbing ghosts in the nursery (Fraiberg, Adelson & Shapiro, 1975). Infant mental health interventions in these circumstances involve complex amalgams of working systemically with infants, parents, and other members of the treating team. It is important to note that for us, the referred patient is the baby, not the parent. Unlike a pure perinatal intervention, the role of infant mental health clinicians is not solely to attend to the mental health needs or distress of

73

the infant's family. This does not mean that the needs of the parents are ignored or neglected. Rather, it is the infant, and working through the infant, that is the focus of the work, and how the work is framed. It is to ensure that the infant is psychologically "alive", both in themselves, and also in the mind of the parents.

To provide some context to where and how this work happens, the Royal Children's Hospital is both a tertiary and quaternary level hospital, meaning that it accepts patients from paediatric and neonatal wards at other hospitals in order to provide highly specialised care. It is also probably fair to say that for some babies, it is the hospital of last resort. This paper focuses on referrals from our neonatal intensive care unit. The Neonatal Intensive Care Unit (NICU) at RCH is a twenty-four-bed quaternary unit for Victoria, Tasmania, and southern New South Wales. The length of stay can vary between days, and many months. The infants are very sick. They may have been born with congenital conditions, suffered physical trauma or infection during the late stages of pregnancy, birth, or very early life, or other complex medical problems. They are fragile, and easily compromised. The babies within NICU are not admitted due to prematurity, although some have prematurity as a co-morbidity. On average, due to the illness severity and level of complications within this population, one baby dies a week, and many of those who live do so with varying degrees of disability. Some of our infants have been identified as potentially having difficulties during pre-natal scans, and in that way, their families may have been able to prepare for what may lie ahead.

However, for other families, the journey to NICU is first flagged at, or soon after, birth. Being a paediatric, as opposed to a maternity hospital, all babies needing our care are transported using the neonatal emergency transport service by air or road, with parents following when they are able. The scenario faced by parents is not the one they envisaged when they embarked on the journey that was conception and pregnancy. Nobody can accurately imagine a neonatal intensive care unit. The need for it is normally for someone else's baby, as opposed to your own. In the course of a pregnancy, a pregnancy that we may perhaps characterise as both physiologically and psychologically "normal", parents go through a variety of phases of imagining, wondering, and projecting. Imagining who this baby may be, what they will become. What they will look like, who will they take after, what they will be good at. The pregnancy is also the time for parents to attempt to consolidate their own imaginings of themselves as parents, drawing on things such as their own experiences of being parented, of watching others parent, or reflecting on their experiences with their own older children. When the birth of a baby coincides with them being acutely unwell, particularly if there is no warning of the potential difficulties prior to birth, it shatters the parental fantasy of what the baby will be like, what the relationship with the baby will be, and the parent's imagined experience of their transition to parenthood.

The circumstances may also disrupt the sense of primary maternal preoccupation as described by Winnicott (1956) with implications both for the mother, and the infant. The necessary medical interventions are a direct impingement on the infant, and the infant themself may not experience a sense of emotional holding. Medically unwell infants often do not, or cannot, display the attachment cues that draw parents to them. Instead, what is present is a baby who is often either in distress, or sedated and muscle relaxed, attached to machines, machines that monitor every function, that sound alarms. A baby whose eyes, rather than meeting the mother, may be shielded from light, denying even that level of connection. A baby who is inside a humidity crib, a physical barrier against touch, or whose open cot is covered in "plastic", literally cling wrap, to retain heat. The reality that some infants do not survive is known and experienced by parents on the ward, who vicariously experience the trauma of other families whose infants, admitted in the same unit, often in the same room, die.

I, Megan P. Chapman (MPC) returned to NICU on a Monday morning to a four-bed room, to see a baby and her mother who I had been working with for some time. The scene I was greeted with was a mother looking shell-shocked, standing next to her muscle relaxed, sedated infant, who was connected to a ventilator and what seemed to be a multitude of monitors, pumps, and machines. The physical state of the baby had not altered since the last time I had seen them. However, two of the other babies in the room had died over the course of the weekend, unexpectedly, despite increased medical intervention. All watched silently by this mother, standing guard over her own infant. "I just kept thinking she's next" was what I was told, and I can never reassure that that is not the case, because there is a significant chance that she may be.

Working with babies who may die involves working with trauma and grief at multiple levels and stages. It seems as if we need to help parents sift through the layers, before we can finally find the real baby, and then they have space to grieve for them. To grieve both for the baby in the NICU, and for the imagined baby who was never born. Acknowledgement of the "unborn" imagined baby, and what they were supposed to be, is an important step in accepting and knowing the baby who is present, in making them known and knowable.

The unpacking of grief is not straightforward. Nor is the identification of families who should be referred to us. We work very closely with our social work colleagues, and have a shared and supportive approach including secondary consultation, clinical discussion, and joint work. Families displaying high levels of distress which is not able to be contained by other members of the treating team are relatively easily identified as ones for whom a referral to infant mental health should be offered. However, some slip through, and the referrals end up coming to us much later. These are families who are often very engaged in the medical needs of the baby. However, this involvement can sometimes be a defence again a psychological engagement with the infant.

Psychological detachment from a baby who may die is a concept that stirs opinions. Is it kinder to allow this detachment? Emotional withdrawal and dissociation on the part of parents, and the infant, is common. On one level, it may be thought of as protective, as it may seem unbearable for the parents to try and understand the world of their acutely unwell infant, the infant they are likely to lose. However, under these circumstances, how can a parent begin to understand their baby? To develop a sense of reflective function regarding the infant's mind, their thoughts, their feelings, their desires, and how these are made known. We currently have a research programme exploring the concept of reflective functioning on NICU, how it is expressed, and what we can perhaps do to help enhance it for these babies and their families, as despite the temptation to allow withdrawal and dissociation to continue, Campbell Paul's (2000, 2014 this volume,) past writings and clinical experience within NICU suggests that it appears important to encourage parents to know their acutely unwell infant, despite the emotional turmoil that knowing evokes. If the infant dies, there exists the experience of the infant being known, and if the infant lives, the trauma of the infant's own experience of that period is not repressed or unacknowledged, rather it is held jointly and understood with the trauma experienced by the parents.

I had what turned out to be a single session with Lisa's parents late one afternoon. Their baby was dependent on continuous positive airway pressure (CPAP), and they were awaiting the results of genetic testing with the possibility being that their only child, a daughter, had a condition that was incompatible with life beyond the very short-term. They had been referred because the mother had not been coming into NICU frequently, and when she did, was not interacting with Lisa. In contrast, Lisa's father was spending significant amounts of time at the hospital, and when he was not there, was trawling the internet for information. This was one of the few sessions that I conducted which was not cotside, which is my preference. These parents preferred to see me in an interview room, away from the main section of the ward. We talked about the pregnancy, about the worries associated with being older having a first baby, and them being in a relatively new relationship with each other. We talked about the distress at being told at a thirty-four week scan that there perhaps was something wrong, and the anguish at contemplating whether to have a late term termination. We talked about the relief at the results of another scan saying all was fine, and then the devastation when Lisa was born and all was not. Her parents talked about Lisa's genes. About what they might mean. About options for palliative care. I queried again, gently, asking them to tell me about Lisa. Again, I found myself back in what felt like a lecture on genetics. It was containing for the parents to reduce their baby to her genetic code. However, they had not either managed to get to know her, or were unable to acknowledge it. I felt compelled to gently reflect that it seemed we knew a lot about Lisa's genes, but I still had not got a sense of her as a person. I also reflected that it was this that perhaps we needed to get to know, that this was not dependent on the results of the tests, but it would perhaps be something that, regardless of the result, they could always know about her. It was though I had begun to speak a foreign language, but one that they learnt very quickly. I had broken the notion that this imperfect child, and the unplanned, inconvenient journey of the parents could be somehow forgotten and life would just return to normal when they left the NICU. I had opened the realisation that even if Lisa died, her memory would remain, and perhaps it would be valuable to be able to remember her for who she was, not just know her genetic code.

When we sift through grief in NICU, it is not uncommon to also find guilt which may also be acting as a barrier to engaging with the infant as a person. Sometimes it is a lingering doubt, usually mothers wondering, sometimes despite medical reassurances to the contrary, as to whether their use of medication such as antidepressants during pregnancy, or a vitamin deficiency, had caused their baby's condition. Sometimes we find more complex scenarios. I was referred a baby who had been in our NICU for a number of months, whose condition was not improving, if anything she was getting worse, and the medical team were still unsure of her underlying condition. This was "touch and go", and I was told on the referral that there was "just something about the mother" which they could not quite define, but could I see her. She was not "difficult", she was attending every day, and was immaculately groomed, polite, and organised. She sat close to her baby, Sarah, and appeared quite attentive. But still, it was thought, given the circumstances, that we should see her. I met a beautiful, engaging, and smiling baby who was neurologically intact yet dependent on a ventilator, who was referencing her mother, following her with her eyes, and reaching for her. Her mother said she loved her. However, the more we talked, I discovered that this had not always been so.

Sarah was conceived because her father wanted her. Her mother felt her life was full and fulfilled by other things, she did not need a baby. But they were getting older, it was now or never, and she was scared the marriage would end if she did not relent. She spent the pregnancy hating the baby, not wanting her, wanting her old life back, planning how to return to "normal" as quickly as possible post the birth, and then Sarah was born and didn't breathe. Her mother felt she had caused this, by not loving her enough, by not wanting her, even though now she did love her, and could not imagine life without her. Her sense of guilt was overwhelming. She was not allowing herself to see herself as a mother, to see that her baby loved her back, knew her, and responded to her. We spend many weeks together, helping see and know Sarah, and helping this mother view herself as a good enough mother, despite the harrowing medical circumstances that were co-occurring. This mother was able to express the anguish of many in her situation, of being asked to chose between letting their baby go, or continuing with invasive treatment which may ultimately be futile, or may impact severely on the quality of life for the whole family, not just the infant. "I can't live if my baby dies, but I can't live if my baby lives". I think that for this mother, getting to know her baby as a person helped her make exceedingly difficult decisions with reference to Sarah and Sarah's needs, as opposed to just her own.

Amongst the grief, I wonder about the role of hope. Sometimes too much hope is viewed as pathological by the treating teams, an inability to accept the acuteness and reality of the situation. I do not see our role as overtly taking hope away. However, through getting to know the baby, this may be the result. The work is sitting with infants and families through periods of not knowing, and helping tolerate uncertainty. Sometimes this work utilises mentalisation techniques, coupled with infant observation, and direct engagement with the infant, with a degree of mindfulness strategies thrown in for good measure. It cannot simply be problem solving or strategy driven.

For some families with religious faith, hope is manifest through prayer. But are the prayers for this baby, or the imagined baby? And where are we left if the prayers are not answered? When it becomes apparent that the infant cannot survive, there is usually some time between then, and death. This time is critical for families to build and consolidate banks of memories. Talking through how these days may look, what the family wants to happen, is an important component of the work. Some families want to take their baby outside into the fresh air. We usually wonder with families who is it important for the baby to meet, and facilitate this if possible. Photos, dressing the baby in their special clothes brought from home, telling the baby the family stories are all part of this period.

The death of an infant in NICU, although unfortunately common, is unique to each infant, as are the needs of their families. When medical intervention is withdrawn, it is common that this is the first time parents have seen their baby's face without tubes. It can be incredibly poignant. Some babies die quickly when care is withdrawn, others linger. I have found myself sitting with families in both situations. Sometimes I am there at the request of the family, sometimes at the request of the staff. Sometimes it feels like I'm emotionally holding everyone. Working with these babies, I spend time with them even when their parents are not there, and it is at these periods that NICU staff often come and reflect on the babies, and their own feelings about them. We usually agree that life is not fair sometimes.

This leads to the final reflection on this work, and a question I am often asked by colleagues outside of it. How do you do it? It is important to have a life outside of NICU. Although the work is about life, death, and facing ongoing disability, it is not your own life. However, it is also important not to pretend that this work does not impact. Supervision and simply being able to debrief about cases with peers is important. Sometimes you need to have a space to just go, think through and process what is happening. Having a small caseload, and not holding multiple infants in this circumstance at the same time is helpful, if possible. But being part of a team is what makes it possible to continue to do this work. Both the mental health team, and the NICU team are skilled at supporting each other through this work. But we also remember the baby as a person, and being able to help families in almost unfathomable circumstances, to be invited to do so, is actually a privilege, and we hope that instead of a ghost in the nursery, we have helped in placing an angel there instead.

References

Fraiberg, S., Adelson, E., & Shapiro, V. (1975). Ghosts in the nursery. A psychoanalytic approach to the problems of impaired infant–mother relationships. *Journal of the American Academy of Child & Adolescent Psychiatry, 14*: 387–421.

Paul, C. (2000). The experience of staff who work in neonatal intensive care. In: N. Tracey (Ed.), *Parents of premature infants: Their emotional world* (pp. 229–240). London: Whurr Publishers.

Paul, C. (2014). Sick babies in hospital. (In this volume).

Winnicott, D. W. (1956). Primary Maternal Preoccupation In: *Through Paediatrics to Psychoanalysis* (pp. 300-305). London: Hogarth.

CHAPTER EIGHT

Infants dependent on technology at home: enabling the staff

Sarah Jones and Robyn Hayles

In our society most infants do not need the intensive care of anyone other than their parents and extended family. However for a small group of infants born with significant physical complications their lives do depend on medical, nursing and family "intensive care".

Advances in technology over the past ten years have allowed children who may have died, such as those born very premature or those with degenerative conditions, to stay alive longer. New technology and improved management mean that procedures are being offered more frequently and are more successful at prolonging the lives of children who may not have lived fifteen to twenty years ago.

"Technology" has been described by the American philosopher, Goldworth, as the,

> application of knowledge in order to gratify human wants and desires. Its success is marked by an expansion of human choices .... (Problems arise) not because the technology fails, ... but action taken produces undesirable as well as desirable results. (Goldworth, 1999, p. 79)

The increasing portability and home usage of the new technology, such as portable ventilators and pumps, is establishing a new population of very compromised special needs children in our community. Previously the small group of these children who did survive resided in acute hospital care. This brings enormous challenges for the children, their parents/guardians and the health professionals. It also produces results which are desired but in need of close examination.

This chapter's focus is on the experience of staff who keep these infants alive by providing the technology within the home. Through the use of a case example of an infant on home based ventilation we will consider the experience for staff working in this changing paediatric hospital in the home system. Following this, the authors examine the evidence from practice based nursing research in this area and the contributions from organisational literature.

This chapter comes out of a reflective collaboration between the manager of a paediatric home based programme and its external staff consultant. The home care programme for medically vulnerable children takes not only the patients out of the hospital but also staff and technology. With all the advances in technological capacity the infant can be overlooked. It is hard to imagine ourselves in the position of the sick infant. How do clinicians, carers, and parents keep these infants in mind, when for the most part the early years are just about keeping the infant alive? How do staff also come to know the impact of working with these children and their parents on themselves?

Much has been written about the psychological impact of severe disability on young people. Over thirty years ago Vanleeuwen wrote "the hospitalised child has many fears: fears of symptoms, pain, damage, exposure, and loss of control; fear of strangers, separation, abandonment and death; fear of the unknown and of his or her own terrible fantasies" (Vanleeuwen, 1983, p. 509). Infant mental health literature has developed this further, exploring the sick neonate and toddler's psychological life (Minde, 1993; Morse, Chapter Four, in this volume). For the infants considered in this chapter, all of them will have had extended hospital admissions. Theut and Mrazek (1994) suggest that hospitalisation can significantly influence the infant's developmental course and disturb the child-parent relationship. They report previous findings that one of the most important determinants in infants' responses to their medical interventions and hospitalisations is the "parents' abilities to cope with their own anxieties during their child's illness" (Theut & Mrazek, 1994, p. 428). If parents' anxieties result in a reduction of emotional support their capacities to modulate the infant's experience is also reduced. Relatively little has been written about the same issues for the technologically dependent infant in the home setting. Whilst this chapter does not explore this further, staff are exposed frequently to these kinds of troubled relationships.

The technological dependent child in the home literature has been the recent area of study by Queensland nurses, Wang and Barnard (2004). They summarise the findings of ninety-seven papers which report the positives for the child dependent on technology; including that home is more emotionally and socially stimulating, child and parent benefit from reduced anxiety, the child acquires social skills by participating in family activities. Parents report satisfaction in witnessing the social and emotional growth in their child. They also highlight literature that indicates that caring for a child who needs life-saving technical support at home can result in undesirable implications for the parents/primary care givers. Parents/primary care givers experience a wide range of emotions such as anxiety, guilt, frustration, and sorrow. They describe the stress for parents in the ambiguity of their positions, "for example, parenting can become confusing because of the nature of medical procedures that parents have to perform and the resulting discomfort and pain to their child" (Wang & Barnard, 2004, p. 9). The authors' experiences and observations are supportive of the literature.

Samantha

Jane and Tom, both in their late twenties, were young parents of a toddler and expecting their second child. At Jane's twenty-nine week ultrasound, her as yet unborn infant was found to have life threatening complex cardiac problems. A few days later Jane went into premature labour and Samantha was born arriving in the world ten weeks early, blue, floppy, and unwell. Her congenital anomalies were compounded by the problems of extreme prematurity. She was transferred from the obstetric hospital at birth to a tertiary paediatric hospital's neonatal intensive care (NICU).

Samantha's immediate physical problems included:

- Chronic lung disease.
- Congenital heart disease.
- Upper bowel obstruction.

Her immediate psychosocial risks included:

- Removed from her mother and father to another hospital immediately after birth.
- Distressed parents whose anxiety impinged on being receptive and attuned to their infant's experience.
- Large numbers of care givers (doctors/nurses) limiting sensitive and reliable attunement.
- Frequent and invasive medical procedures impinging on development of self psychophysiological regulation.

Fourteen months later Samantha eventually was able to leave hospital and go home, supported by the home care programme and staff.

The home care programme

The paediatric home care programme began in the early 1990s. Responding to demands from parents, innovative health professionals and the financial imperatives of hospital administration, the hospital home care programme began with a few patients who had spent all of their young lives within the walls of the hospital. Each year it now supports an average of one hundred and thirty-five children with complex medical care needs. Children remain supported while they continue to meet key criteria of frequent interventional medical care needs, a health status that is complex and predictably unpredictably and frequent hospital admission. Children maybe supported for a few months or many years.

The children supported range in age from birth to eighteen, with forty-four per cent under five years of age. Of this forty-four per cent nearly half are between nought and two years. On average, two to three referrals would be received each year for babies born either premature or with complications at birth. Diagnoses vary greatly with predicament being the commonality—the predicament of complex health care needs impacting on daily living. However in general common diagnosis within the population involves underdeveloped lungs resulting in chronic lung disease, other respiratory complications, cardiac complexities, and various gastrointestinal complications.

It is important, but very difficult for staff to acknowledge, that of the patients who begin on this programme approximately twenty per cent per annum will die. At times death, and its impact on all involved, is denied. Work activities and pressures contribute to this as the urgency created by the hospital system to "get children home" inevitably means that someone else requires staff's physical and emotional energy. There is also some level of unspoken acceptance that for many of these children the life/death balance is so fragile that days of life lived are a "bonus". Quality of life of these children is frequently discussed. Home is better than hospital, but the discharge home is not necessarily the road to recovery. Staff "know" this at one level, and as Menzies-Lyth (1984) described, defend against the reality of this at another. The authors were somewhat disturbed by their own, belated realisation, that they too had omitted mentioning the regular occurrence of the death of a child in the home care programme in the writing of this chapter.

Discharge from hospital to home

Within this particular programme, children such as Samantha are supported by a model of care that is operated by a clinical working team that includes, the parents, medical staff, registered nurses and case managers, usually with a social work background.

When infants with Samantha's level of problems are ready for discharge there are increased anxieties about the departure from the safer hospital to the as yet untested home. This is commonly one of the most difficult times for parents, and most likely for the child, as they face the inevitable loss of the hospital and the relationships developed with key people. There is a large amount of training and practice given to parents and the patient's paid carers about the care tasks required and the use of the technology. For example they need to be educated about the signs and symptoms of when to suction out the tracheostomy, when to provide overnight oxygen and at what level, what the medical danger signs might be and how to respond in an emergency.

To support Samantha at home, trained carers were required seven nights a week. Staff also experience anxiety as they prepare parents and recruit and train carers to take on ever increasing responsibilities of the medical/nursing care. Samantha, at four years of age, had a total of twenty-eight re-admissions back to the hospital. She faced many physical crises, which required both urgent and planned returns for treatment. Staff are often on the professional carriage of the roller coaster of life and death for their patients and may remain so for many years.

A psychosocial consultation to staff: reflective practice

Purpose

Not long after the programme developed management recognised the need for staff to have a regular consultation on their most difficult cases with a mental health clinician with experience of working within hospital systems. The consultation promotes reflective practice; where the advantages of understanding the enormously complex aspects of work and its impact on the staff enhances patient care. Both nurses and case management staff meet together with the consultant. The meetings are voluntary, and open to all clinical staff including management. In general the primary task is to provide opportunities for learning about patients, the families, and the complex systems surrounding each case. In particular the consultations are for the cases where psychosocial issues are at risk of impeding the medical care. There is a secondary role in facilitating working relationships within the teams; working through difficult clinical decisions with the most complex families. The consultation is offered approximately monthly for an hour. Feedback is regularly undertaken by the manager both formally by email questionnaire and directly with staff.

The work

Engaging monthly with hospital staff who are themselves delivering a complex package of care to children with complex medical needs is a humbling experience. They articulate how working directly and indirectly with very sick or severely physically disabled infants and children is both rewarding and demanding. There are constant organisational necessities that have to be managed; an evolving number of complex children with complex diagnoses, referrals increasing per annum and frequent staff changes. All this needs to be accommodated whilst addressing the ongoing work with the very sick infants and children on their caseload. Formal opportunities to deal with the work by thinking about their patients linking it to their own emotional responses, values and experiences in their small work groups are not frequent. This is partly due to the nature of the work taking place outside the hospital. Staff work in the patient's homes also spending considerable time in their cars travelling. Psychosocial consultations provide staff with management sanctioned permission to bring up experiences/conflicts/ intense responses for discussion that are difficult to verbalise elsewhere.

Some of the most painful consultations concern those families whose child's is not so much compromised by their physical condition but by the turmoil in the family circumstances, that frequently lead the staff to say, "Baby X is not even half of the problem."

Cases discussed

The cases staff bring for discussion usual involve:

- Parents' psychiatric diagnoses as they impinge on their child's care.
- A marked lack of acceptable child care being demonstrated by parents/guardians.
- Overwhelming turmoil created by the impingements of the very complex care packages causing families to be angry with "the hospital."
- Cultural differences where the family insist on a life at all costs—even where the hospital have opposed this through legal means.

The authors are aware of a bias in the cases discussed in the consultation. Patients and their families where there are good working relationships and smooth transitions on and off the programme are not the ones presented!

Staff talk of the rewarding differences seeing patients inside their homes when compared to a hospital ward. The staff on the programme have all chosen to work in home based roles, and frequently report the great rewards in the work of seeing and maintaining a child within the family home. They can be empowered by having such an important role in the life of a family. Yet they must also deal with their presence being experienced as an unavoidable intrusion; their witnessing of siblings being overlooked, marriages frayed and complaints from parents' about the lack of privacy when carers are present and constant exhaustion. They are aware of family and financial tensions, preferences for one nurse over another and a very confronting awareness of the visible reminder of the impact a sick child can have on the family relationships and life.

Many psychosocial aspects of sick children are less obvious in the hospital setting. Tensions when the staff are in the home and confronted with "too much information", can lead to them distancing themselves from their own emotional experience and that of the infant/child. Staff can unconsciously defend against getting too close to their youngest patients. This often became evident when we found ourselves immersed in the casework with parents and "forgot" the infant/child. Time and time again we used the consultation for a difficult family problem and then discovered the absence of our attention on the child's experience. In the first year as the consultant began to learn about the programme and the patients this omission was less noticed, however over time it became clearer for everyone what was going on. Could we not bear to imagine the infant's/child's existence? Were we unconsciously colluding with a need to deny the infant's feelings about many of the things done to her? We just could not bring her into our minds. Once we began to find words for this, then members of the group would themselves remind the group the infant/child was getting "lost".

At different times and with different children staff feel the despair of "there is not enough to go around". They can at times feel burdened by being responsible for an assessment that inevitably has limitations. They offer a system for children with protracted medical conditions yet at times they and the families are witnesses to a child's life with little hope of significant improvements. Giving more time to some families, due to greater than normal anxieties, can be difficult to provide. More time and expertise to treat the emotional needs within a compromised infant/child-parent relationship is not yet available. The potential for a child's death is a reality for many of the families. The constant threat of this exposes staff to unimaginable anxieties. These can be expressed by fears of not knowing enough about the child's condition, feeling hospital management "do not know what it is like for us in the home", or being angry and critical of whomever made the decision to prolong a child's awful life by avoiding death. Using Menzies-Lyth's (1984) work it is important to question whether at times the displaced anger reflects unspoken fears of impotence, exposure to too much unabated suffering, hopelessness in the face of impending loss. The consultation frequently does lead to staff acknowledging their feelings of pleasure in their work. This can seem at odds to an angry response when confronted with an angry parent or their experience of guilt when things inevitably go wrong. When this is talked through it is frequently possible to understand what is being projected into them and what belongs to their own experience.

Samantha

The consultations that focused on Samantha began after the first few months at home. The staff who frequently visited noted upsetting interactions between Jane, the mother, Samantha, and her older sister.

Samantha was developmentally delayed due to her premature birth and prolonged and frequent hospital admission, she was receiving oxygen therapy via plastic nasal prongs twenty-four hours a day and received feeds via a tube limiting her ability to move and be moved with ease. She had an oximeter attached to her twenty-four hours a day and when sleeping received respiratory support from a machine providing continuous positive airway pressure (CPAP). Being so aware of Samantha's physical vulnerability and hypersensitivity constrained Jane; she misinterpreted Samantha's emotional cues, and appeared harsh towards her older daughter's spontaneity and need to play and touch her sister. This resulted in high anxiety for the mother ending in tears for the sibling. Samantha or her sister would be constantly being separated to other parts of the house. This caused the staff anxiety and frustration feeling that Samantha was being isolated from her sister and both missing valuable opportunity for development and ordinary playfulness together. The staff had pointed this out to Jane several times but felt she could not take in their suggestions. She wanted some staff to stay longer and appeared brusque and rude to others. The home appeared chaotic and Samantha seemed hard to engage and there was a question of whether she was being more developmentally damaged by the mother's distress and despair. This in turn lead to them perceiving Jane as potentially depressed, hopeless or negligent, and feeling critical towards her.

The consultation began with staff just back from a home visit with Samantha, and the feelings that the programme and the parents were failing her somehow. The questions began: maybe we should change the care arrangements, should we make a notification to social services or a psychiatrist? Tom, the father was working during the day and rarely seen. Staff, following a psychosocial consultation, were able to help Jane put into words how much trauma she had experienced. Parents often deprive themselves emotionally during the prolonged and unpredictable journey to get a son or daughter home. Jane was then able to speak more about her fears of the uncontrollable older child. She had shut herself off from this and became to realise it had found its expression in anger towards the healthier daughter. Staff then thought more with her about how misinterpretations of Samantha's responses were contributing to the anxiety. It was possible to think about ways to help Jane think and experiment with interacting with both children together in a safer controlled way. For example, allocating "girls time" and getting on the floor with both girls, possibly with another adult initially to help contain the situation. This might provide Jane with some different experiences of herself as a mother, with an understanding that both girls needed her and she could be helped to bear their needs. The older sibling was healthily demanding more! In turn she herself came up with the idea of spending some sanctioned time with just the older girl that helped when inevitably the rivalry and envy appeared. When Jane could talk about jealousy with the older child it seemed that she could then attend to both children together rather than only being able to attend to one daughter at a time. Staff reported months later Jane appeared to being able to enjoy her children more and they were less worried.

The consultations are informed by infant mental health concepts, practice based research undertaken by staff members and also by the organisational-systems literature. The chapter concludes with a discussion of how this literature supports the consultations.

The parents' views

One poignant statement captures a parent's anguish: "I worry about myself, I worry about my son and the impact on the other siblings and I worry about myself disappearing as a human" (McDonald, 2002, p. 34). McDonald (2002), a previous member of staff in the programme, interviewed parents who had an infant dependent on technological support at home. She found of the ten families in her study they all valued the programme of care offered; it lead them to have more normality as a family. She also reports that parents "were expected to perform painful procedures on their children which conflicted with their natural instincts to protect their child from harm" (McDonald, 2002, p. 60).

However in her interviews with parents she noted how focused they were on the medical complexity of the children and how little discussion focused on their "developmental" needs. Some parents reported that the model of care provided did not address their "psychosocial needs". Staff themselves are aware they are not providing formal "counselling" in their roles. One of McDonald's findings is that the needs of these families for psychosocial support were not being met (McDonald, 2002, p. 62) There are, as yet, no dedicated mental health services for these families.

Staff know that ultimately they will leave the child's home and the life/death anxieties. The parent can not. She/he is required to focus attention on technology, oximeters, suctioning lines, etc. leaving at times little over for the developing attunement to her infants' communications. McDonald quoted one parent who described the intensity of the experience,

> you're thinking to yourself have I done the eye drops, have I checked the pump to make sure the alarm doesn't go off, is he due for medicine or is he about to have a crisis? So there is constant pressure and … the unpredictability. (McDonald, 2002, p. 32)

The staff views

Case managers are aware of how families find themselves in a "Catch 22". They require the team of health professionals for their child's and family's survival but would never choose to have the seemingly endless stream of people involved in their lives. McDonald (2002) reported that case managers thought the programme had extremely high expectations of parents. "They perceived these parents had to be on the twenty-four hour alert (for years) and spent many sleepless nights getting up to their children. Many of the parents reported each day parents would live with the fear of the unknown" (McDonald, 2002, p. 52).

Staff interviewed by McDonald reported:

> some case managers perceive that they are taking on some of the parental role as they oversee the child's development and decide on what their needs might be … it is hard for them as they do not want to take over the parental role and over step boundaries … There is often a need to offer layers of support around the psychosocial and emotional elements of the impact of the child's care having on the family. It is a balancing act between being available and being supportive to the family and being up to date with what's happening but without being too intrusive and without being more of a part of their life then you need to be. (McDonald, 2002, p. 54)

One of the most commonly articulated fears were that their child become ineligible for the support of the programme. Children may no longer require overnight care attendants monitoring a ventilator, but still be very considerably physically compromised. This is a vexed milestone; it brings some relief in the child's progress yet comes at an emotional and financial cost. Staff who have prepared parents and children for leaving the programme often speak of how disturbing it is to the parents and on occasions be recipients of the parents' hostility.

Organisational systems literature

Menzies-Lyth's (1984) pioneering work on organisational defences within the nursing profession was based on her observational studies in National Health Service hospitals in Britain. An increase in unconscious anxiety was observed when a more concentrated relationship developed between the nurse and the patient. She described how "social defence systems" evolve in order to guard against the impact of working with the ill patient. The term referred to how both the organisation creates a system which influenced the need for staff to unconsciously defend against the true impact of pain, illness, and death. Detachment and minimisation of feelings were observed as ways nurses manage anxieties. "Social defence systems" evolved where detachment becomes an acceptable part of the nursing task, for example a ward's use of restrictive rosters, which give priority to the allocation of duties not to the patient needs. This may mean that when there is a very high level of sick patients expectations about their emotional care are compromised in favour of the procedural tasks, monitoring duties, and paper work. New staff are slowly inducted into the organisational defences by, for example, humour, shared assumptions about the good or bad patient/manager or colleagues and shared assumptions about the expression of emotion etc. Obholzer proposes that what is being expressed is a

> denial, or a repression of the substance of observation. This flight from reality happens gradually and largely unconsciously. In the process of inducting new members the group unconsciously gives the message: 'This is how we ignore what is going on—pretend along with us and you will soon be one of us. It can be called ... institutionalisation. In fact it is a collusive group denial of work difficulties'. (Obholzer, 1994, p. 174)

Menzies-Lyth (1984) brings these difficulties to light in her description of the nursing task: "Their work involves carrying out tasks which by ordinary standards are distasteful disgusting and frightening. The work situation arouses very strong and mixed feelings in the nurse; pity, compassion and love; guilt and anxiety; hatred and resentment of the patients who arouse these strong feelings; envy of the care given to the patient"

(Menzies-Lyth, 1984, p. 5). Staff protect themselves unconsciously from what they witness. The anxiety defended against can be the substance of blame and guilt. It can lead to high staff turnover, denigration of management, and an over identification with the patient.

Dartington (2000) offers further reflection on the nursing task where there is an inherent tension. She outlined the ambiguity in a profession which promotes "a working life dominated by necessity, tradition and obedience". This makes insufficient space for "the processes of reflection about ones' work, its efficacy, its significance; registering the patient's emotional state, the capacity to be informed by one's imagination and intuition, the opportunity to criticise constructively and to influence the work environment" (Dartington, 2000, p. 100).

Paul (2000) writing about intensive care unit work proposes that "fostering a capacity for thought and reflective supervision seems crucial for the ultimate optimal care of the baby and their family" (Paul, 2000, p. 229). There is a question here: that the care of the patient might not only come from technological advances and specialist medical and nursing expertise but also the capacity to reflect on the experience. Paul is an advocate for staff being assisted to bear the load of intensive experiences of life, death and trauma in a neonatal unit. Seligman (1988) supports this by suggesting that professionals observe their own responses to children and their parents; that these can be warning signs of problems to be discussed in supervision.

Whilst these authors are writing about staff engaged in hospital work they may be just as relevant to the newer models of hospital in the home care. As we have shown by Samantha her first four years of life at home was only episodic due to her fragility. For Samantha's life depended on hugely complex care arrangements, which at any time could have failed and lead to her death. Staff were intimately involved with this effort.

Hayles (2001) writes of staff in this programme "moving to a deeper place" with families. Staff find when they can discover this within the clinical relationship it is very rewarding, the greater empathy leading them to develop more sensitive compassion for the child and family experience.

Conclusions

The psychosocial consultation offers staff opportunities more in depth understanding of participants in the family drama as they become involved with their intimate rewarding and distressing messy experiences through their frequent contacts.

Hayles (2001) in her study on nurses' experiences within the model of home care found that the rewards were associated with pleasure the nurses felt when they were "making a difference" in the lives of the patient and the family. The staff help "make sense" of their experience for the family, sometimes they normalise this; other times they need to actively intervene and endure something of the experience themselves. The participants of Hayles' study reflected on "moving beyond the everyday to a deeper understanding". As the nurses experienced the intimate time spent with families their compassion and empathy developed. There was always a conflict however with the experience of "being on a roundabout of compromise". Hayles describes this as being the frustration felt when they had to prioritise patients, could not complete tasks, and placing some patients down the list to address another.

In the case chosen of Samantha to exemplify her experience of a technologically dependent life it was evident to everyone that her sister, only an infant herself, was required to spend long amounts of time away from her parents. This introduces a significant risk to her attachment relationship with her parents. We know from the infant mental health literature that children parented by overwhelmed and anxious parents are at some emotional risk, (Minde, 1993; Theut & Mrazek, 1994) thus Samantha and her sibling were both at risk for mental health difficulties. There is no doubt their own childhoods are irrevocably changed as a result. We hope that over time more mental health resources can be offered to all family members when a child is at home dependent on technology.

As Goldworth proposes, technology's success is marked by an expansion of human choices. These children are recipients of the technological successes. Yet it is incumbent upon all of us in the health professions to examine the outcomes "not because the technology fails, ... but action taken produces undesirable as well as desirable results" (Goldworth, 1999, p. 79).

The authors would suggest that the consultation helps staff to be less reactive to their immediate responses to patients and as a result it develops the staff's capacity for resilience. It assists them in recognising their ability and utilising skills in transitioning acute care into a family friendly environment and supporting parents of children with complex interventional medical care needs. This is another way of saying it enables staff to bear the, at times, unbearable.

References

Dartington, A. (2000). Where angels fear to tread; Idealism, despondency and inhibition of thought in hospital nursing. In: A. Obholzer & V. Zagier Roberts (Eds.), *The unconscious at work* (pp. 1010–1105). London: Routledge, 2000.

Goldworth, A. (1999). Medical technology and the child. In: D. Thomasma & T. Kushner (Eds.), *Birth to Death, Science and Bioethics.* (pp. 79–98). Cambridge: Cambridge University Press.

Hayles, R. (2001). The lived experience of the community based child health nurse practicing in a model of continuous care. *Master of Public Health Thesis*, RMIT (Unpublished).

McDonald, T. (2002). Caring for medically fragile children at home: an analysis of parent's experiences and an evaluation of the Family Choice Program. *Masters of Public Health Thesis*, University of Melbourne.

Menzies-Lyth, I. (1984). *The functioning of social systems as a defence against anxiety.* London: Tavistock Institute of Human Relations.

Minde, K. (1993). Prematurity and serious medical illness in infancy: Implications for development and intervention. In: C. H. Zeanah (Ed.), *Handbook of Infant Mental Health* (pp. 87–105). New York: The Guildford Press.

Morse, S. (2013). I See You—Intensive Care Unit: A case study of Peter. This volume, Chapter Four.

Paul, C. (2000). The experience of staff who work in intensive care. In: N. Tracey (Ed.), *Parents of premature infants: Their emotional world* (pp. 229–240). London: Whurr Publishers.

Obholzer, A. (2000). Managing social anxieties in public sector organisations. In: A. Obholzer & V. Zagier Roberts (Eds.), *The unconscious at work* (pp. 169–178). London: Routledge.

Seligman, S. (1988). Concepts in infant mental health: Implications for work with developmentally disabled infants. *Infants and Young Children, 1*: 41–51.

Theut, S. K. & Mrazek, D. (1994). Infants and toddlers with medical conditions and their parents: Reactions to illness and hospitalisation and models for intervention. In: J. Noshpitz (Ed.), *Handbook of Child and Adolescent Psychiatry*, Vol 1. (pp. 428–438). New York: John Wiley.

Vanleeuwen, J. (1983). Hospitalisation and its meaning to child and family. In: P. Steinhauer & Q. Rae-Grant, (Eds.). *Psychological problems of the child in the family* (pp. 509–526). New York: Basic Books.

Wang, K. W., & Barnard, A. (2004). Technology-dependent children and their families: a review. *Journal of Advanced Nursing, 45*: 36–46.

PART II

INTERVENTIONS IN CRYING, FEEDING, AND SETTLING DIFFICULTIES

CHAPTER NINE

Reflux and irritability

Brigid Jordan

Persistent infant distress is often presumed to have a gut cause and interventions usually involve digestion and feeding—weaning, formula changes, gripe waters, colic mixtures. Infant irritability is commonly attributed to oesophagitis presumed to be caused by pathological gastro-esophageal reflux (including "silent reflux") and treatment with anti reflux medications has become popular, despite the lack of evidence about its efficacy. All infants reflux to some extent. Frequent or prolonged episodes of acid reflux may cause irritation or inflammation of the lower oesophagus, which may have a role in infant irritability.

The lack of empirical knowledge about the role of reflux in infant distress prompted a prospective research study of otherwise healthy infants admitted to The Royal Children's Hospital for investigation of persistent irritability. This was the Irritable Infant intervention project, The Royal Children's Hospital, Melbourne, and of whom the investigators were B. Jordan, R. Heine, M. Meehan, L. Lubitz, and A. Catto-Smith. One aim of the study was to identify clinical predictors of pathological reflux. The other aim was to evaluate the effectiveness of anti-reflux medications in infants who had mild to moderate (but still within the normal range) gastroesophageal reflux.

Only nineteen of the infants who presented to the hospital had pathological reflux as measured by twenty-four hour oesophageal pH monitoring (Fraction Reflux Time greater than ten per cent). This is likely to be a much higher incidence than in the community—as parents who brought their infants to the emergency department had usually seen several doctors; a quarter had had previous admission to a hospital or mother–baby unit for irritability; half the sample were over three months of age and the group included an equal number of first and second born infants.

This study found no correlation between the amount that the infant cried and reflux measured by pH monitoring. One third of the younger infants and two thirds of those aged over three months of age were reported to have feeding difficulties and seventy-three per cent had sleeping problems. However, feeding difficulties, feeding refusal, feeding refusal when hungry, back arching and extending the head were not predictors of pathological gastroesophageal reflux. The only significant clinical predictor of pathological gastroesophageal reflux was vomiting frequency (not volume). Infants who vomited more than five times a day were more likely to have pathological reflux (Heine et al., 2006).

The study also found that anti reflux medications were no more helpful than placebo medications in reducing the amount that infants with normal reflux cried. Maternal report of improvements in infant crying or other aspects of behaviour (ability to be consoled, routine, response to comfort) were similar for infants who had been on anti-reflux or placebo medications.

If not reflux, then what?—"But I know that my baby is in pain…"

Crying has been described as an "impoverished" and graded signal—crying reflects the degree of distress and not the cause of the distress. It may be helpful to have a framework for understanding infant irritability that can accommodate an appreciation of the infant's emotional as well as physical experience.

When there is no identifiable physical abnormality or organic cause with an available medical remedy for the infant's irritability, the clinical task becomes how the clinician and parents can help the baby cope with their discomfort and distress. The irritable infant may be struggling to cope with physical sensations and experiences (digestion, elimination, normal reflux, tiredness, hunger) that fall within the normal range but are experienced as too startling, overwhelming, or frightening. The infant's response needs to be understood in the context of the emotional development of the infant and the developing infant–parent relationship. Social and cultural beliefs, as well as the parents' own psychological style and family experience, will influence how they understand, react to and help their baby deal with distress.

Persistently crying infants are a heterogeneous group. The factors that exacerbated crying initially may not be the factors that are perpetuating it.

One of the tasks of earliest infancy is to for the infant to anticipate and make links with the maternal care that satisfies the infant's needs. Thus, when things go well, the infant learns that hunger is ameliorated with a satisfying feed, that tiredness disappears with sleep, desire for emotional contact is met by holding and talking, boredom alleviated with play or change of environment. It may be more helpful to think about the mother's role in helping the infant deal with the infant's own anxiety, rather than necessarily seeing the infant's distress as caused by maternal anxiety. Maternal depression, anxiety, a tentative pregnancy, unresolved feelings about the baby's conception, loss or grief or other emotional conflicts may complicate this process.

It has long been argued that attachment behaviours (sucking, clinging, following, crying, and smiling) have a biological base and ensure the infant's survival by promoting the infant's close proximity to a parent. An infant whose cry is responded to in an inconsistent manner—at times picked up immediately, at other times left to cry for long periods—will not have learnt to anticipate a graded response to their needs and is likely to feel insecure and uncertain about their needs being met. Their insecurity and anxiety may prompt crying as an almost universal response to any upset. If multiple formulas and soothing regimes have been tried, or the infant has been alternately left to cry alone or comforted, it is easy to imagine that they have difficulty in achieving a sense of agency and containment and that this might exacerbate a frightening view of the world. Parents who are frightened about their babies becoming "too dependent" may need developmental guidance explaining that infants need to build a sense of security and trust in a responsive world before they are able to manage more on their own and settle themselves.

It is hard for the infant to be convinced that they are all right when parents are frantically worrying whether they are in pain or unwell and anxiously changing from one soothing strategy to another such as patting to rocking to walking the floor. Rather than reassuring the infant that they are all right, that the upset can be survived and managed, the infant may get the message that there really is something to worry about and an escalating cycle of anxiety and crying ensues. Helping the parents to read their infant's behavioural cues, including the cry, as an indicator of the infant's emotional state and reactivity and ways of self-regulating may be helpful. A baby who is easily overwhelmed may need more buffering and gentle, graduated exposure to new situations or change in pace such as to changing nappy or the bath or being put to bed. A baby who frantically looks around the room when distressed may need to be held in a position where their mother's face is available for them to lock onto and to be gently engaged in cooing and talking about their distress. A baby who quickly retreats from the impingements of the world, including parental attempts to soothe, and who seems unreachable, may need gentle rather than vigorous reminders from the parents that they are still there. Infants who are easily disorganised and not very adaptable may need predictable routines. The introduction of a predictable routine of feeds and settling can help the world become less chaotic and frightening and make the baby's cues clearer to read and the parent's messages to the baby clearer to understand.

Parents may also need to persist for longer with attempts at comfort and not to give up too easily in the belief that what they are doing is "not working". Sometimes parents have become so governed by a campaign to soothe the baby and avert their crying, that they spend the whole day trying to "down regulate" and "not over-stimulate" the infant, reducing the infant's contact with the world to a bare minimum, and not responding to the infant's interactive overtures or providing sufficient play opportunities and experiences. This exacerbates the crying as the infant becomes bored and lonely and cries to try and make contact with the parents. Alternatively some parents try to distract their infant with yet another toy or activity which often works momentarily and achieves a short-term lull in the crying. However, the infant does not learn to deal with anxiety and frustration, and becomes increasingly reliant on illusory distractions that have an increasing threshold before they provide even a brief respite from the crying. These infants might be able to let go of their preoccupations with what happens inside their body as they become less frightened and more interested and fascinated in a deeper engagement with the world around them. Consistent approaches to soothing the infant that recognise the emotional quality of the infant's crying and attune to this will help the infant learn to anticipate that the distress can be survived.

Reference

Heine, R., Jordan, B., Simpson, D., Lubitz, L., Meehan, M., & Catto-Smith, A. (2006). Prevalence and clinical predictors of pathological gastroesophageal reflux in infants with persistent distress. *Journal of Paediatrics and Child Health, 42*: 134–139.

CHAPTER TEN

Ooey gooey group: a behavioural interactive group for parents and young children with feeding problems

Libby Ferguson and Sue Morse

The Ooey gooey group is a mealtime playgroup run by two speech pathologists at The Royal Children's Hospital, Melbourne. The group comprises toddlers and young children with feeding problems along with their parents, most often their mothers. The children come to the group with a history of complex medical conditions and are reliant on tube feeding for most of their nutritional needs. The children have in common a reluctance to eat an appropriate amount or range of foods. Some have neurological difficulties and all have developed an unhelpful pattern of behaviour around food and mealtime. Food refusal for these children ranges from gagging on particular foods to complete refusal to allow any food into their mouth. The group meets weekly at lunchtime and comprises a play session and a meal.

The name of the group, Ooey gooey group, reflects its acceptance of messiness along with the development of comfortable familiarity with the sensory aspects of eating. Many of these children have learned to associate discomfort and unpleasantness with eating and drinking. Food intake has become "medicalised", measured and worried about. Neither parent nor child looks forward to mealtime with pleasurable anticipation. Rather, they anticipate struggle, anger, disappointment and a whole range of emotions and behaviours not conducive to pleasure and satiation of hunger.

Children attend the group at a developmental stage often vexed with fussy, changeable behaviour. It is a time when they are still endeavouring to establish a sense of autonomy and separation from their primary attachment figure. Along with eating, the toddler is trying to become autonomous with toileting, dressing and bath time etc. It is also a time of curiosity and social exploration. The group capitalises on this drive for independence and supports the parent in allowing their child to take risks and extend boundaries. An aim is to replace panic and alarm with curiosity, playful exploration, and mastery.

The group provides a place for the children to experience food and eating at their own pace within an encouraging and motivating environment. The food is usually provided by the therapists and chosen to match the child's capabilities. It might be that the child is afraid to chew and swallow solid food because of a history of gagging or choking. Some children will have poorly developed oral motor skills and remain stuck at a level where they feel safe and past which the parent is frightened to go. The group aims to replace anxious anticipation with an expectation of pleasure. The child and parent's prior experience has often contributed to a classically conditioned link between food and unpleasantness.

The group is lead by two speech pathologists with experience in the fields of oral motor behaviour, medically complex children and infant mental health. The therapists model eating behaviours, often playfully and with enjoyment, and encourage the child to follow. Explanations with the parents happen at the time rather than following the event. Having fun enables the child to tackle new behaviours and to imitate adults and other children in a safe environment. In this environment, parents feel able to try a different approach to mealtime with their child. They also feel free to initiate discussions in an accepting environment. The group provides a place where risks can be taken. The children and parents take on new challenges and the therapists risk looking inexpert and at times a bit silly. While the general routine of the group is set, (i.e., moving from play to lunch to play), rather than prescribing the individual steps, the therapists enter into spontaneous and dynamic exchange, incorporating what the children bring to the situation. Parents and children find themselves in predicaments, manage to survive them and come to their own solutions.

Play experiences, in the group, are not specifically based on eating and mealtime. The children might at times play at feeding each other, the adults or dolls and teddies. They might also take up physical challenges with balls and cars. They practice negotiating for possession or dealing with dispossession of a toy. Parents join in the play or watch and reflect on the achievements of their own or another's child.

The group process offers the possibility of identification, self-reflection, generation of solutions and encouragement and support from the group. Parents develop an empathy with the other children and the mothers' difficulties, and through that with their own child. Being part of a group reduces the focus on individuals. A similar process occurs with the children as they identify with each other, take risks, compete and follow each other's lead. Behaviours are practised in play and interaction before they are brought to the table.

Children have come to the group because of their refusal to eat. Resistance to food and eating was measured with the Feeding Resistance Scale (Chatoor et al., 2001). Preliminary evaluation of the group has been encouraging. Measures of feeding resistance, range of food consistencies accepted and total food intake are done prior to and following attendance at the group. Preliminary results, on a small number of children, suggest that feeding resistance is decreased and an increased range of food consistencies is accepted. What we observe early in the group is that the children happily anticipate coming to the table to eat and show pride in their developing ability to manage food and mealtime. They develop social relationships with the other children, the parents and the therapists and within this safe environment feel more able to explore their environment and the messy, pleasurable environment of mealtime.

References

Chatoor, I., Ganiban, J., Harrison, J. & Hirsch, R. (2001). Observation of feeding in the diagnosis of posttraumatic feeding disorder of infancy. *Journal of the American Academy of Child and Adolescent Psychiatry, 40*: 595–602.

CHAPTER ELEVEN

In the nurse's consulting room

Michele Meehan

*The experience of weaning: psychic trauma
and relationship disruption*

As a clinical nurse consultant in maternal and child health, much of my day-to-day work is with infants with day-to-day problems. It may seem trivial to think of weaning as trauma, but the depth of emotion seen in two cases of undesired weaning makes a good platform to consider the psychic trauma experienced by infants in adjusting to "our" desires. Weaning a baby from the breast during a hospital stay goes against all notions of attachment, wellbeing, and security. However situations arise when it may be necessary, desired, or unavoidable.

The meaning of the breast to the baby, mother and father may often be a far cry from that attributed by the health professional. Too often breastfeeding may be seen as merely a food, and persistence with breast-feeding an "interference with good management", at best a whim of the mother, at worst an obsession. Eating is fundamental to life, but the infant enters life dependent on the mother providing food for survival. Feeding is therefore an interaction between mother and child, with the development of feeding and eating skills dependent on the growth of this relationship.

The progress from one stage to the next relies on the infant signalling his readiness and the mother responding and encouraging the development of independence. If they are not in synchrony in this process, feeding problems may arise. In the earliest relationship feeding comes to mean more than the giving of nourishment, for in the tie forged between mother and baby, feeding symbolises love. Emotional conflicts may therefore be played out in the act of feeding. The mother in terms of her emotional needs may misinterpret acceptance and rejection of the food by the baby. What then if the baby finds enjoyment of feeding is removed and a less than satisfactory substitute forced on him?

To understand the distress we need to understand the meaning of feeding. It is not just good health, nutrition or food, but may even seem a matter of life and death. To feed a baby is to keep her alive, and daily weight gain is a phenomenon of these early months and years, a sign to parents that they and their baby are doing well. To be a good parent is to nurture and help your baby grow both physically and emotionally. The dependence of a baby on his parents for food is part of the development of trust and love in this relationship. Feeding, especially at the breast, is often synonymous with offering comfort, and the predictability of receiving food when a baby signals that they are hungry enhances their sense of security and trust.

The meaning of the "breast"

The motivation for the decision to breast-feed or not is different for many parents. The decision to breast-feed may be made because it is promoted as best for the baby; it is a commitment gladly undertaken, a gesture of effort, time, and emotion, ensuring the baby's wellbeing by giving the best possible nutrition. Pleasure in being able to nurture, to enjoy the baby's pleasure as well as the time together during feeding, may be synonymous with the decision to breast-feed. While it may not always be easy, the struggle may seem worthwhile. The predictable availability of the breast and its food is linked for the baby to all things, mother herself, comfort, food, pleasure, love, physical contact, and learning.

The meaning of weaning

Weaning has many aspects. "Substitution of milk other than breastmilk" and "physical separation from the breast" are not just definitions, they are also developmental progress: a sign that it is time to move on, an ability to take other food, an interest in the outside world. The separation involved is a sign that the baby is ready to separate, and the mother is feeling right about letting him go. Weaning involves a loss of the intimacy of babyhood and the exclusiveness of feeding and nurturing. It is also a transition time: an acknowledgement that the baby is growing, that time is moving on. The baby's independence is recognised, there is a need to accept that the baby does not need the same, that the parents are ready and want her to move on and grow up.

When is the time to wean?

The mother and the baby, not outsiders, usually make this personal decision. It may be based on past experience: if breastfeeding was for a short period with the previous baby, the parents may want to do it longer the next time, or they may believe that a certain age is a good time to wean. Weaning is usually when the mother is ready, sometimes also when the baby signals readiness. Sometimes the baby's signals of his readiness may come as a shock to the mother. But the hardest time is when breastfeeding is no longer possible although still greatly desired. When feeding is going well the decision or need to wean may be devastating to a mother but too often we presume the baby will go along with our decision.

However what does the baby say about this? In a strong statement of independence she may categorically declare, "NO WAY!!"

Case studies

Alan was experiencing a cessation of weight gain over three months, and at eleven months of age refused any other food; his mother had been trying to introduce other food for the last five months. The constant breastfeeding was tiring her and his feeding had developed into constant attachment to the breast. The response to the plan to wean, while causing mixed feeling from the parents, was absolutely clear from the baby: absolutely negative. Alan was furious. He refused a bottle/cup/food, refused to have his mother holding him when she would not let him feed, hit her and pulled her hair. He screamed and threw things at her when he woke in the morning, His mother was distraught about his distress, and became tearful whenever he behaved like this.

Colin's response was somewhat different. He was a premature baby who had been slowly growing and developing, gradually increasing the amount of breastfeeding he could do. This was then stopped and he was offered a bottle as his mother felt that he might be discharged home from hospital sooner. His response might be termed "passive aggression". He seemed confused, refusing the bottle, but then not demanding feeds. While he had started to wake three-hourly for the breast he now needed to be woken. He stopped gaining weight, and took a long time with the feeds.

Too often the decisions regarding feeding are made around the needs and/or difficulties of those caring for the baby. Infant mental health clinicians need to promote thinking not only about the baby's reaction to changes in feeding but also her contribution to the feeding interaction. How can we help both mother and baby in these situations? What response from us will help the baby and her parents?

Unfortunately the baby's refusal to wean is too often seen as a win/ lose situation. "If you give in to your baby, you'll never get there." By helping the mother understand and accept the baby's response whether it is angry, passive or distressed, and by validating the strength of the baby's reaction, the issue of who "wins" is diminished.

Rather than trying to address why the baby was behaving like this, perhaps thinking about "what" the baby was doing would lead to an understanding of the best approach. What he was doing was demonstrating his extreme anger at what was happening. Talking to the mother and baby using language that is genuine is important: "He's really angry with you refusing him the breast", rather than laughing at his "tantrums". Too often strong emotion from babies is seen as amusing by adults and not acknowledged for what it is—an honest expression of feeling. By ensuring that there is time for the mother to spend with the baby other than feeding attempts, the relationship does not deteriorate into a battle of wills. Allowing or introducing aggressive play with older babies, acknowledging their anger through play, hammering, throwing games and drumming, allows suitable aggressive outlets.

On one occasion while I was talking with Alan's mother, he wanted to feed, and she refused, putting him in the cot with some toys. His response was to fling a ball at her; I caught it and flung it back to the foot of the bed. This developed gradually into a quieter response of a tossing and catching game in which he let his mother join. If parents respond to this play and verbalise the anger, the baby may feel less compelled to act this out in the feeding situation. Similar responses of banging a tattoo on the bed in rhythm to his kicking helped acknowledge that anger was OK, and we would continue to interact with him.

We need to consider how to replace for the baby and the parents that which is lost with the loss of breastfeeding. The loss of security by the change from the normal routine/familiarity is emphasised by the change in feeding—"What does this bottle have to do with my being hungry!" There are feelings of unfamiliarity, and the need to learn new skills both by the baby and parents, especially by the mother who may never have given a bottle. The subsequent feelings of loss of confidence in the parenting role may lead to the baby being affected by parents' hesitancy and distress. Helping the family through this stressful time takes patience, empathy, and support.

The father's needs were also huge, as he was seen as the one to intervene with the baby as well as to support the mother. Active involvement by Alan's father was a strong feature. He had been as committed to the value of breastfeeding as his wife and found it hard to reassure her when he felt the loss greatly. He was thrust into the role of supporting her, and being go-between to the hospital staff when Alan was most adamant about refusing the bottle. Alan's father took over a lot of Alan's care and encouraged his drinking and self-feeding skills. He found it hard to balance doing things for Alan while trying not to feel that he was taking him from his mother. He stayed at night to attend to him and ensured that they had time all together when it was not meal time. He was sympathetic and caring to his wife, listening to her doubts and assuring his support in any decision. At one stage he stated that he would help her with her decision, if he could work out what it was! She laughed and agreed that she wanted to wean and that they would do it together. This seemed a turning point for her in not being so tearful over Alan's behaviour.

The outcomes for these babies were that we were successful in achieving weaning Alan, and establishing cup feeding and self-feeding of solids. Colin went back to the breast and everyone just had to wait! The true success can only be measured by the ongoing relationship between the mother and baby.

The distress around weaning can be severe both for mother and baby, and this stress can make normal behaviour and decision-making impossible. Acknowledging by discussion the strength and motivation of the individual's contribution (both parent and baby) to the breastfeeding relationship should be a vital ingredient in management advice and ensuring a caring response to weaning decisions whether voluntary or not.

Child's play

We are so used to seeing children and infants play that we tend to overlook its importance. How often do we hear the phrase, "It's child's play"? Any busy active baby demonstrates that it is anything but simple and straightforward. Play is the child's daily work and part of their development. While it is easy to understand that children play for pleasure, they may also use play to act out the struggles they face on a daily basis (Winnicott, 1964), and to make life real and meaningful. Through play, children can learn to deal with and feel in control of real experiences, fears as well as aggression. There is a great drive to persevere to a desired end, to overcome difficulties and to concentrate on the matter in hand. Play is therefore a powerful and expressive tool by which we as clinicians can assess, engage, intervene, and understand children's daily struggles.

What constitutes play?

Babies come into the world with a general readiness to engage socially (Murray & Andrews, 2001). The baby begins to discover his environment and capabilities by touch, taste, sight, hearing, smell, and movement. Play is not something parents generally need to worry about "teaching" their baby. Any interaction between the child and the outside world may be deemed play. A child or baby who is engrossed in something usually gets absorbed intensely in what they are doing. Opportunities for play behaviour enable the child to seek levels of stimulation that lead to cognitive development, or to avoid or cope with unpleasant stressful situations. Play may be as simple as the infant following his mother's face as she turns away to pick something up, or reaching out to touch a rattle shown to him or her. Focusing and paying attention to toys and people as well as everyday objects is the basis of understanding the broader world. Providing an object for the baby's viewing, seeing if he can follow it or reach out to grasp it, is all play that aids the baby's cognition. The baby using his voice to babble is "playing" with the sounds produced. Our talking back, imitating, gives meaning and engages him in play.

Play is an infant's tool, and when we relate to the infant with play that is thoughtfully about him, the infant has a sense of being "met" and this conveys a message to him or her (Thomson-Salo et al., 1999). Young children may play out their anxiety and new experiences through play. The infant or young child, struggling with unpleasant feeding experiences (e.g., excessive vomiting) may respond by only feeding while distracted by toys, or "switch off" and stare at an object to help "get through" the experience. Alternately they may "play" with the bottle before they settle in to the feed. Expecting them to feed "properly" may impinge on their way of developing confidence about the coming feed. By being in control of what goes in may make it easier to take in more.

Talking about play

The mother or father brings a host of already existing behaviour patterns to their interaction with the child. Their personality, attitudes toward life and the baby, the degree of turmoil in the family life, their health, and expectations of the baby affect the approach to the baby. The baby's characteristics and individual differences, degree of irritability, responsiveness and habituation (ability to ignore impinging stimuli) will also affect any interaction.

How can we think about play as a way of understanding the struggle for parents and their young baby? When talking with parents who describe a long day of difficulty, asking about what space there is to play may reveal more of what is contributing to the baby's struggle (as opposed to the parent's). Does the parent try to play? Often the difficulty with feeding/crying/settling to sleep has meant that when the drawn-out battle and anxiety is over, there may be little time or inclination for play. On the other hand, ensuring that play is not used as a "trick" may be a beneficial interaction for both mother and baby. Does the baby enjoy it? If the baby is reluctant to interact with the parent, looks away or is late or slow in smiling, then there is little positive feedback for the parent's efforts. We need to ensure that we do not only talk about what the parent should be doing.

In assessing the play experience of mother and baby, it is helpful to think about what can inhibit playfulness.

- Immobility. This may be due to illness or disability. But the child who is always in a stroller may also be unable to reach all the stimulating things around, or the baby in a cot may not be able to reach the things that she can see. Without the chance to interact or handle toys, the baby may limit her capacity to be absorbed in the outside world.
- Dull or repetitive environment. If there is nothing in the environment to look at, listen to, manipulate, or investigate then the child has nothing to play or explore. The trend to remove all stimulation to ensure dropping off to sleep may be counterproductive if there is little for the baby to focus on as he tries to regulate their state. Parents may also not realise how the baby is developing and still present toys more suitable for a younger baby.
- Overstimulating environment. On the other hand too much noise, too much handling, too much movement may mean that the baby retreats from the world to help down-regulate, and ignores the parents' comforting that could be helpful. The baby may end up being overstimulated, for example rocked vigorously and jiggled to try to "calm down", a contradictory response. The baby then does not engage in play or seek it out when it would be offered and most helpful. Also excessive pain, distress, or difficulty accompanying a "normal" event for example, feeding, bowel action, or going to sleep, may mean that the baby tends to switch off from the distress and in the process may not be available to take in the comfort offered.

Parents, overwhelmed with their own emotions, birth trauma, postnatal depression, family health or financial concerns may have little emotional energy for play. Babies who are very clingy and difficult to settle may interpret being put down to play as a signal that the parent is leaving, and cling even harder.

Play as a diagnostic and intervention tool

Talking about play and engaging the baby in playful interaction and talking about the baby's response illustrates that the baby is expressing more than just his or her mother's wishes. A baby has their own agenda and contributes their individual character to any activity. Only by experiencing "with" the baby can the nature of the play be assessed. It may be that through playing with the baby one can get a feel for the baby's response to events and share this with the parent. One six-month-old baby to whom I was showing a toy truck as I talked with her mother about her feeding, just looked at the car, pushed it a little then went back to what she was doing. I said to her mother that she did not seem to want any help! She replied that she felt the baby could get on without her, in fact she felt very cut off and distant emotionally from the baby and said, "Maybe that's why she doesn't feed very well." This proved to be a turning point in understanding what was going on and suggesting what approach to take.

Even a one-off response that is different can change a baby's mindset. If a baby experiences a different response to his behaviour, for example stopping the feed when they turn away, rather than pulling them back to the task, this allows them to learn, "Well, I do have some control here, so maybe I don't have to be so forceful."

If we talk about the baby's responsibility in any interaction and not just the mother's, then we add a wider field of interaction to discuss. We need to become comfortable with engaging the baby while the mother is just "sitting" there when we are engaging with the baby. Talking about what play the baby is doing, and using play, may broaden our assessment and especially intervention in understanding children's daily struggles.

Enough is enough

Sleeping, feeding, crying, and behaviour issues present in a variety of ways. Two babies were referred to me with similar issues and an idea of "overindulging" them seemed a way to help them move forward. Both babies were about eleven months and presented because of clingy and demanding behaviour: both would cry as their mother attempted to put them on the floor. As a result they were carried around most of the time, which was not acceptable to the family. Both were boys of married parents; Ben was a first child while Will had a six-year-old sister.

Will was striking in his aversion to strangers, his clinging to mother and demanding needs. I found him wary and slow to engage. He stayed on his mother's lap with his dummy (he was sleepy but had not slept in the car on the way to the hospital, a seventy minute trip). His mother showed me that if she made a move to put him down he grabbed hold of her; I therefore suggested that she wait while we talked for a bit. His sister had made herself at home with the food and tea set and was busy preparing lunch for us. As we talked of how draining

Will's behaviour was for her, especially with two children at home on the school holidays, he slid down and stood at her knee. He sat down then pulled himself up on a chair that I had near us and laid his head down turned away as though having a nap. I approached him, talked quietly, and stroked his back. He turned his head and looked at me. I then picked up a soft toy lamb and a cloth cube with a bell inside. He looked at the lamb and I said that it was sleepy too and laid it beside his head. I very gently banged the cube on the chair in a double rhythm. He smiled at the noise of the bell and I got more vigorous as he "woke" up more. He let me pat his back in time to the bell and laughed. As this went on for a few minutes, I then picked him up and sat him between my knees as I knelt on the floor with him facing his mother, away from me. He was looking around and I talked about what his sister was doing, but made no effort to move him. He initiated the move away, heading off to her, taking the doll that she had set at the table. He was interested in the food, so I sat him at the table with her and they remained playing there for the rest of the session.

His mother said he would never do this and she had been surprised that he had let me approach him. It was obvious that he made no attempts to engage his mother until he was happily playing and she responded warmly. I told his mother that I thought the more demanding Will became, the more she felt pressured to "get rid of him", so the harder he clung to her, and so on. To expect him to suddenly change was a big ask, especially as he felt that if he was upset this was where he needed to be because that is what always happened. While acknowledging that a main issue here for his mother was her postnatal depression (mentioned by the referring nurse) I felt that she also needed a strategy to help make a change rather than only address her projections.

I suggested that while it sounded horrifying, what she could try was to not put him down as soon as he was settled. When he grizzled or cried, she could pick him up and sit or turn him to "take in the world" rather than cling to his mother and "see" only his mother as the solution. To sit as I had done and show him the world waiting for him and let him be the one to say, "I want to go". A similar strategy she could try was taking him out in his pushchair (where he was happy) and when he got home (when he would immediately start crying) leave him there until he wanted to get out. In a way she would be saying, "You can stay here as long as you like"; his thinking may then become, "I can get as much of Mum as I want, so maybe I'll go off here for a while." He could then carry in his mind the memory of having her whenever he needed her.

A week later his mother reported that she had been able to do this, and that when he started grizzling she started by asking, "What do you want?" instead of "What's the matter now?" and if she waited a few minutes, Will would often go off to play. The pram walks were very successful and she was getting out more and feeling better. He looked much more animated on arrival and greeted me with a grin behind his hand. He pointed to the stove and the pots and demanded to get out of his pushchair.

Talking about the problem would not have been as effective. By actually sharing the difficulty from his mother's and Will's point of view, a broader picture was seen, and a strategy developed. I suggested his mother pre-empt his demand for attention, by going to him when he is happy, then not let him go until he asked to be put down, to talk about what was going on elsewhere in the room and let him demand involvement. This one-off "change" endured, perhaps because as his mother felt that there was hope for change, Will coped without needing his mother in this strange situation, and we were able to talk about what this had felt like for his mother as well as for Will.

This idea of overindulging was also successful with Ben whose mother said he was "an embarrassment" at playgroup or family outings, as he would only stay in his mother or father's arms facing the wall or away from everyone. In contrast to Will, Ben had no idea about playing. While he was sitting on the floor (again with slow coaxing and pessimism from his mother) I rolled a ball to him and he looked at it, then at me and did nothing. He made a similar response to any other toy offered. It seemed that his parents themselves played with the toys and showed him what they did. At no time in the session did they attempt to play or talk with him and both stayed on their chairs even though I was on the floor. I spent a fruitless hour trying to get him involved but with only a little success. I discussed that I felt he needed to feel comfortable to play and not just to cling. His parents said that they could do this at home, but asked what about playgroup and said that they had a big family get-together the following weekend. I talked about how Ben's separations were always at his mother's instigation and he seemed to have no role in asking to leave, that just when he was settled his mother tried to put him down. Playgroup was the next day so I suggested that she keep him with her firmly on her lap with an arm holding him tight while she talked about what the children were doing. If he looked interested in something she could get it, and play with him on her lap—and only if he wanted to get down should she let him. The next week as they came into the room he scrambled out of his father's arms, crawled over to the box, and brought out some balls. His mother immediately got onto the floor and sat there playing with him or just watching as we talked. He was busily interactive, laughing, and happy.

These two cases highlighted the dilemma that parents find when they are trying harder and harder to remove a "limpet": the more they push the harder the baby clings.

Working directly with the infant can make rapid shifts while the ongoing therapy for mother and baby can stabilise the relationship. As a nurse, parents come seeking "intervention" for their baby and are not often ready to address their emotional issues or the relationship. Being able to bring in concepts of the infant's mind and possible thought/ emotional processes, that the baby has ideas about what is happening and is not just being "difficult, clingy or stubborn" is a good step to further exploration of the relationship as a duo and not just a list of "Good mothers should." Membership of the infant mental health programme reinforces the dual role nurses can take in directly intervening with the infant, and being able to address the mothers' emotional issues at the same time.

Infant mental health: more than advice

Infant mental health should not be considered an arena solely for mental health professionals. Nursing care in the broadest sense, that is, caring for the patient and her family, means that nurses are in the unique position to being able to assist parents while addressing the issues presented by the baby. However, the idea that the baby can trigger change herself should always be considered. By looking at the issue from the baby's point of view and discussing their needs, behaviour and response rather than the idea of what the mother (or the nurse) can do "for" or "to" the baby, acknowledges that the baby themself is able to evoke change.

Patrick was born after a full-term emergency forceps delivery for meconium aspiration, with resulting respiratory distress requiring his being transferred from a country hospital to the city. His father worked for the armed services and the family was stationed in a town 1,300 kilometres from the nearest paediatric centre. There was no extended family nearby to help, so that his mother, Angela, was alone for most of the first few weeks he spent in hospital.

After his initial discharge, Patrick required a further four or five re-admissions for ongoing problems. His parents requested, and received, a compassionate transfer by the armed services so that they could be nearer his maternal grandmother and a specialist paediatric centre.

Angela had been ill during the pregnancy, which left her with severe arthritis. When I first met them, Angela and her baby had been home for only eight consecutive days since Patrick's birth fourteen weeks pre-viously, and her arthritis was slowly improving. As a hospital-based clinical nurse consultant, I was asked to see them because of the prob-lem of frequent breastfeeding, hourly at times, and concern about his slow weight gain.

The usual advice

Patrick's frequent feeding was assumed to be due to Angela not pro-ducing sufficient milk—a reasonable assumption, given the distress, separation, illness, and interruption to breastfeeding in the previous few weeks. The usual advice: to increase supply by increasing the number of feeds, was obviously out of the question in this instance. Other advice previously given to Angela was to increase the intervals between feeds so he would be hungry enough to take a bigger feed, which would allow her supply to build up a little. This advice, however, had been unsuccessful as he cried if not put to the breast and became distressed and tachypnoeic, causing Angela to give up.

It was clear that the intervention of giving advice was not helping, and all the advice that I might give had already been tried. So if the basic advice was right for mother, but not possible because of Patrick, then it was clear that we needed to look from Patrick's perspective to see if there were other options.

More than advice

Tschudin (1987) describes counselling as listening well, then talking in such a way that the other person finds his own solutions by listening to himself talk. Listening, reflecting and responding to Angela and

Patrick's story identified that Angela was adamant that breastfeeding was the right thing for him. But she was very worried that she would stop lactating; which is why she kept putting him to the breast to be sure that he got whatever milk she had. Patrick settled at the breast, so it was the best way to prevent him becoming too distressed, and so the cycle went on. Angela's anxiety meant she felt she had to keep putting Patrick to the breast, and he felt he was only reassured there. Therefore, any advice that had been given did not acknowledge Angela's concerns, and failed to take into account Patrick's behaviour.

The link between a mother's emotion and her baby's behaviour or mood is well documented (Ainsworth & Bell, 1970). Tschudin describes listening to the person as a whole, not just to the words spoken and the problem presented. By talking to mothers about their experience of caring for their baby, nurses should be open to the emotional messages that mothers give. The initial response to a mother's dialogue may set the scene for whether a topic is taboo, not appropriate, or not something to be raised immediately. The question for a mother will be: "Does this person want to hear my emotion?"

Putting it into practice

In developing an interview counselling style, it is important to have questions and responses that elicit further information, that encourage shared confidences and respond to strong emotion rather than gloss over it. Rather than taking a history, the nurse could start by saying: "Tell me what has been happening?" The use of a mother's words and where they start the story might indicate what is the most important part of the story. The point at which a mother starts the story is a good place to explore the emotion she expresses or that is felt in response to her story, by encouraging further elaboration, or even by commenting on, for example, that it seems too distressing to talk about.

Angela began by saying that since Patrick's birth, time had seemed to stand still. She said: "I don't know what day it is or really when any event happened. It's all blurred into one." Her words evoked a picture of endlessness, and I reflected this back to her. When I asked her to tell me about the first few days, her response was emotional: she had been worried that he would die. "I almost couldn't be with him," she told me. I commented that this was not how she felt now. "No, I don't want to let him go."

I ASKED: "What do you think would happen?"
ANGELA: "Well, nothing really, I guess."
I THEN ASKED: "But you feel you have to have him with you now?"

Daws (1993) suggested that the feeling of "not having enough for the baby" was a reflection of not feeling able to give enough care, and of the baby "asking more than I can give" of time, effort, and emotion. To express to health professionals the pressure of the baby's demands through breastfeeding might seem more acceptable for a mother to say than, "I've had enough of the baby." Fear of not having enough to give might be voiced in terms of not having enough milk to give. If we are able to hear and accept such ambivalence in a new mother, expressed through the feeding difficulty, or feeling empty or depleted through the baby taking "too much", the mother may feel supported enough to continue. Pines (1989) described the anxieties of new mothers and the confusion they feel which arises from both the physical and psychological adaptation to birth. This is exacerbated when the baby is ill and/or when a mother's health is slow to return to normal. A fear of losing the baby during pregnancy or a difficult birth can leave unresolved anxieties that are carried through to the feeding and caring experience.

Separation

One of the tasks that a mother must perform is to separate gradually from her child and at the same time encourage her child to separate from her. The baby must slowly learn to tolerate frustration, to substitute transitional objects for the mother's presence, and to hold the memory of her when apart. By doing this, the baby is able to achieve steps to eventual independence and a separate identity. However, if there have been threats to the survival of the baby, it is more difficult for parents to reassure themselves, and the baby, that everything will be all right.

Therapy

Therapy to achieve such changes also has a place in helping to promote some understanding and resolution of Angela's inability to achieve this separation. While for some parents, separation may be longed and aimed for, for others as it may symbolise bereavements and other intolerable losses they have experienced the anguish feels too great (Pines, 1989). Angela returned to the city to be near her mother and benefit from her support. When questioned about her relationship with her mother, she laughed and said, "Oh, she's great, but I'm still her daughter." Further exploration of this relationship revealed that she always deferred to her mother for advice about caring for Patrick, believing that "she knows best". Angela also felt ungrateful if she did not take her mother's advice. This ambivalence in the mother/daughter relationship seemed to be reflected in the mother/son relationship with Patrick: wanting him close, but wanting him to get by without her, too. A mother's distress at what is perceived to be an over-demanding baby may give rise to an overreaction of keeping the baby too close, that is, to protect the baby from her wish to go.

Patrick's experience

So what was Patrick saying and how could he be the subject of this intervention? By speaking to Patrick we can see his response, his gaze and reaction, as well as his desire to share his experience. We can describe to his carers a picture of an experience as chaotic as his mother's had been. In the midst of different caregivers, illness, and surrounded by distress, the mother's breast and her presence had become the one constant comforting factor. Patrick was clearly saying that he wanted the breast, that what he was hearing from his mother was, "If I'm upset this is what I need." The strong message that Angela gave was of her need to hold on to her baby in order to be sure that he stayed alive, and Patrick responded by staying close and needing her breast to settle. There seemed to be no other arena of communication for either of them.

Patrick's contribution

By exploring what Patrick could do, we expand the picture of him as a growing developing baby, not a tiny, totally dependent, fragile one. Asking about his development elicited the news that he was starting to smile. I explained to Angela that while this was late, this was understandable given his recent experiences, and that smiling now might be his way of saying that he was relaxed, or well enough to start taking notice of the world. Angela said that he was interested in the chain which she wore around her neck, that he held it when he was being fed. By using the chain and his smile, we used the feeding time to encourage his looking and talking with his mother.

She talked to him about her chain, telling him that his hand held it so strongly now. He was getting better and coming home with her soon. He stayed looking at her instead of dozing off and he fed for longer. After the feed ended he spent a short time awake just listening to his mother talk to me. With my emphasising his need now for cognitive development, demonstrated by his interest in the environment and socialisation, Angela could offer something good, other than the breast, and as he became more interested, could extend the play periods and give him another parameter of comfort. This gradually led to longer periods of separation from the breast as well as not immediately feeding him. The longer space between the feeds allowed extra milk to build up and he could have longer, bigger feeds. Angela was able to follow Patrick's signals rather than try to do things for him. Patrick very rapidly spent longer periods awake, fed better and gained weight within forty-eight hours.

Exploring and confirming these underlying issues identifies the need for different interventions and an extended range of skills on the part of the nurse. For effective listening both to the baby and the parent, the first step is to feel comfortable in our communication. Being alert and empathic to the emotional messages of mothers' discourse, the baby's responses and their timing can help provide another way of thinking about the problem. However, the emotions raised by discussion may be hard to bear, and may generate feelings and emotions in us for which we are unprepared.

I discovered this ten years ago when I noted that many of the families whom I saw had a common theme—a poor relationship with the mother's mother. Sometimes she had not listened to them, sometimes she had abandoned them (through despair, postnatal depression, or poor attunement), sometimes she had died; in some cases there had been an abusive relationship. As my work continued, I found myself becoming more distressed by the stories, and when talking of the cases with our infant mental health team I would frequently become very emotional. One of the members suggested that perhaps the source of my distress was my own mother. It took this discussion for me to acknowledge that previously I had let remarks pass, such as, "Well, my mother's no help" or "My mother's in Queensland" or "She died a few years ago". Unconsciously I protected myself from thinking about my own parents' deaths when I was a child, and what that loss meant to me then, and now, as an adult.

Other professions have a culture of ongoing supervision and consultation. Nurses should consider incorporating into their culture supervision or support from a mentor. In organisations where no formal support structure exists, this could involve finding a counsellor through their general practitioner, community centre, or professional network.

Interaction skills

Nurses who are comfortable reflecting the emotions of a story rather than asking another question, find that this slows the history taking, and allows time to think of a new perspective. Many nurses have developed phrases or questions that reflect their own style. Some examples of these are:

- "You sound very distressed/sad"
- "It sounds as though it was terrible! Frightening/worrying"
- "What were you feeling then?"
- "What did you think would happen?"
- "It sounds as though you may be blaming yourself for something?"

Another important skill is learning to say nothing—to be comfortable with silence. Too often when we ask a hard question we then leap in while the client is gathering courage to answer. "It's hard to talk about it" is an authentic acknowledgement of the client's struggle. It is also one which shows the client that you can tolerate the emotion of the struggle, and assists you over the silence if it feels that it has gone on too long.

A final skill required is to feel okay about not finding a solution. Counselling is about helping clients to find the answer for themselves. "Solutions" often serve to help health professionals feel good, as if they have done something. Approaches which let the client lead the contact include asking, "What do you think you want to do next?"

With Patrick and Angela's story, we talked about what might be happening for Patrick: it was his mother who described his interest and talked to him of her chain. We made no plan but to see what else he was interested in and that I would see her again.

There will always be cases requiring counselling and therapy which are beyond the nurse's skills and experience; however, skills and knowledge that all nurses should have are:

- the ability to recognise "this may be too much for me"
- knowledge of your local services
- the ability to refer with confidence.

Conclusion

Our interpretation of the nature of nursing is reflected in the role that we choose and the interventions that we use. Infants, children, and families need nurses who feel that they are doing a worthwhile job and feel appreciated. By thinking of the infant's contribution, by responding to and talking with the baby, a nurse can only increase the range and depth of their skills in helping babies and their families. Thinking about enhancing the connection with patients, through moving past advice and extending the use of counselling and therapy in everyday work, might be a way to greater personal growth, fulfilment and reward, and one that gives greater satisfaction, while benefiting those for whom we care.

References

Ainsworth, M. D. S. & Bell, S. M. (1970). Attachment, exploration, and separation: illustrated by the behaviour of the one-year-olds in a strange situation. *Child Development, 41*: 49–67.

Daws, D. (1993). Feeding problems and relationship difficulties: Therapeutic work with parents and infants. *Journal of Child Psychotherapy, 19*: 69–83.

Greenspan, S. (1981). *Psychopathology and Adaptation in Infancy*. New York: International University Press.

Murray, L. & Andrews, L. (2001). *Your Social Baby*. Australia: Acer Press.

Pines, D. (1989). On becoming a mother. In: P. Ashurst & Z. Hall (Eds.), *Understanding Women in Distress* (pp. 35–44). London: Routledge.

Thomson-Salo, F., Paul, C., Morgan, A., Jones, S., Jordan, B., Meehan, M., Morse, S., & Walker, A. (1999). 'Free to be playful': therapeutic work with infants. *Infant Observation Journal, 3*: 47–62.

Tschudin, V. (1987). *Counselling Skills for Nurses*. (2nd Ed). London: Ballière Tindall.
Winnicott, D. W. (1964). *The Child, the Family & the Outside World*. London: Pelican Books.

PART III

INFANT–PARENT THERAPY

CHAPTER TWELVE

Talking with infants

Robin Wilson

W hen an outsider sees a baby, they can bring hope to the baby through a new observation of the baby's mind, and the baby can be helped to understand their experience of the world through different eyes.

This "outsider" can be a doctor, therapist (or even friend or neighbour) and the interaction might only be a very brief one for it to be helpful to a distressed infant. I can give an example from my personal experience many years ago. I remember waiting with my own ten-month-old daughter in hospital just before she had an eye operation. I was worried and unable to play with her in the pre-operative ward that morning, and I sat beside her cot looking away so that she would not see my distress. Whimpering and clinging to the cotside, she stood looking miserably around the ward and her eyes met those of the father of an older child. They began a game of peekaboo together and continued happily interacting until she was wheeled away for her operation. I too was able to relax and smile at them and to feel that everything would be all right. I still feel grateful to this stranger for helping my daughter and me to cope with the anxiety of waiting for her procedure.

It is an example of an outsider being available to the baby to help her to deal with distress (in this case by playing a game about separating and being reunited).

Similarly, in our mother baby clinic, distressed mothers are often too preoccupied with their own problems to be available to their baby and to think about what is happening in the infant's mind. Our speaking to the baby directly about his feelings can have a powerful effect. In these situations it is a challenge for us to keep the baby in mind and to find a way to make contact with the baby. Some babies will seek engagement with an outsider and are able to use them readily, while other babies are withdrawn or easily overwhelmed, and might need to be approached slowly.

The following two examples are from my work at the mother baby clinic where I think it was important for the baby to feel understood by me. The first is a twenty-two-month-old baby, Bella. She had been a happy baby whose mother and father, despite their struggles, had been able to think about her in her early life, and care for her well. Being resourceful she was able to respond in a very positive way to one brief intervention. The second case is of a baby, Minnie, whose difficulties in her relationship with her mother began at birth, when her mother became depressed. Minnie too appeared depressed, and it took many months of visits to me before I was able to see a change in her mood and behaviour.

Bella's reaction to a violent conflict

Bella had always been a happy, active, adventurous infant who showed no stranger anxiety. Her Indian father and Australian mother did not plan to have children, as they had only recently married, but were happy with the pregnancy. Bella's mother suffered severe morning sickness but she related this to the stress of her Indian mother-in-law's prolonged visit, and to her husband's sudden plans to go and live in America, which he had subsequently abandoned. Bella's birth and delivery were uncomplicated and she was a healthy breastfed baby whose development was normal. She was much loved by her mother and her father. Her parents however, began to have marital difficulties and when Bella was eight months old they separated for one month. When she was fourteen months old, her Indian grandmother came to live with the family. At that time her parents began to argue again. Her brother was born when she was seventeen months old. Two months later Bella developed a sleeping problem after having slept well until this time. She became extremely difficult to settle and would cry for several hours from her bedtime onwards, eventually falling asleep exhausted about midnight.

When Bella was twenty-one months old she witnessed her mother and father arguing fiercely one night. Her father punched her mother in the face, and she fell to the ground. Three days later, her mother left her father and took the two children to live with her parents. Bella's sleeping problem became much worse: she cried loudly in an extremely distressed manner and would wake several times at night screaming and calling for her mother. During the day her behaviour appeared normal, and she responded happily to the extra attention she received from her grandparents and aunts. One day, however, Bella's mother was lying on the floor, and her grandmother prodded her playfully with her foot. Bella was watching and began to cry and could not be comforted. She remained distressed for several hours to the puzzlement of all the family, as it seemed a serious response to a trivial incident. Bella's mother who had been attending the mother baby clinic for a year to discuss her marital difficulties had only occasionally brought the children along and at this point brought Bella again.

Intervention

When I saw Bella, aged twenty-two-months, I was struck by how sad she looked. She appeared to be avoiding eye contact with me, which was unusual for her. As her mother told the story of Bella's unexplained distress, Bella brought me a small plastic ball from the toy basket. I cupped my hands together and let her put the ball into them. She stood and watched my hands as I held the ball. I asked her mother if she had discussed with Bella the fight with her husband and the subsequent separation. She said she had not done so because Bella was too young, and she did not know what to say to her and wished to protect her from distress. I remarked to Bella that her mummy and daddy had been very cross with each other and that her daddy had hurt her mummy. I said to Bella that she must have been very frightened when this happened, and perhaps she had remembered that when her grandmother touched her mother with her foot. Bella watched me silently and then took the plastic ball from my hand and gave it to her mother.

Two weeks later I saw Bella and her mother again. Bella no longer looked sad, and her mother reported to me that she was now settling to sleep better. Bella's mother had started talking to her daughter about her separation from her husband. Bella came over to the toy basket and picked up two small teddies. Once again I put out my hand as she came over towards me as if to give me the teddies. Bella looked me in the eye and brushed past me, and gave the teddies to her mother. She turned towards me and smiled, and I smiled back.

Discussion

Bella's mother thought that she was too young to understand the concepts which her mother and I were talking about. However Bella picked out a small ball and gave it to me to hold, as if to see whether a part of her could be held and understood. She then seemed able, at some level, to have been able to hear about her parents' anger and her own fear when I spoke to her, and to understand these.

At our second meeting she chose two teddies from the toy basket as though she were able to make a more mature and integrated choice. She brushed past me quite deliberately, as if to tell me that she knew that I wanted to help, but that now her mother was able to bear her own anger and sadness and Bella's as well. Bella no longer avoided eye contact and we acknowledged our understanding of each other by smiling. Bella's anxiety had lessened as she had felt understood and her sleep had improved. Although she and her mother are still angry and sad about their loss, they are able to deal with it in a more open and honest way.

Minnie's depression from birth

Minnie and her mother were referred by their local general practitioner to the mother baby clinic because of maternal depression, excessive crying, and feeding difficulties. Minnie was a very much-wanted baby. Her parents married two years before her birth in Scotland, where her mother, Jill, aged forty-two, had taken a teaching position. When Jill and her thiry-four-year-old husband, Ian, married they began to plan a family but soon found that Jill was already menopausal and no longer ovulating. They travelled to Australia where Jill knew a woman who had offered to give her an egg. Through the IVF programme, this egg and Ian's sperm were used to create an embryo, which was to become Minnie. The pregnancy was a very difficult one and Jill suffered from fatigue, reflux, and nausea. Jill became increasingly irritable and disenchanted with Ian. Minnie seemed to be healthy and growing well but was sensitive and responsive "in utero". She would move quietly when she was stroked gently but she reacted violently if the obstetrician tried to examine her or listen to her heart. Minnie's birth was by a planned Caesarean section at thirty-eight weeks. She cried at the moment she was born. Ian bathed her and wrapped her and she was shown to Jill who thought that she was wonderful. But she was unable to attach to the nipple, did not suck strongly and fell asleep exhausted and hungry after a feed. Her mother began the long and laborious task of expressing milk by electric pump, which took nearly all day and, because she was attached to the pump, someone else had to feed Minnie by bottle. Minnie became extremely distressed and cried inconsolably when she was fed or handled by a staff member. But despite the feeding difficulties, Minnie put on weight and was discharged with her mother from hospital at eight days.

On discharge from hospital Jill "fell apart". She was crying all day, unable to sleep at night and felt constantly unable to cope with Minnie's feeding programme. Each feed consisted of time at the breast, followed by a bottle of expressed milk followed by a complementary formula feed. Jill also constantly shouted at her husband for his ineptness and lack of support. Minnie's grandmother (Jill's mother) came to stay but she too was out of tune with Minnie (she banged doors and entered the room in a way that startled Minnie) and was soon sent back home to the country. From the age of about two weeks, Minnie would vomit during and after her feeds. Jill took Minnie to several specialists. A paediatric gastroenterologist diagnosed reflux and Minnie was prescribed various drugs in turn. She cried and was difficult to settle after feeding but between feeds was quieter. Jill, however, felt very strongly bonded to Minnie.

Intervention

Minnie was ten weeks old when I first saw her. Jill arrived twenty minutes late for her appointment saying that the taxi driver had dropped her at the wrong building and had become angry with her and thrown her things onto the footpath. Jill told her story in a flat and resentful way. I was aware of a growing feeling of annoyance with her. However my feelings about Minnie were quite different. Minnie appeared large and round and looked robust. She looked at me directly with her big eyes while lying in the pram. Jill picked her up and spoke to her soothingly, patted her and called her "gorgeous". Minnie appeared to hold herself stiffly but smiled weakly at me, then looked toward her mother and smiled. She continued to smile looking from her mother to me, and back again, as if to connect us. Jill asked if she could heat up a bottle and handed Minnie to me. Minnie did not "mould" into me but held herself very stiffly. However, she became enlivened as I held her and made small "ooh" sounds. Jill appeared pleased that Minnie and I were communicating.

While my initial response to Jill was to feel angry with her and I was tempted to refer her on, in effect to "get rid" of her as everyone else had (e.g., the taxi driver and other doctors), these feelings were steadfastly contained in the countertransference and Jill, who had considered going elsewhere, returned with alacrity as she felt her own angry and sensitive baby feelings to be held in a new way. I continued to see Minnie and Jill weekly until Minnie was five months old. I have no doubt that Minnie was also depressed for her first few months. Her face looked sad when she arrived and she often posited her milk. She cried in a strange, flat little voice for a great deal of the early sessions. She was easily startled if I approached her too quickly or spoke too loudly.

However, Minnie was extraordinarily responsive to me when I spoke to her. She looked at me in a very "knowing" way, vocalising back to me with "ooh" sounds. When her mother picked her up, she twisted her body around to look at me and reached out her arms as if she wished me to pick her up. On occasion I remarked to Jill that Minnie appeared to be reaching out to me. Jill agreed and said, "I think she wants to go to you," and handed Minnie to me. Minnie stood up in my lap, smiled when I spoke to her, said "ooh" and looked from me to her mother, as if pleased with herself. She also appeared to want to connect her mother and me, by looking from one to the other in a happy way, in contrast to her rather flat, distressed mood when she arrived. Jill too brightened up when Minnie responded so well to me, and did not experience this as a rejection from Minnie. These interactions with Minnie were in stark contrast to my conversations with Jill. I encouraged her to talk about her early life, and her family and relationships. She was an unhappy third child of a rather punitive, fundamentalist Christian minister and his country wife. Through her life, Jill had difficulty with friendships and angrily blamed others. My gentle attempts to look at her paranoid feelings, or her rage with her husband, were met with silence or appeals from Jill not to upset Minnie. Jill turned the lights out in the room or opened the door if the conversation headed toward her anger with Ian. She then arrived very late to our next session, as if threatening not to come back.

The central issues in assessing Minnie and providing therapy were firstly her mother's depression and her angry rejection of her treating doctors and nurses and second, Minnie's depression which was undoubtedly a response to her mother's. A major factor was Minnie's response to me and her eager participation in the therapy. Minnie's reaction had interested me and when Jill and Minnie came back, I was able to focus on Minnie and continue therapy with her, albeit gently, because she was very sensitive. In this therapy, my attention was on Minnie by talking to her gently and trying to put some of her unique baby experience in words. Although avoiding Jill's gaze, Minnie would, as time went on, engage her mother after looking at me. Gradually their relationship became more comfortable and Minnie's depression, crying, and vomiting improved. At five months Minnie slept for ten hours at night. Jill was more able to cope and although still depressed, she did not feel overwhelmed.

Conclusion

These two infants are very different but they were both caught up in marital conflict. As Daws (1989) pointed out, "When parents have an estranged relationship, the baby's experience will not only be of a mother being in difficulties with being emotionally available to him, but he will also sense that his parents are not performing this for each other" (Daws, 1989, p. 191). The infant may experience a range of feelings such as fear and anger or even a sense of being the cause of the parental distress. There may be no one available to empathise and understand the infant. This is when an infant can sometimes use a person who is removed from the conflict and available to think about his or her experience. Our work with the baby can be particularly important when there is marital conflict.

Bella had good self-regulation and was a settled toddler who slept well at night. After a violent exchange between her parents there was a change in Bella's sleeping pattern and her behaviour. She was probably angry with her parents and frightened to go to sleep at night. Her mother brought her to see me in the hope of gaining some understanding of Bella's distress. Although Bella had not yet developed sophisticated language, she responded very well to my attempts to put her emotional experience into words. She indicated to me in her symbolic play that she felt held and understood. A significant difference was made in one visit.

In contrast, Minnie's distress began from birth, or possibly even earlier, in the pregnancy. Minnie was a "much wanted" baby whose mother had gone to great lengths to conceive her despite waiting until she was in her forties to plan a baby, which was a clue to her ambivalence about a having a child. At birth Minnie was healthy and robust but immediately suffered feeding difficulties and was struggling to be nourished by her angry mother. Fraiberg (1980) wrote that, "In every nursery there are ghosts. There are visitors from the unremembered past of the parents" (Fraiberg, 1980, p. 164). Minnie's mother had suffered in her own childhood but was unable to see Minnie's experience, and was unwittingly recreating the horror for Minnie. Through capturing my gaze and looking from me to her mother, Minnie seemed to be entreating me to help her and her mother, and to link us. Gradually Minnie warmed up and as her mother was able to see her experience, and Minnie's depression, although it took many months, lifted.

References

Daws, D. (1989). *Through the Night. Helping Parents and Sleepless Infants.* London: Free Association Books.

Fraiberg, S. (Ed.), (1980). *Clinical Studies in Infant Mental Health.* London: Tavistock.

CHAPTER THIRTEEN

When twins present: creating space to be seen

Teresa Russo

W hat is it, as if it is only one thing, that ensures for one infant, despite trials and tribulations, a sense of possibility and capacity to engage with the world, and yet for another—often despite care and concern—a sense of exclusion or impenetrability about the world, and yet for even another the resultant anguish of the seemingly constant companion of fear and anxiety? What shapes the infant's options, his or her tomorrows?

Over an eighteen month period I had the experience of working with several sets of twins—some came for one or two sessions, some for a few weeks and some stayed for twelve months—and certain questions presented themselves again and again, uniquely experienced but hauntingly similar; questions of passivity and activity, of collusion and withdrawal, allies and enemies. With each set of twins came a mother, concerned, interested, frightened, in varying proportions but fortunately present and willing enough to venture into the world of her infants' minds and thus her own.

This experience of twinship uniquely placed in the broad swathe of humanity, two infants born at the same time into the otherwise unremarkable realm of family, a family of current circumstances and past histories. Two babies: for parents a double blessing perhaps, yet combined with concerns about how to provide doubly; for the infants themselves the usual task of establishing a place in their parents' minds and in the family order.

However, for the infant in twinship there is the added dimension, not faced by the singleton, of the ever present reality of the actual other, constantly there from day one to give tangible form to phantasies and thoughts of devouring greed, threatening deprivation, murderous rivalry; thoughts if not given a place to mellow will become unthinkable thoughts that limit the possibility of an encounter with a satisfying tomorrow. Ann Morgan would remind us that in the beginning, the mother's mind "is" the baby's world. Can there be room for two babies in that landscape?

Rosie rang. Could she come and talk? The twins she said were like chalk and cheese. The babies were thirteen months old. Katie, solidly confident but Jess not so. Poor sleep, frequent overnight waking, clingy, sometimes angry, often inconsolable, refusing food. The sleep school was fully booked for the next three months—testament it would seem to the wild night life of so many infants and the concomitant bleary-eyed days of their parents. But it was more than that—for Jess no words or gestures to tell what she wanted and she seemed smaller and hunched over unlike her robust communicative sister. Rosie was worried. What if … an unmentionable doubt seeped through her dulled voice. Her question hung in the air. We made a time and during weekly visits over the next six weeks the following drama played out.

Week one

They arrive in the double-stroller. Rosie helps both girls out and from the outset Jess, after an initial searching appraisal, actively engages me, much to her mother's surprise; grinning, bringing me things, somersaulting, the occasional twirl—doing "tricks", her mother says a little warily. I play with Jess, showing my pleasure at receiving her gifts, exploring interestedly with her the things she brings, admiring her physical feats. But there is an air of anxiety that contrasts with Katie, who contentedly explores with appropriate referencing to her mother. Rosie tells me a little about the arrangements at home, that she had returned to part-time work and that her husband cares for the children during those times as he is able to work from home. For the most part the session feels very benign, everyone is "nice", the infant who is "the problem" plays and I begin to wonder whether there is much of a problem at all. I find it difficult to get a foothold and begin to feel a little superfluous. Towards the end of the session I leave the room to get my diary, acknowledging the girls and telling them I would return. On my return Jess is in her mother's arms, upset, angry, refusing to look at me, turning away, shaking her head. Rosie says that she wanted to follow me. I feel an emptiness, a pain, demolished, caught in a strange world somewhere between regret, guilt, shame and sadness; I don't know which way to look. I stand still, waiting for Jess to return, till she is ready to re-engage. Rosie tells me this is what happens at home and it often slips into inconsolable rage. At those times she tries to placate with food and drink, which Jess will taste and then reject and the rage escalates. In the end Rosie feels she has no other choice but to ignore her. Jess can remain sullen and withdrawn for hours.

My thoughts dwelt on my experience of emptiness, demolition and having to wait and I felt that Jess had communicated her experience to me. Had there been a time for her of having to wait unbearably long, of having felt betrayed? It seemed that Rosie also carried a sense of demolition, that her capacity to mother this infant had been derailed. Rosie had brought the children along but she was not keen for anything difficult to be seen and was probably concerned that she was about to be exposed as a bad mother. So she was a little thrown when this infant came in and started to play happily enough, it seemed, with me until that last interaction. I think that possibly what was difficult and painful to bear was buried, and in this first session I was drawn into colluding, partly defensively I suspect, with that, with the niceness, and it may have needed to be like that for the infant to get across to me her experience.

Week two

Next week when they arrive, the girls are keen to play. From the heavily laden stroller, Rosie unpacks containers of fruit and biscuits and cups of drink as if preparing a picnic setting. A happy tranquil scene, but with the feel of a Hitchcock movie, birds hovering. Rosie mentions Jess's "upsets", about not being able to settle or comfort her even though she offers her food and drink, and as Katie approaches, pointing at a drink cup, Rosie says approvingly that Katie is more able to express her needs and wants with gestures and sounds. Right on cue, as Katie absorbs her mother's approval, the scene plays out. Jess becomes irritated. Rosie, kneeling on the floor, offers food, item after item. Jess crawls onto her mother's lap, crying, becoming more and more distressed, rage building. Rosie looks up at me despairing, and a hint of something that looks like shame. She says she has nothing to offer her; she seems to have forgotten that she has her voice, her touch, her thoughts. I notice that though Jess arches and cries she does not try to leave Rosie's lap. I say this to Rosie. She looks at Jess and offers tentatively, "Good girl, it'll be all right," and though Rosie reminds me of a small, frightened creature approaching danger, she stays with Jess, stroking her hair. Then strikingly the baby's cry changes and a mournful lament fills the air. Rosie recoils and says in a haunted voice that this is what she sounds like at night. Even as she stays with her it seems that Rosie does not know this infant all over again. Every now and then Katie comes over, pats Jess and then moves on, concerned yet strangely unmoved. Jess's crying eases. The session ends and both girls settle into the stroller though Rosie notes that Katie seems unfamiliarly hesitant.

Again Jess had powerfully communicated her experience, this time of despair, of mourning a great loss, an experience complicated and intensified by Katie's presence and approval by her mother. The balance was skewed—this trio felt less like a threesome and more like a powerful alliance between Rosie and Katie with Jess hung out to dry and yet Rosie's response of "unknowing-ness" seemed overwhelmingly disabling. Again powerful projections emanated from the distressed infant, this time of helplessness and terror, projections which seemed indigestible for this mother. Yet with support Rosie was able to stay with the distressed infant.

Week three

On their return the following week, Rosie tells me in a strangely subdued way that the world has changed but I hold my breath wondering in which direction the planet is heading. She settles down onto the rug watching the girls as they move around. She tells me that Jess now is much more settled during the day, sleeping through at night. Something niggles at the back of my mind. What is it that Rosie has begun to digest that leaves her so subdued even as she sees Jess begin to improve?

Together, mostly in a comfortable silence, Rosie and I watch the girls; occasionally one of us would comment and share a thought on something that one or other of the girls was doing; when they play with the baby dinosaurs, burying them in the playdough, I murmur to Rosie "Well that's one way to deal with too many babies!" Jess brings me the Babushka dolls, curious at how they come apart and stack back together and I wonder with her. The two girls play at hiding baby dinosaurs in a tub of playdough then searching for them again; sitting on the small chairs, hopping off then climbing back on, giggling. They play around each other, not quite with each other, every now and then touching base with their mother. Towards the end of the session Jess climbs up onto the couch and tosses all the cushions onto the floor. She grins. Her mother smiles warmly at her.

For Jess it seemed clear that her experience of being tolerated the previous week by her mother as she, Jess, exuded fury and hate, had had a profound effect, a relief to find that she was tolerable and that her mother was not irreparably damaged. As the balance shifted, something between the two infants was beginning to playfully come alive.

Week four

As Rosie wheels the stroller in, Katie is eager to hop out and play with some wooden trains but Jess remains slumped in her seat. Rosie seems hesitant. I sit down opposite Jess and say that I think she wants us to wait for her. She turns her head away, glancing back surreptitiously. She puts her hands up in the air and pulls the safety-bar down to a level that obscures her face. I peer over the top, wondering and searching as I say, "Hiding—where's Jess?" She pushes the bar up then down, glances up over the top and grins. We play the game a couple of times and then Rosie joins in and continues the game. As I step back I notice that Katie stands silently watching. Jess lets her mother know that she is ready to hop out and I talk with Rosie about a different pace for each child.

Katie has resumed her play with the small wooden train carriages that have magnetic connections; she joins them but they come apart as she pulls the train along; she becomes very distressed. I commiserate with her and talk to her about there being one, two or lots and spread my hands in a gesture of everything falling out; maybe she wants there to be only one and I wrap my arms around myself. But when they come apart there are lots of pieces and I drop my hands out again. Her mother comments that this happens a lot at home, that she wants things in the right place and gets very distressed if things are out of order.

Within the safety of the therapy playroom, it felt that as Rosie had more space in her mind to think about difference so did each of the infants seem to have space to explore their own internal worlds and in particular those aspects that stirred up painful feelings—for Jess it seemed to be about how could she be seen and for Katie something troubling was only now becoming visible.

Week five

On entering, Katie seeks out the trains and plays again but rather than distress this time she seems just mildly annoyed, as she herself pulls the carriages apart before putting the train back together again. Her mother says there has been a lot of this at home this week; working it out, she says. She also talks about the changes in Jess, that she is more confident and starting to vocalise. Rosie says that she herself is more at ease now in coping with both the girls. She is grateful for the help in thinking about the girls' experiences and when she suggests that next week will be their last visit I am not really surprised but I am disappointed. I think I understand how difficult this has been for her but I do not want them to leave.

Something felt unfinished.

Week six

The girls play comfortably, sitting for a while at one activity and then moving on. In particular I note Jess's relaxed confidence, no need for "tricks" to please me, no manic air of defiance to propel herself into activity. Rosie tells me that it has been a tough week and something crystallises for me. I realise that I have often been baffled as Rosie starts to talk because I have no sense whether what I am about to hear will be hopeful or horrendous. I wonder if this masking reflects her efforts to remain calm in the face of the overwhelming experience of two babies and all that their care entails, and what of an infant's experience of this state of mind, of an unreadable mother?

Rosie continues. The girls had a routine physical check up this week only to reveal a finding in Jess that led to multiple appointments and urgent hospital investigations. As Rosie watches she muses that Jess has not been at all concerned, that her night sleeping remains undisturbed; Rosie and her husband however were desperately worried. Then after a pause she tells of a previous hospital experience when the twins were five weeks old. Katie was desperately ill. For five days her survival was in doubt and Rosie stayed in hospital with Katie. Jess was at home without her. Rosie thinks now that this was when the sleeping troubles started. It is as if she has only just been able to make her way back to those dark five days (with the safety of this being the termination session), and from that dark space she is able to voice the question that she has not been allowed to think, the question perhaps that created a roadblock for Jess into her mother's mind:

"What if Jess, being the baby she is, has caused damage to Katie?"

At first I am puzzled by the question, confused. Surely Jess was the baby she had come about, the one that she was worried would not eat or sleep or talk. Then I feel outrage. What does she mean, "caused damage to Katie"? What had Jess become in her mother's mind when it seemed that Jess would live when Katie might die? And what had Jess imagined that she had become in her mother's mind? And then I think about the terrible dilemma that Rosie had faced and what now seems like her struggle with her ongoing fear or mistrust of this baby and her guilt. I think something becomes clearer in both our minds.

* * *

Rosie's absence from Jess and the long days at the hospital for Katie created a severe disruption for both these five-week-old infants, a disruption that was compounded further for Jess by her experience of losing a safe place in her mother's mind, a mother who was totally preoccupied with the distressing possibility of a baby dying. As for Katie, a whole other story was evolving in tandem, a story with a flavour of control and rigidity as she tried to make sense of falling apart, trying to hold her world together.

Rosie's return from the hospital with a recovered Katie offered little consolation for Jess who struggled to find a place to process her own confusion about presence and absence. But Rosie's question provided some illumination. Perhaps something from Rosie's own past, perhaps something that evolved between Katie and Rosie in hospital, perhaps something within Jess herself, contributed to that which Jess became in Rosie's mind, an ever present and ongoing threat to the other's survival. As Jess failed to find a firm footing, a resonant self, in her mother's mind, she was at grave risk of teetering into a world of limited tomorrows.

This difficulty in finding a footing was almost re-enacted with Rosie's finishing the therapy just as an understanding was coming together in my mind. But this time it seemed that there was now enough space in her mind from the work of the previous sessions to enable a greater freedom, not just to see the twins differently but also to think what had previously not been able to be thought. As I engaged with the infants and their mother, it had been possible that some of these powerful feelings could begin to be known about and made sense of by me and then unconsciously communicated back to both them and their mother. What was difficult and painful to have to bear in the countertransference seemed to have been taken back by them without the need for it to be verbalised extensively as they were able to take it in and build on it between sessions.

CHAPTER FOURTEEN

Play dough, pooh, and general practice: communications of a two-year-old child

Teresa Russo

Where to begin? General medical practice—the world of eleven-minute consultations. But general practice is also the place where, over time, practitioners come to understand more of the complexities of ordinary lives—lives that often impress with their courage and resilience. An appreciation of the family circumstances may give some insight into contributing causes to physical symptoms yet attempts to achieve change may not be so successful—symptoms may shift from organ to organ system or even to another family member. Infants and children with feeding and sleeping problems, with rashes and allergies, with pains, constipation and headaches may present and not infrequently general practitioners may feel powerless to offer relief.

The young patient I would like to discuss took me on a journey and along the way I came to better understand how bodily experiences and a developing sense of self can become enmeshed and entangled with emotional turmoil and can solidify into physical symptoms.

Jane and Helen

Jane, aged two and a quarter years old, presented initially with sleeping difficulties and later, with severe constipation and a painful, blistering rash. She was seen at the hospital outpatients' department and treated for four months with enemas, suppositories, and ongoing laxatives. Despite this, her symptoms of holding on and hiding when she defecated persisted. All this occurred in the context of disputed access visits with her father.

I first met Jane and her mother, Helen, when I was asked to see them by another general practitioner in the practice. My colleague was concerned that Helen was depressed and was having difficulty tolerating her daughter who had become very unsettled and clingy at bedtime. Jane's parents had separated when she was two months old. Her father, Mike, had continued to see her frequently, often three days a week. When Jane was around twelve months old Helen decided to visit her own mother overseas as she desperately craved the support of her family. Helen and Jane were away for three months. The visit was not very successful. On their return to Australia everyone was angry and Jane's relationship with her father was clearly disrupted. Mike's visits became very irregular and at the time of the first presentation around sleep difficulties, Mike had seen Jane only once in the preceding six weeks. Jane missed him terribly and at night time desperately clung to her mother.

My first two meetings were with Helen alone as she felt that there were things she needed to say that could not be said in front of Jane. I later came to understand how Helen's difficulty in allowing any angry feelings to be spoken of contributed in part to Jane's anxieties and impacted on the child's attempts to control and manage her bodily experiences. Helen spoke of her early childhood, of her parents separating when she was three and not seeing her father again after the age of five. Since having her own child, Helen saw her mother as having adopted "the victim" role. Helen had returned to tertiary study and worked part-time to earn some extra income. Distressed, she described Jane occupying her bed at night and restricting any opportunity "for a life". She angrily raged about Mike whom she believed was trying to punish her by not spending time with Jane. Her resentment and ambivalence were powerfully palpable. On our third visit I finally met Jane, a very bright and engaging little girl who enjoyed exploring, playing, and drawing. She seemed clearly able and willing to make use of anything I had to offer, and I was acutely aware that this was not the little girl I had expected to meet!

After this visit however, Helen cancelled the next appointment and I did not see Jane and Helen again for four months. But as circumstances spiralled out of control, Helen returned with a distressing story. Mike was depressed, behaving erratically and often verbally abusive. Helen had taken out an intervention order. Access visits with Jane now occurred at the police station and these were conditional on supervision by Mike's parents. Helen described these meetings as a war zone; legal battles loomed. It was during this four-month interlude that Jane's constipation manifested as a clinical problem. My colleague had referred her to the hospital for management. Sleeping difficulties persisted and despite continued use of laxatives, Jane was reluctant to open her bowels, insisting on wearing a nappy and always holding on and hiding when she needed to defecate. Helen was furious and, through clenched teeth, she described patiently trying to manage Jane's "constipation". Once again everyone was angry and Jane was suffering. Fortunately, enough of her own childhood informed Helen so that, every now and then, when the rage settled, she was painfully aware of Jane's experience and would waiver between blaming herself for behaving as her mother had or bitterly resenting the situation she found herself in.

Most telling during one session was Helen's description of an overwhelming moment at home where she had sat and cried helplessly. Jane had approached her and gently caressed and consoled Helen:

"Don't cry Mummy. I'll look after you."
"It shouldn't be like that for a two-year-old," Helen sadly told me.

In the room between us was a shared image of Helen as a young child supporting and parenting her mother.

I offered Jane and Helen regular sessions where together we could play and talk and think about what was happening for Jane and her experience of the obvious turmoil in her life.

Ongoing therapy

Over the next four months I saw Jane and her mother weekly. The box of toys I kept for her included play dough and animal cut-out shapes, house furniture including an oversized toilet, a range of dolls (mother, father, girl, babies), a set of three Babushka dolls, and a container of animals including a lion, a large cow, three dinosaurs and an angry-faced rubbery hand puppet. Jane's use of these objects showed repeated themes and she came to use particular items with specific meaning.

In the first play session we got straight down to business with Jane demonstrating that she needed and wanted to be heard and understood. She came in carrying a baby doll from the waiting room. Curiously this was the same doll that she had brought on her last visit four months ago. Quite coincidentally I had in my collection of toys an identical doll. On entering the room she looked around at the toys, picked up the identical doll and quite poignantly and gently fell to the ground, letting the two dolls slip from her hands. It was as if she trusted that I would under-stand her as she demonstrated how insecure, both inside and out, her world felt. I sympathised that she must be hurt to fall down like that, to which she responded with a big grin and jumped up and went in search of more toys. The dolls remained on the floor in the middle of the room, a paralysing reminder of her pain, while the rest of the session swirled around the room at whirlwind pace. As she left she efficiently collected her doll and returned it to the waiting room. The "falling down" proved to be a recurrent communication, as Jane often used this to remind me that, despite my wish for it all to be better, her struggle was ongoing and that for now she required my continued support.

She would bring so much each session that there were times when my head was spinning. In the first session a very small baby doll was repeatedly dunked in the toilet, the Babushka dolls got stuffed full of play dough, the large cow with the very big udders stomped all over the angry rubbery face, the family of dinosaurs was viciously attacked by the cow and at one point Jane instructed us all to make angry then happy then sad faces, rapidly alternating. Finally, as Jane discovered that the toy table had a wobbly leg, she wondered aloud whether I would be able to fix it, and just to make sure I got her message, she herself wobbled and fell to the ground.

Every act, every movement seemed to have meaning and often I was not quick enough to give voice to my understanding. Initially this caused me a great deal of angst—I wanted Jane to know that I under-stood what was happening for her. Of course, I was also acutely aware of her mother sitting in the room wondering what on earth I was play-ing at. The sceptic in me wondered if I was not reading just a bit too much into Jane's play. At these moments when my confusion was about to engulf me, Jane would give me a glance and with a half smile, as if she knew how I felt, would reassure me. I eventually came to tolerate these occasions and began to trust that just knowing about and appreciating Jane's experience was in fact communication enough. She just needed me to know.

But there were also times when words needed to be spoken and on those occasions Jane would push me, until I managed to get it right. This often seemed to be when the "unmentionables" needed mentioning particularly in front of her mother—being allowed to say that she felt angry or that she liked being with her father. Sometimes it was just wanting to know more about her own body, what was inside, where babies come from or about the new man in their lives who for some odd reason slept on the couch when there was clearly room in her mother's bed for him.

In the third session Jane was playing with the girl doll who, she said, wanted to get messy in the play dough. Meanwhile Helen was telling me that her boyfriend had stayed over and Jane had happily joined them in the bed in the morning. As Helen was talking I became aware that Jane was at my lap agitatedly trying to get my attention. She was rattling a closed container and anxiously asking, "What's in there? What's in there? I can't open it. Can't open it." I helped her open the container and much to my surprise inside was the bowl of play dough with the undressed girl doll stuck in it. "What's in there?" Jane again badgered me. This time she wanted an answer. Instinctively I replied, "Sometimes babies are inside mummies' tummies." With this, Jane gave a satisfied nod and took the girl doll off for a bath.

These early sessions seemed to be about sorting out the difference between play dough, pooh, and angry mixed up feelings; about working out what was inside and what was outside, what belonged where and how to manage it all. Her play with the Babushka dolls was one example. She would furiously stuff the dolls full of play dough and then anxiously and bitterly complain that they were too full and would not fit together properly. On one occasion she became quite distressed that the small doll could no longer fit inside the larger doll with all the play dough there. "Too full of angry feelings," I commented and her distress eased. Gradually over several sessions she came to limit the amount of play dough so that the dolls could easily fit together. Later on still, as her emotions became more "fluid", the tough sticky play dough was replaced with water.

By the second session Helen reported that the sleeping problems had eased considerably, with Jane sleeping in her own bed. By the fifth session Jane was wearing panties and "weeing in the potty". Helen had also noticed that Jane was more assertive and angry lately and more able to tell Helen of her displeasure. The hiding and holding on, however, would fluctuate, often depending on the situation with the access visits, Mike's mood state, Helen's work pressures or how many letters from the lawyers had arrived that week.

I felt pleased with the overall progress but I was soon to be made aware that I too was holding back, that I had not yet accepted that Jane's relationship with me was an important element in the whole process.

"Messing up"

Finally I had to accept full responsibility for my involvement. One week I forgot the special box of toys but, as there were other toys in the room, I made no specific mention of it. It was an irritable session and Jane, grizzly and whinging when it was time to leave, had a minor tantrum. I realised that I had never seen her behave like a two-year-old before. The following week Jane, wearing her "I'm a Superstar" tee shirt, marched arrogantly into my room. She had brought two jellybeans from home. She ate one and in a severe, no-nonsense tone of voice said, "The other one is for later. None for you." Then placatingly, as if fearing retaliation, "I might bring you one next week." She immediately drew a large circle with squiggles in it and took it to her mother.

> "What is it?" asked her mother.
> "It's a potty with wees," stated Jane.
> "And poops?" asked her mother hopefully.
> Irritated and cross Jane snapped back, "No poops, just wees."

Helen said that it had been a bad week with lots of holding on. Everything this session went wrong. The play dough was too hard. The lid was stuck. The pens would not work. My interpretations were rejected with a resounding silence. Then with a black pen she scribbled on the dolls, then all over the cow and all over her hands. I felt at a complete loss. I had no words. Jane then marched over to the basin and ordered me to put some water in the basin. There was no plug. I felt incompetent and stupid. "Like last week" she scornfully said, perhaps referring to our use of a scrunched up paper towel to plug the drain. I had forgotten. She stood at the basin and, Pontius Pilate-like, washed her hands, mocking me, as I too tried to deny my involvement.

I stood in silence, helping with the water and soap, and then it occurred to me. Her words "Like last week" brought it to me ... "Last week I forgot the toys. You've been angry with me so you've been holding on to your poohs." And with that I felt her resentment and anger dissolve. Her body eased and her shoulders relaxed. As I was able to say it, so she could know it and did not have to keep acting it out. She could hand it back to me. With that she then washed the cow and the dolls and at the end of the session as she was leaving, she looked back over her shoulder and said, "Thank you for helping me wash all the dolls."

Several weeks later Jane brought in from the waiting room several train engines and their carriages and trucks, all disconnected. "How do they join up?" she asked as she struggled with hooking and unhooking. Her mother meanwhile was telling me that it had been a big week—mediation through the courts, Jane being looked after by Helen's new boyfriend one evening while Helen studied, and baby-sat one evening by the new boyfriend's parents to allow the couple an evening out—as well as Jane's usual two days in family day care. Throughout the session Jane returned to the trains, lining them up, joining them, hooking them together. "Can they be all together?" she asked. I commented to Jane that there seem to have been lots of people in her life this week coming to look after her. She took all the trains over to the basin and submerged them in the water. "Too much water—can't see. Less water ... more water" she muttered and instructed me. As she merged them all in the water there was a sense of learning to cope with all the overflowing emotions—with a little help from me to control the water level. "Lots of parts to look after," I said. Jane then took the trains out of the water and wrapped them in paper towels and carefully dried them. "It's hard to look after all these people," I commented and I was left with such a sense of responsibility. It was Jane who felt she carried the burden of responsibility for all these people in her life.

The next session Jane entered the room carrying the collection of trains all connected up and demonstrated for me how well they travelled along the ground.

> "Look at all the trains. All together," said Jane.
> "You're feeling very good today," I smiled.
> "Yeah," said Jane's mother. "Tell Teresa what happened this morning, what you did."
> In a very soft voice Jane said, "Poops in the potty."

Discussion

The first few visits with Helen alone were, I believe, the basis of the trusting therapeutic relationship that was to evolve between Jane, Helen, and myself, providing a milieu in which Helen was allowed to sit back and, for a short time each week, safely relinquish control. Equally Jane was able to use this space to do things that she was not allowed to do at home: to speak of unmentionables, to explore her anxieties and come to know a little about her anger. She felt free to experience her own body with pleasure and, importantly, to express, in the presence of her mother, her love and compassion for her father. She was able to consider and tolerate the vast array of conflicting feelings and loyalties that she experienced in relation to the various people in her life and moved some way towards integration. Within this proceeded the normal development of a toddler, her evolving linguistic and cognitive capacities, increasing motor capabilities, issues with control involving her struggle for mastery, ongoing separation-individuation and psychosexual development.

As Jane and I became more confident about each other, the theme of the sessions began to shift and, as she became "de-parentified", she began to bring more about herself. In her drawings she would often ask me to trace around her hands or her feet, defining her evolving sense of self. She would enjoy making imprints in the play dough of her hands and feet, enjoying her ability to impact on her world. She would proudly show me her new dress or smart tee shirt and then undress and immerse herself in water play. During later sessions she would confidently ask to go to the toilet. As she became less fearful that her "messy poops" would make her unlovable, she became more confident in showing me her "real" self.

General practice with its structure of continuity of care allows the opportunity over time of listening to the life stories of our adult patients and, particularly in those patients with some degree of anxiety and depression, an appreciation of the impact of early childhood experiences on the development of physical symptoms as well as mental health issues can be better understood. In this context then, as a place where patients of all ages can be heard, general practice is well situated to allow early recognition of developing difficulties as well as being an ideal forum to practice early intervention with our youngest patients.

CHAPTER FIFTEEN

Tom's perfect world

Julie Stone

Tom died three months after his third birthday. His death was expected. Kathie Waters, a senior infant mental health clinician and I, in my role as infant psychiatrist, worked together with Tom and his family in the final months of Tom's life. Our work was part of a community based mental health programme for children under five and their families.

A social work colleague working with one of the specialist medical teams in a children's hospital referred the family. She told us that Tom's mother, Lisa, was struggling. Our colleague asked for our help because she said she felt "out of her depth". She was unsure how to help Lisa or how to respond to Lisa's request for help with preparing Tom's older brother, Nick, for Tom's inevitable death, a death that might be five weeks, or five years, away.

When we first met Lisa, Tom, and Nick, Nick was solemn and silent. He looked a very sad five-year-old. Tom was much brighter, though his smile seemed permanent and rather mask-like. Lisa was tearful and troubled and worried about her boys. Her opening request was about Nick. She explained she did not want "to leave him out". She badly wanted to "get it right" for her sons. She told us of her mother's experience of having an ill sibling. Her mother was said to hold onto some resentment toward Lisa's grandmother because she favoured the ill child and her mother felt overlooked. Lisa was troubled that Nick might come to resent her. How could she help prepare him for his brother's death? The unspoken question loud in my ears was "how can I pre-pare myself for my son's death?" Lisa wanted to know how she could care for Tom appropriately balancing his needs with Nick's. She wanted help to find room in her mind, her heart and her daily demands, for both her boys.

During this first meeting, after some shared time, Kathie and Nick left us to explore other spaces and possibilities within our workplace. Nick seemed keen to get away from his mother's talking and we won-dered if he would become more enlivened in a different space.

Tom stayed with his mother and me. He explored the toys that I brought to him and listened carefully to our conversation. I included him, of course. At one point, I said, "Mummy is just telling me how very sick you have been and that she is not sure how long you will stay with the family." Tom looked at me wide-eyed and interested. His mother quickly interjected, "Oh, I don't think he understands." I smiled at her and said that I suspected Tom understood quite a lot, and he was certainly very interested in listening to all that we were talking about.

I asked Lisa how much she and the children's father, Peter, talked with Tom and Nick about what was happening in their lives? She answered, "Not much really." In essence this is what Lisa wanted help with—what to share with her sons and how best to express it. She wanted assistance to be a good enough mother for both her sons.

From this first meeting, Lisa made a commitment to our work together. She brought her sons to see us weekly and courageously engaged with talking about and thinking about her experience. Over time she devel-oped a greater capacity for thinking about the world from the point of view of her sons, and she began to understand how her experience directly influenced her sons' experience.

Lisa was frail and frightened. In her family of origin she had learned the art of avoiding thinking about all things uncomfortable. Distraction and/or dismissal were their way, so our work together was confront-ing. Over time, Lisa said she came to experience thinking and talking about the things that she was worried about and troubled by, as com-forting and supportive. When we said our goodbye she remarked, "I do not know how I would have survived without you."

Sharing an hour with Kathie and I became an important aspect of the boys' week too. Despite Nick's sometimes-grumble in the early days, both boys looked forward to visiting the clinic. They quickly learned to use us, and what we had to offer them, fully and thoughtfully.

The boys' father worked away. It was some months before he came to meet us on a visit home. He was reluctant, watchful, wary, and uncomfortable in the first meeting. He seemed tense and ill at ease. We did not think we would see him again. However, over time and as Tom became more and more unwell, Peter embraced our work with his family whole-heartedly and demonstrated that he wanted to be part of it too. He brought a liveliness and an irreverence to the work which were great assets. They were assets because they did not take up all the space and because they were great leavening agents.

The early presentation led us to formulate that rather than preparing for Tom's death, what Lisa was really struggling with was allowing her younger son to truly come alive to her. It was painful and difficult for his mother and the world to see Tom for who he was, to embrace him as Tom, rather than a "poor wee thing" or the family's tragedy.

Tom was two and a half years old when we met. With his tiny withered body, he looked like an eleven-month-old babe. His mother carried him on her hip and was used to moving unnoticed as a mother carrying her baby. However, as Tom's language progressed and developed, Lisa became increasingly uncomfortable because she felt people stop and stare at her and her talking boy, who clearly was not a baby, and yet looked so like one. She found their curiosity irksome and embarrassing.

There were so many contradictory forces: Lisa's wish for Tom to stay as a baby, Tom's wish to explore and discover the world; Lisa's wish for Tom to stay close, Nick's need for his brother to separate from his mother a little so that there was more room for him. The boys need to struggle openly with their rivalry for their mother's attention opposed to their mother's need to have them always in harmony. For Nick to be able to both hate and love his brother free from an impossible expectation that he would always be a good boy and look after his little brother. For Tom, to be able to strut his stuff and to protest about some of the things he could not do.

One of the therapy rooms was called the "pillow" room, which was inspired by the lively work of a late colleague, Margaret Fay. It was a space with lots of cushions, mattresses and soft balls of all sizes: a safe place for rough play where no one would be hurt. Nick was one of many children who loved the pillow room.

A rhythm for our work evolved. We would all meet in the largest family therapy room with its comfortable chairs for children and adults and lots of room for sitting and playing on the floor. In the centre of the room there was a children's height table and on the wall a children's height white board, and shelves of toys, blocks and a dolls' house. After this initial "catching up" Kathie and Nick withdrew, usually to the pillow room, for thirty minutes to do their work. Then we came together again, to talk and play together and to each share aspects of our work, if that felt important. Finally we would play involving both boys, particularly focusing on their relating to one another and speaking about and giving words to their battle for their mother's, or Kathie's or my attention, if one ensued.

Tom, Lisa, and I stayed in the therapy room. We would all sit on the floor, or we would all sit at the small table to talk and play. I often needed to divide my attention between Tom and his mother as their agendas ran in parallel. On one occasion Lisa was telling me how she had been to a birthday party for a three-year-old. She said how sad it was and how unfair. She complained that other three-year-olds were developing and growing and Tom was not. As his mother was saying this to me, Tom was creating a wonderful drawing, all the while telling me the story of it. I said to Tom, "It sounds like you are wanting mummy to know that you are growing and developing—drawing and making stories—learning lots of new things, even if you cannot do some of the things that other boys and girls do." He nodded and smiled at me.

The next week Lisa came in laughing. She said Tom had spent the entire week drawing, drawing, drawing!

After a couple of weeks of Nick and Kathie disappearing and returning to us, red faced and clearly having had a lively time, Tom made a wordless protest. Kathie asked him if he was letting her know that he wanted to go into the pillow room too. He nodded vigorously, and said, "Yes!" clearly delighted that Kathie had understood his protest.

Lisa was wary of Tom venturing into the rough and tumble of the pillow room. However, she agreed to "give it a go" if we thought Tom would be all right, if it would not be "too much" for him. Despite Tom's pronounced limitations to independent mobility he entered vigorously into doing what he could, showing us how he could kick and roll and throw, and so a dialogue began, describing Tom as the rolling boy, the kicking boy, the balancing boy. With each named accomplishment Tom's smile grew broader and brighter. Nick needed help to accommodate his brother in this space that had previously been his private space where he was the only boy. Finding a place for some of the feelings that are part of ordinary family life was necessary and helpful, not all of the focus could or should be on Tom's illness and his dying. Rivalry and competition belonged to brothers and to living.

As well as some new-found physical prowess, Tom also discovered play dough. He delighted in making and creating shapes with his mother and me and vied with Nick for the favourite shape-cutter when Nick and Kathie returned to join us. One afternoon, sitting at the table in the therapy room with Lisa and me, engaged creatively with the play dough, Tom looked at me, smiled. He said, "It's a perfect world." His mother looked up, startled and asked, "What did you say Tom?" He smiled at her and repeated, "It's a perfect world." Lisa was amazed. She looked at me and said, "I have no idea where he heard that, and I have never heard him say it before." It was a precious moment. Tom, a little boy, present in the moment of creative engagement, at one with his life, a perfect moment.

On another afternoon, I went to the hospital to meet Tom and his mother after a review appointment with the specialist. Peter was away, and Lisa was worried about the meeting and what it would tell her about Tom's future. I packed up some of Tom's favourite toys from "our" room, including the play dough. We sat together in a make-do private space where the three of us could be together. Lisa was very distressed. The last-ditch effort at treatment was not working and Tom's functional capacity was deteriorating. The physicians did not know what else to try. Lisa sat weeping and telling me about her fears, while Tom sat with me on the floor industriously making shapes out of the play dough. When particularly pleased with how one turned out, he would offer it to his mother. He made a butterfly and sat it on the back of his hand. Tom held it up to his mother who was crying and talking intently to me. He sat there patiently, waiting for a space to share with her. "Mum, mum," he said in his effort to get her attention. Then, more emphatically, he said, "Mum, open your eyes!" I heard him calling his mother's attention to him: here, now, alive.

This stays with me a poignant reminder of the fine balance between present and future, between life and death, between embracing one moment rather than fearing the next. In the week following this meeting

Tom suffered a brain haemorrhage. It left him with a left hemiparesis and without speech. He smiled much less often after this, and when his face did lighten with a small smile, it was lopsided. This event, followed by a ten-day hospital stay during which Tom and his family celebrated his third birthday, marked the beginning of the final stage of Tom's life. It was a painful time and also an important time. It was a time for Tom and his family and those who loved them to prepare for the end of his life, which, although ever present, now became more real and very close. Peter came home and stayed with his wife and sons. Lisa mourned the boy she had lost: Tom the talking boy, Tom the laughing boy, Tom the lively boy.

Following his discharge from hospital, most of our work was done with Tom and his family in their home. However, Tom did visit the clinic one last time. His father took some photographs of Tom in our therapy room and in the pillow room and Tom showed us all that he was pleased to be there.

Although in a different key, and with a different pace, our work continued to be about holding present and future in mind, simultaneously: striving to embrace the moment, as well as planning for the future. Not an easy task.

How does one talk to a three-year-old about dying? Lisa telephoned distressed and upset after one of the visiting medical team had used the word "dying" in front of Tom. She asked what she should do. I suggested we talk about it together with Tom during my visit (Kathie was on leave) the following afternoon. When I arrived, Tom was sitting on the couch with his mother watching television. I sat on the floor near to him and said simply, "Hello, Tom". He held my gaze intently. Peter, who was about to collect Nick from school, said, "Wow, Tom is really looking at you intensely!" Lisa responded by saying to Peter, "I think it is because Julie talks to Tom. Most other people just talk to us now."

After Peter left, I asked Lisa to turn off the TV. I sat holding Tom's hand, talking with him. I told him his mummy had telephoned me because she was upset with some of the talking people were doing around him. I told him that his mummy and daddy did not want him to be frightened, that they would stay with him. I explained that his mother was upset because she did not know how to say goodbye to him. She was very sad because three birthdays did not feel like enough; there were so many things she wanted to share with him. Softly, gently, quietly I shared with him the thoughts that came to me; snippets of conversations that

I had had with his parents, things that we had enjoyed together. Lisa sat by his side, with her arm around him, weeping quietly. Tom held my gaze, his eyes fixed upon my face, listening to what I was saying. I was watching carefully, attuned to Tom's expression, ready to read any communication from him that said he had had enough. The three of us sat together for a long time   ten minutes, maybe more. Then, at some signal, a subtle shift in Tom's energy, we moved, together, to the floor. Lisa placed Tom between my outstretched legs, and Tom leaned into my abdomen. Together the three of us began playing with the play dough and shapes that Tom's parents had bought him for his birthday. Tom directed my industry and placed his able hand on mine to help with the cutting.

When Nick returned from school with his Dad, they joined us on the floor. Peter entertained us with making a moustache, big red lips and some green snot to run from his nose! The boys were delighted.

Before I left, Tom sat on my knee as his father showed us the photographs that he had taken during his final visit to the clinic. We shared those and the images from Tom's birthday, and images from a recent family holiday. Then Tom indicated he needed to return to his mother's arms and I said my goodbye. I was about to go to a meeting overseas, and I knew that I might not see Tom again. I said, "Goodbye, Tom, I am going away for three weeks, and I may not see you again." Lisa was anguished and said, "Don't say that, I want you to see him again." I replied, "Of course", then repeated my goodbye to Tom and said I would be away for three weeks.

Tom died two days before I returned to work. Kathie had been a regular visitor to the family during these last days. Lisa telephoned to let her know that Tom had died—the day after her last visit.

At Tom's funeral Peter spoke so lovingly of his sons. He honoured Tom and he honoured Nick in a way that clearly articulated his ability to keep both his sons in mind. He said too that a lot of living can happen in three years and that being Tom's father had changed his life; it had widened his heart.

My heart has also been widened by the journey with this family.

Kathie and I continued to see Lisa, Peter, and Nick weekly from some months. During this time Nick engaged in some important work with Kathie. He used his work with her to help make sense of some of his mixed-up feelings about being the living brother and his fears that all the goodness had been buried with Tom. Nick was able to think and to talk about wanting his mother to see him and his wish to be allowed to be alive and lively. He wanted his mother to be alive and lively again too. Both he and Peter, his father, knew that this would take time, and they were prepared to be patient with her.

Life and death, endings and beginnings, pain and sorrow, joy and laughter: Tom's short and perfect life left a rich legacy for those who knew him.

CHAPTER SIXTEEN

Babies in groups: the creative roles of the babies, the mothers, and the therapists

Campbell Paul and Frances Thomson-Salo

B abies and parents spend quite a considerable time in group contexts, and babies have been in group situations or interacting with each other since the beginning of time. In this chapter we look at some ways that four kinds of groups using a psychoanalytically informed group therapy model could be therapeutic. In an earlier paper we discussed the development from 1990 of a mother–baby therapy group particularly from the perspective of the way a baby might take the lead in therapeutic work and is therefore present as an equal member (Paul & Thomson-Salo, 1997). Since we started that group there have been many developments, with an increasing acknowledgement of broader social relationships, and of connectedness with babies. In this chapter we'll consider developments in therapeutic work with infants in groups that retained the idea of viewing the baby as subject in his own right. Three others groups grew out of this model which we describe as, the "very" premature babies group, the Stargate infant–parent group for infants who were in care for the first time, and the Peekaboo club for mothers and infants who had witnessed violence in the first year of life.

The *Mother–Baby Therapy group* synthesised developments in the areas of psychoanalytic group work and psychotherapy with parents and very young infants within the first year. We will describe some clinical findings, particularly the interactions between infants and therapists and those between the infants themselves. Interactions which we think contribute to some resolution of the difficulties will be discussed briefly. We think that the group is innovative in that we have not been able to find any accounts in the literature of a mother–infant therapy group where the focus is as much on the infant as on the mother. There has been growing emphasis on the infant's contribution especially since Klein's (1948, 1952) insights into the infant's internal world, and this is reflected in a rapidly expanding body of experimental work on the capacities of the infant. The idea that very young infants can be engaged in their own right in therapeutic work has yet to be fully explored.

Literature review

Christie and Correia (1987) who ran several slow-open groups for neurotic and borderline mothers whose children's problems appeared to be related to unresolved conflicts in their mothers, described how, as the mothers work through conflicts around ambivalence, there is a freeing of warmth and constructive resources in them and in turn they become freer to allow forward movement in their children. A number of clinicians have described their work with closed time-limited therapy groups for mothers who are depressed after the birth of their infant (Bailey, 1981; Holden et al., 1989; Meager & Milgrom, 1996). Other clinicians have run groups for depressed mothers where the infants accompany the mothers but the infants have not been engaged as members in their own right. Currently there is an increasing readiness to set up groups for mothers who are depressed, either along psychodynamic lines or more structured groups, usually time-limited, and often with a planned programme of topics for each session. (Clark et al., 1993; Conte et al., 1990; Gruen, 1990, 1993).

Another group with a similar approach to our model was run by Siksou (1990), a psychoanalyst working with a midwife co-leader, which was offered to mothers the week after they gave birth. It is an open group of about thirteen mother–infant dyads with a core of six to ten dyads, and is presented as a group that will help mothers with their difficulties. Initially, when a main theme is the fear that the infant will die, Siksou's stance is a facilitating one, and in time the mothers' identifications become benign and supportive. For the more peripheral members of the group the experience will be one of brief support. In the ongoing work there is no focus on the infant's contribution.

Over the last decade an increasing range of psychoeducational groups for infants and their mothers or sometimes their fathers have been developed by other practitioners, as for example Smith's (2004) PAIRS groups that are time-limited, semi-structured and build in a separation model. There have also been a number of groups for fathers and infants in varying contexts from antenatal educational classes to fathers in prison.

Rationale for psychoanalytically oriented mother–baby therapy groups

When infants present with a psychosomatic symptom, they often improve without their mothers' issues being addressed and we are interested in trying to bring about change for the infant in the present as well as a more long-lasting change in the mother. Clinical experience suggests that otherwise such infants might present with problems later on, for example, infants with feeding difficulties may present later with anorexia nervosa. We therefore see the group as having a preventive function. In addition, we offer something quite substantial for the infant. Green (1980) argued that the infant may feel with a depressed mother that the infant has a dead mother, and there is the possibility of therapeutic interventions to lessen this effect.

The group is a place where women can share what has been an overwhelming experience, explore their ambivalent feelings and start to redefine their sense of self to include the concept of "mother". It provides them with a place to start separating their past anxieties and conflicts from their view of their infant so that this can become more realistic. Group work may particularly be indicated for those mothers who present as cut-off in a way that might lead to their being difficult to contact in individual work, and also for some mothers who have difficulties with their anger and may therefore feel more supported in a group (Durkin, 1954, 1964; Hopkins, 1993, personal communication).

Siksou (1990) suggested that mothers in a group can more readily accept confrontation by the other mothers than if they were in individual therapy. We have wondered whether the mothers' experience of guilt and feelings of blame is less persecutory in a group, and also whether there is a greater possibility of a therapeutic identification with the baby and other mothers. We have also thought that the therapist's countertransference might be more usefully available in a group.

It seems likely that in selecting women and infants for our group we reach a group who need something more long-term. The infants are usually three months or older when they come into our group so that we may be seeing pathology which is on the way to becoming established.

We believe the mother–baby therapy group model has the potential to be applied to a range of different populations. The first criterion is that there is distress for the babies and/or their parents and the parents are able to see their baby as in need. Other criteria are flexible depending on how the group has been set up. Usually parents need to be able to understand what we hope to achieve in the group. Occasionally we have worked with parents who suffer severe mental illness who find it harder to see what it is hoped to achieve.

Organisational set up of the groups

We will describe the set up and running of the group as it applies to the original mother–baby therapy group, and then describe variations in the subsequent three groups. This group runs weekly and lasts for one and a quarter hours. The infants, referred by various clinicians, present with a number of difficulties, such as feeding and sleeping disturbances, as well as more serious concerns such as failure to thrive and profound gaze aversion. There are four to five mothers and their infants, and the group is available to them for as long as they feel it would be helpful. It is set up as a slow-open group; six months is an average length of stay. Together we meet the mothers and infants to prepare them for entry into the group. Our guidelines are that they should feel free to say what comes into their mind; that we advise against socialising after group sessions to facilitate sharing confidential information in the group, and we ask for a reasonable period of notice when they want to terminate. We obtain their consent for the group to be videoed, which we do to help us with what we have missed as we have a special interest in infant–infant interactions, and also for teaching purposes. We are able to make the video-ing arrangements fairly unobtrusive. There has been a brief follow up six- eighteen months after they leave the group to help us understand what part the group played for them.

We have not arranged parallel therapy for the mothers in a formal way, though it is available for some, and while there may be advantages in setting up a parallel group for the fathers, we have not done this because of what we felt were boundary problems in entering a therapeutic relationship in another context with the mothers' partners.

It seems helpful to have a male and female co-therapist. We do not have defined roles, but offer ourselves as a thinking parental couple who are different from one another with different contributions that the group can use from us. Having two group leaders helps with the experience that, with the infants present, it often feels chaotic in the group. In the group room, we provide basically the same few carefully chosen toys each week, to offer as uncluttered a physical space as possible.

Because of its size the group may appear vulnerable, through illness in the infants or the mothers' difficulty in making a commitment to longer-term therapy when so much in their lives is in flux. The group is, however, surprisingly hardy which is linked with the place it has in our minds; the infants are also very much contributing members.

Clinical guidelines

We have four main guidelines in our interpretations.

First we try to create a space by not providing direct instructions or guidance. We share Winnicott's belief that "the answers" are in the mothers and that there is no single "right" way to parent.

Second, we try to interpret group process rather than to work with individual mothers, and, where appropriate, we take up the negative transference. When we work more with an individual mother it is partly to do with viewing her as speaking for other members and also that it would feel somewhat artificial at that moment to make a group comment.

Third, we attempt to keep the focus on the infant's communication and the mother–infant interactions as much as on the mother's experience of being a mother.

Fourth, seeing the infants as being of equal standing in the group we address comments and interventions to them when it seems appropriate.

Rapid changes in the infants

Rapid change can be a feature of therapy with distressed infants and their families, and can be understood as one outcome of the plasticity of the infant if the environment begins to change. The mother's psychic adaptedness to her infant as well as her wish to get it right are also important. Mothers usually start in the group with a relatively positive attitude to us. As Gosling (1981) pointed out, very small groups have more benign expectations, and less regressive features and less expression of aggressive expression, and where there are more benign expectations, the results seem to be more positive.

> In seven-month-old Ian's first session his body tone was flaccid, he could not sit up and he looked like an infant who was depressed. His mother was severely depressed. She thought that every time he looked at her she had to smile, which led to rather fixed smiling on her part. He did not look at us or the other infants very much, unless we were active in eliciting his gaze or Mary, who had been coming for some time, was persistent in reaching out to touch him and vocalising to him. He often withdrew into holding or mouthing a toy. By his second session, however, Ian was a transformed child, he sat upright, and was more engaged with the group leaders and Mary; he smiled, moved, and vocalised with pleasure, and communicated what he wanted. It seemed that the new experience of the group and its interventions had promoted change for Ian and his mother.

Daws (1995) pointed out that in infant–parent therapy small changes have the possibility of setting in motion more widespread changes. It is worth highlighting that in the group, there are not only the interventions by the therapists—the infants cannot fail to be aware almost immediately of the response of the other infants. We think it possible that where infants feel held by the group setting they may process difficult feelings for one another by projective identification.

Group themes: maternal themes

Schindler (1966) described the clinical finding of the transference to the group as mother, which suggests that the group experience predisposes mothers to be able more quickly than in individual therapy to work on aspects of their relationship with their own mothers, and of the meaning of motherhood. The main themes have to do with conflicts over the losses that they feel they have experienced in relation to themselves, their infants, and their partners, and of a good internal mother.

The birth story, the impact of the birth on the mothers' psychosomatic integration and ambivalence about their relationship with the baby's father are prevalent themes. They convey the disparity between societal expectations of perfect motherhood and their own sense of incompetence and despair, as well as being competitive in their neediness with their own children. There is a longing for a reparative relationship with their own mothers; often they have little practical or emotional support from them. Some aspect of these themes may be present in nearly every session and are worked through in each mother's time in the group.

> In the course of the work Celia's view of Mary changed. She became softer and warmer towards her, and talked with her rather than at her. She stopped dreaming of coffins flying off and came to feel that she was bonded to Mary. She was less intrusive and was happy to let her play with other children, commenting on how well she was doing it. She said with feeling, "The surprise with the new baby is at how much you have to go outside the family for assistance and a lot of family assistance can be pretty damn useless." Talking about hating her adoptive mother and other childhood experiences which she had felt as rejections led in time to the group helping her redefine her relationship with her adoptive mother. It was more of a feeling that she had to create rather than recreate an internal good mother. The group constituted a good mother, in that it was non-judgemental and containing. During sessions she could say things that she felt were trivial or hateful and it was acceptable. By the end of her stay there was an actual reconciliation with her adoptive mother and Celia identified with some of her good aspects.

Infant–infant interaction and infants' themes

Although there is a considerable amount now known about the infant's cognitive capacities it is still not widely thought that very young infants are emotionally interested in their peers. There is, however, from early infancy, awareness not only of the parents but also of peers. Based on Rochat's (1998) conceptualisation we have come to think that in the group situation the infant sees herself reflected in the other infant, the peer, and thereby comes to know who she is, a separate person from the other infant.

There has been little research published on infant–infant interactions but pioneering work from Selby and Bradley (2003) illustrates the power of infant–infant interaction in the early months of life. Mueller and Vandell (1979) report that as infants master a particular motor or vocal skill they begin to direct that behaviour to an available peer. For example, with infants who are frequently together, extended looking at the peer in the first two months is reported. Touching the peer is reported at three to four months. From about six months onwards infants become more actively engaged with each other. They smile in response to their peers' coos and vocalisations. By seven to eight months as they become more mobile, they approach, follow, and reach for peers. From around nine to twelve months more clearly "social" behaviours develop with increasing frequency. Ten-month-olds have a marked propensity to look at their mother when alone and at a peer stranger when s/he appears. With both mother and peers present, the infant directs more looks, touches and proximity-seeking behaviour to the peer, not the mother.

Around nine to twelve months the "offer" and the social "take" are observed regularly between peers who know each other. The offer is by hand, whereas previously infants have done it by gaze or sound. These offer and take behaviours are thought to be most important because they maximise the likelihood of evoking feedback from the partner, whether peer or parent. With this feedback the possibility of sustained encounters can be enhanced. During the nine-to-twelve month period infants who know each other have been observed playing games with each other, such as run-and-chase, peekaboo and ball games. With the acquisition of these behaviours of vocal exchange, offer, approach, and smile, the repertoire for the infant's social encounters is fairly complete. It is clear that interactive play is present in the first twelve months. Montagner (1989) in stressing that peers are important in installing behavioural organisers highlights the specific importance of the infant's action of offering to others.

Considering the infants' evolving interactive and internal processes in the group, the infants' awareness of and empathy for the other infants' feeling states seem quickly apparent on entry into the group. We provide a quiet reflective space and try to keep the focus on interpersonal matters rather than on actual things, to facilitate the development of empathy, and the infants use the space in their own particular way. If one infant in the group cries other infants can often be seen looking anxious or upset. From a very early age they show pleasure in interacting with other infants, and activities and games are increasingly elaborated with them. From a very early age the infants give clues both that they miss the other infants if they are not there, looking round for them and being low key for a time, and that they remember the activities they had been engaged in with them, by starting off with the same activity.

The Group is a playground where they can work out developmental concerns. For example, after a toddler had pushed over twin girls smaller than himself we raised with his mother that she had not talked to him about her pregnancy. He then laid a doll in the centre of the floor, and the following week he began the session by laying a doll on the female therapist's lap.

The infants at times express their ambivalence and concern for their mothers. Each mother/infant pair brings their anger and battling into the group, which provides some containment as they struggle with their difficulties. Infants may hit their mother or avoid her or have temper tantrums. If the mother's anger towards the infant comes through in what she says this resonates with the infant's feelings, and the infant needs to cling to her or act it out in his activity. Gradually as mother and infant work out some of these difficulties the infant's concern for the mother can be seen slowly growing. From her longitudinal study of six pairs of same-aged babies (five of whom came into the study aged between six to twelve months), Urwin (1990) reported that as ambivalence towards the infant's mother increased by the end of the first year there was also increased ambivalence towards the other infant of the pair. We have not seen this as clearly demonstrated in our group and think that jealousy and other conflicts might be heightened in the way Urwin studied the pair relationship (with the infants playing together but not in the presence of their mothers) whereas the group setting allows other possibilities.

Therapeutic interactions and interventions

The fact that the infants' ages range from three months to about a year means that practical aspects of infant care may feature quite considerably, or even dominate, the sessions. Infants sometimes need their nappies changed in the group; they are fed milk or biscuits or vomit this up; they may be tired; they may sometimes cry inconsolably; they need to be held and walked around by their mothers—all this often gives sessions a very chaotic feel.

Initially we were puzzled about why in some sessions we had not made many transference interpretations, and why we had not more vigorously taken up what could look like attacks on the process, for example if the mothers were late. We did not think that it was simply collusion on our part. The transference may not always be so clear when there is so much happening physically and verbally, and although there may be regressions and anger expressed about their children, the mothers cannot completely put on one side their mothering role as their infants need them to continue functioning as mothers.

The therapists' ability to bear and contain the "actual" as well as the "psychic" mess and pain brought by the mothers and the children, the crying and demandingness, the illness at times in the mothers, and the many difficult feelings communicated by projective identification, is crucially important, and may have a more important function in a group of mothers with their babies than if our group were composed entirely of adults. Being able in the countertransference to bear the confusion and chaotic states, we provide a containment that acts as a non-verbalised interpretation: what has been brought is bearable and knowable. It is noticeable how, after a session where some of the chaos is contained and not acted on, the following session is calmer or leads to further development of material such as a mother's anxiety that she might abuse her child. We hold the child in the mother and the real child, and think about them in a way that allows the mothers to find the answers within them. Our thinking about the mothers helps them to think about the baby. One mother said that she thought we were "reparenting" her and was horrified that we should think that the answers were in her, partly because she did not feel she had any answers and felt what was inside was so bad. By the time she left, she had come to feel there were no "right" answers and no longer felt herself to be the mother of a bad child. The mothers were able to feel we had some faith in their capacities for change and to love and care for their infant.

Whatever rivalry there is for the group leaders' attention, the mothers can be verbally supportive to one another. Quietly supportive gestures go on between them. It is usually a sign of some internal change when the mothers start reaching out to other mothers' infants.

Apart from providing a containing space for the mothers to project their internal world which is also a physical space where mothers can watch the play of their children together unfolding, we try to interpret group themes and the negative transference when it impacts on the therapy.

We have the expectation that when the infants form significant relationships with their peers this could be as positive a therapeutic experience for them as for their mothers. To facilitate their interactive empathy, the group toys are arranged between the therapists so that the focus is between us and not all around the room. If children are having difficulty in engaging in the group we might initially try and facilitate this. We might, for example, make a comment such as, "How would your child feel about another child being away for a week?" We try and create an atmosphere where the mothers talk about how the infants might be thinking about each other.

We do not deliberately offer ourselves as models for the mothers but try to respond from a position of having the infant and her mother at the centre of our thinking. Holding the infant's gaze while we think about and respond to him is, we think, one of our most significant interventions. There is increasing awareness of the importance of gaze in early infant communication and interaction (Paul, 1991; Riess, 1988). It is an enormously significant experience for infants to know that they have succeeded in capturing the gaze of another. We also talk about the infants and talk and interact directly with them.

The infant's transference and countertransference

Infants transfer onto us and the other group members feelings and ideas which derive from their caregivers. The therapists become significant to the infants before the other mothers do and how infants initially behave with the two of us is transferred from how they are with their mother.

Some infants relate positively to us from the first, as though they have left aside the difficulties with their parents, and are ready for what we offer. But it is not the extremely intense and immediate transference which Watillon (1993) describes, although over time it can build to that. In Watillon's view, at some point in the first therapeutic consultation the infant externalises the conflicts with the parents in a dramatisation which she can interpret to the parents in order to free development, and the infant senses very quickly that Watillon can act as a container. Her consultations seem, however, to be mainly with older infants, and to constitute brief therapy rather than gradual therapy with the infant over time. The children in our group often end up gravitating to Campbell Paul partly because he represents an interested and available father figure.

By projective identification we have had to bear very difficult feelings about some infants and their mothers that they could not bear to know about. Sometimes we comment on a child's activity to try and help the mother "see" it, if for example the child is vocalising more but her mother comments adversely that her language is delayed.

Therapeutic action

What had not previously been focused on before is using the infants' activity as part of the process of the group. In pointing out the part that the infants' activity plays, we are likely to be addressing one of the following four aspects. Firstly it reflects or illustrates the conflicts and anxieties of the mother(s). Secondly, it enacts for the mother(s), for example where the mothers talk about their difficulties in expressing their anger and the children behave aggressively. Thirdly it helps in a defensive manoeuvre, as sometimes when mothers find a topic difficult the children create a hullabaloo, which puts an end to exploring anxiety-provoking material. Fourthly, it counterpoints, for example when the mothers are talking about something sad but the infants seem able to have fun. We increasingly use the children's activity as a basis for a "group as a whole" interpretation (Foulkes, 1964). Not only is it a way of interpreting issues without sounding trite, but it came to seem technically preferable at times to say, for example, "All the children seem to be cross today" rather than saying, "There seems to be an issue of aggression here." It provides a medium for the mothers to focus on what is happening in their own psyches in a way that might otherwise not be so available, and to facilitate changes in their perception.

The presence of infants in the group as members in their own right faced us with the difficulties that they were experiencing and with the need to consider whether the usual group techniques had to be adapted in view of their developmental status. If we did not respond to an infant who had made an overture to us, would that be experienced by her as rejecting? We thought about the times when we initiated a gesture or action, and came to view such times as a communication to the infant and to the group that we were thinking of the infant's experience and in effect commenting on it. We came to view the responses that the infant evokes from us as enabling us to communicate our understanding to the infant and to let the infant know that we believe that some of the answers are also in the infant. We feel strongly that infants need a response from us which is affirming and growth-promoting. It may be worth clarifying that what we are calling play constitutes very minimal action on our part, that we rarely move around in a session.

> When Tom, aged seven months, and his mother Brenda joined the group he was rigid and unsmiling, with his arms held out at right angles to his body. Brenda had lost her first child in a cot death when she was a year old and had been unable, in anger, to begin mourning. Her relationship towards Tom was a very conflictual one and we learnt that when she looked at him she saw her daughter's face. When Campbell Paul moved his own fingers we noticed that Tom watched them. Campbell then touched Tom's hands and talked to him and gradually Tom could mouth Campbell's thumb. Still holding Campbell's hands he was able for the first time to relax his own arms, as if able to loosen a rigid "second-skin formation", and bring his hands together. As he did so he smiled. His mother played with him for the first time, lifting him up in the air and smiling at him. Whereas before his outstretched arms had got in the way of turning round to his mother for comfort he could now use them to find where she was and he began vocalising.

When a therapist responds to something in the child with their own activity and this is done in a thoughtful attuned way it has the potential to bring about change very quickly. Rayner (1992) suggested that the pleasure between mother and infant at the height of attunement may be a kind of pre-verbal affective insight, in that what was in one mind is experienced in two, which can then bring about change in the self. This would add to our understanding of relatively quick behavioural changes. We think that an infant's attunement with another infant has a similar potential.

Developments in group therapy: the very premature baby group

A group of parents whose babies had been born before twenty-eight-weeks gestation sought to meet together to discuss the experience of having had a premature baby and its impact on relationships within the family. The mothers of the babies had each attended a maternal and child health nurse centre in the same locality, and a psychotherapeutic group for babies and parents was established, with Rosalie Birkin as the co-therapist, and with the nurse facilitating the process. The mothers had already described to the nurse the trauma that they had experienced while their baby had been in the neonatal intensive care unit (NICU). They described a harrowing and lonely experience. They often felt unable, for a number of reasons, to talk with other families, and yet they could see the pain and distress that their own infant appeared to suffer.

The closed psychotherapy group was established for the mothers and babies, with some separate early evening sessions for the fathers and the babies as well. Guidelines for this group were established. Parents were encouraged to talk about whatever they wished to discuss, but then what was discussed would remain confidential within the group. They were encouraged to play and interact with their babies as they would ordinarily, and we were interested to observe and facilitate interaction between the infants. In this way there were similarities with the community mothers' groups, but we anticipated that the mothers would feel more comfortable with a group of their peers who had undergone similar experiences in NICU.

There were four families and six babies (there were two sets of twins). An analysis of the themes that the parents discussed showed that they included feelings of isolation from their own family and from other families in the NICU. It was clear that the task was one of survival, and they were not keen to share their experiences or talk with other families at times of such intense emotion. The birth story and the account of time in the NICU were avoided in the group as mothers feared it would be very traumatic in the retelling. In time however they felt they needed to know something of each other's experience, so they arranged to present a brief account, in turn, over several weeks. This seemed manageable, and brought them to a shared understanding. Other themes included:

- Fear of breakdown and of damage to the couple's own relationship
- Ambivalence about their own very vulnerable baby
- Loss of control over everyday decisions about their baby, and fear of loss of control over major decisions, such as whether intervention or resuscitation should occur at particular times

- Inability to talk with other parents, fostering envy and fear of other babies and their families
- Fear of their own intense feelings, including anger that seemed to be an intermittent but distressing feeling since it seemed unjustified and the parents wondered how they could be ungrateful and very critical to the staff who gave so much to their children
- Trauma, and significant post-traumatic stress disorder symptomatology, including intrusive memories re-experiencing episodes of danger and very powerful identification with their baby's resilience: "She experienced so much but she was a real battler."

The opportunity of this group enabled the observation of the powerful interactions between babies, including the intense relationship that formed between twins. The parents in the group felt it was important that other parents and professionals working with such vulnerable babies should be aware of some of the feelings that they had been unable to tell the staff about at the time their baby was in hospital. A follow-up of this group was developed in the neonatal intensive care unit providing a twelve-session educational and psychotherapeutic group to parents while their babies are in hospital.

The Stargate infant parent group

For a period of time a number of infants were seen as part of an innovative project which provided a comprehensive emotional and developmental assessment programme for children when Protective Services had been involved, and they had been removed from their parents' care because of dangerous and abusive actions (see Milburn, 2005). We met with some of these parents and infants for a therapy group which ran in parallel with the assessment. This group aimed to provide infants and parents who had been separated an opportunity to be together in a controlled environment allowing for some continuity. We tried to use the same set of guidelines as in the basic model.

Even in the more extreme situations where for example a mother seemed to be colluding in the infliction of massive injuries on her baby, being present in the group with other parents and infants with the therapists helped her see that despite her personality difficulty she still had something to offer her baby. She would still have a relationship with her for the rest of her life, which was an argument for providing help for her now. The mother has to be there in her role as a mother: despite all that happened there is an expectation of responsibility and the capacity to care as a parent and she is still the mother to her abused child. While this group only took place for a short period of time, the staff found it supportive while the families waited for other services to be arranged and infants with a developmental delay began to move forward.

The Peekaboo club group

Building on this group experience with parents of deprived, neglected, and abused infants a new initiative was recently launched. We acknowledge the contribution of the facilitator, Wendy Bunston, Royal Children's Hospital Child and Adolescent Mental Health Service, Melbourne, whose enthusiasm and drive saw the establishment of the Peekaboo club. Wendy Bunston had, in the suburbs of Melbourne, provided within the mental health services a child-focused programme for families where family violence was a major issue, which had tried to help mothers understand the experience of violence in the children's homes. The group therapy model was seen as an ideal way to provide a non-threatening way for mothers to talk about their experience while engaging and playing with their own babies. The group aims to provide the mothers with a safe therapeutic context where issues of violence can begin to be explored in a group where the infants are also related to in their own right, and both mother and infant are provided with experiences of pleasure. Clinicians need to feel comfortable to explore issues the violence with the mothers, otherwise these may be avoided. While the numbers are small, there was improvement in how the mothers scored on the scale for depression in pre- and post-test measures and the infants who had been developmentally delayed began to move forward (Bunston, 2006).

Reflections

We have wondered whether the mother–baby therapy group is protective of parents abusing their children at a later date. Providing some mothers with a place where they feel safe enough to raise protective issues and also helping to facilitate being more in touch in a loving way, more empathic, with their infants, may be the greatest single safeguard against later abuse. Research in the area of postnatal depression points to the increased risk factors for neglect and abuse for those parents who experience difficulties in the early months of their infant's life. This highlights the importance of intervention which is early and sufficiently far-reaching. A related question may be whether being in the group enabled this protectiveness by giving more insight into her own emotions and differentiating her own needs from those of her infant and to seek further support from within her family and therapists. The containment provided in the group is likely to enable some mothers to feel that it is a place where quite considerable disturbance can be held.

We feel that a mother and her infant have been able to benefit from the group when there is more ease in communicating in the relationship and more enjoyment in doing so. This presupposes that there would be more empathy on the mother's part than there had been on entry to the group. We have noticed that when mothers leave the group and reflect what they have gained from the group, they often mention a different view of seeing the child, that is, not so much in terms of the child being naughty but a child whose needs can be read and understood.

Conclusion

We have tried to show something of the therapeutic interactions that occur in groups between the infants, the infants' contribution to the group process, and how these might come to have a therapeutic effect. We have also argued that some of the innovations in technique have come about through following the infant.

References

Bailey, V. (1981). Groups for depressed mothers. *Group Analysis, 165*: 165–166.

Bunston, W. (2006). The Peekaboo club. *The Signal*, 1–7.

Christie, G. & Correia, A. (1987). Maternal ambivalence in a group analytic setting. *British Journal of Psychotherapy, 3/3*: 205–215.

Clark, R., Keller, A., Fedderly, S., & Paulson, A. (1993). Treating the relationships affected by postpartum depression: a group therapy model. *Zero to Three, 13*: 16–23.

Conte, B., Moltz, E., & Solomon, E. (1990). Training and supporting leaders of mother/baby groups: the P.A.C.E. approach. *Zero to three, 11*: 17.

Daws, D. (1995). Infancy and psychoanalysis, discussion point at the first Colloquium of the Australian Association of Infant Mental Health (Victoria) and the Melbourne Institute for Psychoanalysis.

Durkin, H. E. (1954). *Group Treatment for Mothers of Disturbed Children.* Springfield, Il: Charles C. Thomas.

Durkin, H. E. (1964). *The Group in Depth.* New York: International Universities Press.

Foulkes, S. H. (1964). *Therapeutic Group Analysis.* London: Allen & Unwin.

Gosling, R. (1981). A study of very small groups. In: J. Grotstein (Ed.), *Do I Dare Disturb the Universe? A Memorial to W. R. Bion* (pp. 633–646). London: Karnac Books, 1997.

Green, A. (1980). *A Private Madness.* London: Hogarth.

Gruen, D. (1990). Postpartum depression: a debilitating yet often unassessed problem. *Health and Social Work, 15:* 261–266.

Gruen, D. (1993). A group psychotherapy approach to postpartum depression. *International Journal of Group Psychotherapy, 43:* 191–203.

Holden, J. M., Sagovsky, R., & Cox, J. L. (1989). Counselling in a general practice setting: controlled study of health visitor intervention in treatment of postnatal depression. *British Medical Journal, 298:* 223–226.

Klein, M. (1948). *Contribution to Psycho-Analysis.* London: Hogarth.

Klein, M. et al. (1952). *Developments in Psycho-Analysis.* London: Hogarth.

Meager, I. & Milgrom, J. (1996). Group treatment for post-partum depression: a pilot study. *Australian and New Zealand Journal of Psychiatry, 30:* 852–860.

Milburn, N. (2005). Protected and respected: addressing the needs of the child in out-of-home care. The Stargate Early intervention Program for children and young people in out-of-home care. *Journal of Paediatrics and Child Health, 42:* 309–310.

Montagner, H. (1989). Le role d'un espace experimental structure dans l'emergence et le development des systemes de communication des jeunes infants, paper presented at the World Association of Infant Psychiatry and Allied Disciplines Conference, Lugano, 1989.

Mueller, E. C. & Vandell, D. (1979). Infant–infant interaction: a review. In: J. D. Osofsky (Ed.), *Handbook of Infant Development* (pp. 591–622). New York: John Wiley.

Paul, C. (1991). Le bebe qui voit, mais ne regarde pas. *Devenir, 3:* 62–78.

Paul, C. & Thomson-Salo, F. (1997). Infant-led innovations in a mother–baby therapy group. *Journal of Child Psychotherapy, 23:* 219–244.

Rayner, E. (1992). Matching, attunement and the psychoanalytic dialogue. *International Journal of Psycho-Analysis, 73:* 39–54.

Riess, A. (1988). The power of the eye in nature, nurture, and culture. A developmental view of mutual gaze. *Psychoanalytic Study of the Child, 43*: 399–421.

Rochat, P. (Ed.) (1998). *The self in infancy: Theory and Research.* Amsterdam: Elsevier.

Schindler, W. (1966). The role of mother in group psychotherapy. *International Journal of Group Psychotherapy, 16*: 198–202.

Selby, J. M. & Bradley, B. S. (2003). Infants in groups: A paradigm for the study of early social experience. *Human Development, 46*: 197–221.

Siksou, J. (1990). Therapies en groupe des troubles precoces de la relation mere-bebe. *Devenir, 2*: 35–47.

Smith, J. (2004). No place in the world: unwanted, rejected babies find mothers in Dandenong PAIRS groups, paper given at the ninth Congress for Infant Mental Health, Melbourne, January 2004.

Urwin, C. (1990). Getting to know the self and others: babies' interactions with other babies, paper at fourth European Conference on Developmental Psychology, Scotland.

Watillon, A. (1993). The dynamics of psychoanalytic therapies of the early parent-child relationship. *International Journal of Psycho-Analysis, 74*: 1037–1048.

PART IV

INTERVENTIONS WITH INFANTS WITH PROBLEMS OF RELATING

CHAPTER SEVENTEEN

Infant–parent psychotherapy in a community paediatric setting

Mary Brown

This chapter explores the role of infant–parent psychotherapy in a paediatric practice by describing the experiences of a mother who thought her infant son was developing autism. It concerns the role of understanding maternal projections in the genesis of psychopathology in infancy and the task of the clinician to unearth and change distorted projections which may interfere with the parent–infant relationship and, as a result, impair the infant's psychosocial development.

Ghosts in the nursery—the role of maternal projection in symptom formation in childhood

When feelings or images that belong to one person are transferred on to others this projection or projective identification is often a socially adaptive reaction, but if the projections are substantial and disregard the specific individuality of the other, such distortion of reality interferes with the relationship. When such pathological projections occur in a relationship between a parent and infant, the parent endows the baby with characteristics that are at odds with the baby's nature. The strength and nature of their projections determine to what extent parents are able to recognise the infant's own individuality (Brazelton & Cramer, 1990). Distorted identifications can undermine the relationship and parents may react exclusively to the intentions which they lend to the infant, but which in reality emerge from their own psyche. A situation can therefore arise where "symptoms" in the child may be highly expressive of the parent's unconscious conflicts. In the words of Brazelton, a paediatrician involved in infancy research, and his colleague Cramer, a psychiatrist:

> These projections are often revealed in the parent's description of the infant's problems; but sometimes it takes a long time before the plot 'behind the scene' is uncovered. This is achieved only when the parents reveal the link between their perception of these 'problems' and their own past. (Brazelton & Cramer, 1990, p. 135)

Selma Fraiberg used the term "ghosts in the nursery" to describe such projections, likening them to "visitors from the unremembered past of the parents; the uninvited guests at the christening" (Fraiberg, 1987, p. 100). Like the good fairy or the threatening witch of fairy tales, these ghosts can cast good or bad spells on the child. Normally the child has such a strong claim on the parent's love for his or her unique self that the ghosts are banished from the nursery. However at times the ghosts may take up residence at the baby's side attracting more of the parents' attention than the real baby. In such situations "parents relate to the ghost who is interposed—like a screen—between themselves and the child" (Brazelton & Cramer, 1990, p. 139). Such an intrusive ghost creates a major source of mismatch between parent and infant. The parents are unable to react to the infant's signals because they are busy communicating with the ghost. The presence of these ghosts may impede the development of the infant in unacceptable ways who sometimes seems engulfed in the parents' difficulties and shows early signs of emotional disturbance.

Fraiberg designed an infant–parent psychotherapy intervention model to address the problems that arise from such distorted relationships (Fraiberg et al., 1980). In this model, the problem requiring therapy is seen as a serious conflict within the parents and between the parents and their baby, in which the baby has become a representative of an aspect of the parental self that is repudiated or negated, or the representative of figures or situations within the parental past. The aim of therapy is to identify those aspects of parental psychological conflict that are impeding the formation of stable bonds between parent and baby and hindering the child's development. These conflicts are resolved by examining the past and the present with the parents to free them and their baby from old "ghosts", the distortions and displaced affects that have engulfed the baby in the parents' difficulties. In this model, both parent and baby are the patients and the focus is on the relationship. The therapeutic work moves back and forth, between present and past, parent and baby, but always returns to the baby. As Fraiberg argues:

> No baby can wait for the resolution of a parental neurosis which is impeding his own development. He must have our help too. And we have learned from our work that it is possible to give help to the parents concurrently, with great benefit to both, and that the baby can be brought to adequacy even when his parents have not yet resolved their own personal conflicts. (Fraiberg & Fraiberg, 1980, p. 53)

With increasing acknowledgement of the role that the infant him or herself contributes to the relationship through his own idiosyncratic behaviour and vulnerabilities, the importance of work directly with the infant is becoming increasingly recognised. Greenspan describes the important role of direct work to compensate for what the child might fail to contribute to sustain a good relationship (Greenspan et al., 1987). Direct infant work also has a function where the parents are unable to use their thinking to make links with the past, as described in the Fraiberg model, and the infant cannot wait for the resolution of parental difficulties (Paul & Thomson-Salo, 1997).

Nadia's story

This is an account of the work with a mother, Nadia, and her nine-month-old infant son, Karl. They presented in my consulting room in a community-based paediatric practice because Nadia suspected that Karl was "developing autism". The general practitioner referred them to me after Nadia told him of her concerns that her infant son was showing the same pattern of development as his two older brothers, aged eight years and six years, who had both been diagnosed as having "high functioning autism". The eldest child was five and the middle child four years old when a Melbourne-based autism assessment team made this diagnosis. By this time, both boys were attending regular classes in a primary school in their small home town with the help of integration aides; the eight-year-old had made excellent progress with much improvement in his social relatedness since being in the school environment.

Karl's conception was unplanned. There had been talk of her husband having a vasectomy, but Nadia said she had thought she would like another baby some time. So, when she found out that she was pregnant with Karl, she was not unhappy about having a third child. The pregnancy and delivery were uneventful and all was well for the first few months of Karl's life. However at about eight months of age Nadia suspected that he was following the same course as his brothers because of "his fascination for toys with wheels and other spinning objects, his eating habits and the way he shook his head".

Clinical assessment

When I first met Karl, he appeared to be showing normal signs of social relatedness and behaviour. In particular, he did not show any deficits in sociability, or reciprocal verbal and non-verbal communication, which are the main characteristic symptoms of autistic disorder. During the assessment, he would endeavour to get my attention and enjoyed activities such as bouncing up and down on my knee, clapping hands, playing peekaboo and similar joint activities. On occasions he would tend to withdraw into himself and become engrossed in a toy, particularly little cars with wheels, when he would lie on the floor on his side and run the cars up and down in front of himself, making no sound. But it was never difficult to distract him from this activity to engage him in interactive play.

However, from the outset, it was readily apparent that the pattern of Nadia's interactions with Karl was quite unusual. He generally seemed to be ready for social contact but Nadia was so focused on her thoughts about autism that she did not observe his need to be in touch with her. She initiated very few interactions with him. If he approached her, she held her hands in such a way as to look as though she was pushing him away. Her arms were rarely open and welcoming and, when he got onto her lap of his own accord, she was slow to put her arms around him. Poking him, flapping her hands at him, kissing the soles of his feet, and patting him on the head as one would a dog were characteristic of her interaction patterns with him.

My initial impression of Nadia's unusual pattern of interaction with Karl was reinforced over successive visits. In play she presented him with seemingly endless toys one after the other in rapid succession without making any effort to interact with him. She remained physically distant from him and used a plastic hockey stick to push the toys to him, seeming to expect him to know what to do with them without ever demonstrating how they worked. Many of the toys had rolling balls, wheels or spinning parts. She made very little eye contact with him. When he used vocalisation, she made little or no effort to talk to him or interpret his language. For instance, at twelve months he started to make the sound "up", which could be interpreted that he would like to be picked up. She replied with, "That's your new word, isn't it?" but without reaching out to lift him up she merely leant forward and kissed his feet. Most times she expected him to play without assistance and, when she did join in, she often played alongside him rather than with him. Her occasional attempts at interactive play were intrusive; she would rattle or jangle bells in his face and interactions tended to begin and end abruptly.

Nadia described the children's father as a recluse with poor communication skills, working in isolation as a forestry fire officer. She described him as quite restless, changing his place of work often. But meeting him for the first time, I was surprised to find him quite sociable and easy to talk to. Although he fathered all three children, he was unaware of the existence of his first son until the child was two-years-old. He then resumed a relationship with Nadia and they subsequently married and have remained together since.

Conceptualising Karl's difficulties

My impression was that Karl was not autistic, but had a significant delay with expressive language development. He also had a tendency to withdraw and become self-absorbed in repetitive play at times. I felt that Nadia was over-interpreting the evidence for autism by focussing on some of the stereotypic behaviours characteristic of autistic disorder. She seemed totally unable to observe the very positive signs of social relatedness that Karl displayed in his interactions with people and I was concerned about the quality of the relationship between mother and child.

Nadia's only prior experience of parenting was with her older autistic sons. How this would impact on her mothering capacity for subsequent children was unknown but it is likely that her way of relating to Karl would be coloured by her experiences of her interactions with the autistic boys. These experiences with the older children, together with her knowledge that siblings of autistic children are at significantly greater risk for exhibiting autism, were considered to be factors influencing her interaction style. Her conviction that he was developing autism was very strong. I postulated that because of her strong belief that Karl was autistic, despite there being considerable evidence to the contrary, Nadia might be treating him in a way that could produce behaviour consistent with an autistic child. By projecting her own fears about his development on to Karl, I felt that it could have a deleterious effect on his social development. After observing Nadia's interactions with him, I considered that his episodes of withdrawal were possibly an autistic defence, which he had developed in response to a lack of positive feedback and encouragement from her.

At the same time as I had these concerns, I recognised that Karl was in a high-risk group for developing autistic disorder, even while the aetiology is unknown except in a minority of cases. However, there is strong evidence that genetic factors are important and research suggests that siblings of autistic children are at significantly greater risk for also exhibiting autism with a recurrence risk of between three and eight per cent in families with one affected child. So, with two siblings already diagnosed, I would expect a mother like Nadia to be acutely vigilant and possibly more astute at detecting early signs of autism than an outsider such as myself.

Treatment intervention

I organised for Karl to be assessed by the regional Early Intervention team as soon as possible. They agreed that his main problem with development was delay in expressive language and a speech therapist began a weekly home-based intervention. In the meantime, I arranged to see Karl and Nadia for monthly treatment sessions.

Mindful of the role of maternal projection in the genesis of psychopathology, in this case the possible development of autistic defences in Karl, I aimed to modify Nadia's projections using infant–parent psychotherapy and direct infant work. The intervention drew on a case report in which Zeanah and colleagues (1988) described the evaluation and brief treatment of an eight-month-old girl whose parents were concerned that she was autistic. Their concern was raised because they felt their daughter's behaviour was strikingly similar to her older, autistic sister's behaviour. The intervention helped her parents to develop more satisfying and effective interactions with her and by the age of eighteen months the infant had recovered from a serious early disturbance in social relatedness. This was achieved through positively connoting the child's behaviour and the parents' behaviour with the child, modelling pleasurable interactions with her, challenging the parents' representational distortions of her and providing non-specific support of availability. Although the central therapeutic effort was to change how her parents experienced and related to her, the therapist also engaged the infant directly through the sessions.

I decided to use a similar approach. My aims in treatment were twofold. The first was to change Nadia's perception that Karl was developing autism. I hoped to achieve this by exploring her negative projections and by helping her to see the positive signs in Karl's development to counteract the power of her projections. My second aim was to give Karl an experience of interaction with adults that was interactive and fun and at the same time would encourage his language development. This would be through sessions with the speech therapist and direct play with Karl and myself in the course of the consultations.

Therapeutic process

I had monthly consultations of an hour's duration with Nadia and Karl from the time that Karl was nine months old until he was just over two years of age and the family moved away from the area. As evaluation of the intervention was used as part of a case study for a higher degree in infant mental health, the majority of consultations took place in the family home and were videotaped. This is not my usual mode of practice and at times provided some technical challenges for me. The home setting also meant that there were other distractions; the consultations often had a social element to them as Nadia often prepared refreshments for my visit and wanted to show off her craftwork. However, I think that the home setting generally proved to be less threatening for them than the more formal setup of a paediatric consulting room. A therapeutic alliance was established and both Nadia and Karl reacted positively to my visits. Karl rapidly became confident in my presence, always responding warmly after a game of pretending to be shy at the start of most sessions. Towards the end of the treatment period, he would cry sadly as I departed. I used a mixture of assessment and therapeutic activities throughout, with the initial sessions more focused on information gathering and developmental testing and the later ones more directly therapeutic.

Challenging mother's thinking patterns

My initial hunch that Nadia was over-interpreting the evidence for autism was borne out and my concern that she might project her fantasies on to her infant with detrimental consequences for his development seemed well founded. While I frequently attempted to challenge her representational distortions by interpreting Karl's behaviour as normal, particularly his social relatedness, Nadia did not seem convinced and had it fixed in her mind that he would become autistic when he was two years old. There were many signs that he wished to be near her and engage with her, but she ignored him. For instance, when she was in the kitchen Karl tried to climb up to the bench to see what she was doing, but Nadia felt that he was being a nuisance and was unable to see situations like this as a positive sign of his sociability. When Karl was nineteen months old, I used the CHAT (CHecklist for Autism in Toddlers), a questionnaire for infants aged eighteen-months that has been shown to predict a definitive diagnosis of autism by thirty-months (Baron-Cohen et al., 1992; Baron-Cohen et al., 1996). The key items assessed are pretend play, protodeclarative pointing, joint-attention, social interest and social play, which are common deficits in autism. Karl's normal performance on this screen was shared as further evidence to Nadia of his normality in these areas of development.

Nadia's background was explored and I attempted a weaving of past and present, trying to make links between her own childhood and the here and now. She spoke dispassionately about her own childhood and teenage years, describing her mother as someone with a drinking problem who was quite unable to show affection. Her childhood sounded empty and joyless, there were no toys, nobody who played with her, and no celebrations of birthdays because of her parent's strict religious beliefs. It sounded as though there was no fun in her life. At one stage, she revealed a dream that she remembered having as a teenager. This dream appears to be very significant in trying to make sense of her later experience. She dreamt that she would have three boys with special talents. She did not know the term "autism", but knew that there would be something different about the boys, that they would have super abilities in certain areas. While she remembered her childhood experiences, she was unable to get in touch with her own painful memories at an affective level and could not use the space for thinking and making significant links to what was happening currently.

Changing mother's interaction patterns and affect attunement

Nadia's skills at interpreting non-verbal communication were very poor. To overcome this, I attempted to interpret Karl's attempts at communication. For instance, when he said "up", I suggested that wanted to be picked up, and when he screamed piercingly when she made sounds that he found unpleasant, I interpreted his reaction as possibly due to fear, but certainly something that he distinctly did not like. I modelled interactional behaviour informally on many occasions. I used developmental testing procedures and free play situations for this sort of guidance and encouraged her to copy, although she sometimes missed the point. More didactic guidance was given by the speech therapist about communication skills and it was in these situations that it was clear that Nadia followed advice in a rather non-reflective way. For instance, during a bubble blowing game, we suggested that she say the word "bubble" as the bubbles floated through the air. She followed the advice and repeated the word quite often, but not necessarily when there were any bubbles in sight. On another occasion after she had been told to use some sign language to help stimulate language development, she made a round shape with her hands as she asked Karl to get a ball from the toy cupboard. However, he was already in the toy cupboard with his back to her and the aim of the exercise was lost. We encouraged her to make play with him interactive, rather than just putting the toys in front of him and expecting him to know what to do with them. She did become more responsive to his approaches over time, but her play skills remained elementary and lacked rhythmicity and turn taking.

Direct work with Karl

As time went by, I spent more time in direct work with Karl. Nadia was a mother obsessed and, at times, oppressed by autism. The flatness of her affect and her depressed demeanour meant that the richness and range of experiences available to Karl was seriously limited. Many times he experienced a very passive reception to his own efforts to engage with his mother, which would have violated the expectations of closeness and warmth that an infant normally has in such interactions. I thought that his tendency to withdraw and use repetitive non-imaginative play was a defence he had developed to compensate for the sadness and loneliness he experienced from her lack of responsiveness to him. This aspect of his behaviour was at times worrying, but it never became fixed or generalised and with the minimum of effort it was always possible for me to engage him in some activity to interest and enliven him. Playing with him and talking to him directly became more important parts of the therapeutic process. For instance, if he became a little self-absorbed and reverted to playing with his cars and spinning their wheels, I tried to tune in to his feelings and put a name on his experiences of loneliness and being left out and invited him back into the world of relating with a person. He invariably responded quickly. Non-interactive throwing of blocks or toys was converted to putting the items into a toy box incorporating both interactive play and turn taking between us. Games like peekaboo were firm favourites with him. Experiences such as these validated Karl's experiences and emotions, as well as providing some fun in his life and simultaneously acted as a model for Nadia in ways of interaction.

Outcome

By the time he was two years old, there was very clear evidence of delay in Karl's expressive language development but there was no indication of impending autism. He was very adept at the use of gesture, both to indicate his desires and to express joint interest in something, and his episodes of withdrawal were infrequent and never became generalised. For Nadia, the intervention resulted in a subtle change in her thinking by the time Karl was two years old and a general tendency to be able to see the real baby rather than the child of her dream. However, she still had some expectation that autism would develop. It was hard to budge her conviction because of her belief that the problems "really come out after they're two".

Implications for paediatric practice

The story of Nadia and Karl shows the importance of unearthing the plot behind the scene. It illustrates much about the power of maternal projections in preventing this mother from seeing her real infant as distinct from the imaginary infant of a childhood dream. Cramer and Brazelton (1990) wrote of "imaginary interactions" where the parent projects their internal conflicts on to the infant who then lives out the conflict through "symptoms". Cramer (1987) described the process as follows:

> Parents constantly submit each of the infant's behaviours to influences stemming from their own private set of expectations, ideals, prohibitions, predilections, and so on. Through this process, various aspects of the infant's repertoire are selected and enhanced, while others are censored and extinguished. ... Tremendous pressures are applied on the child's productions and states, embedding them instantaneously into a web of meanings predetermined in the parent's mind. (Cramer, 1987, p. 1044)

Knowing the thoughts and fantasies behind the presenting symptoms helped my understanding of their significance to Nadia and particularly her resistance to changing her thinking pattern. Her expectations of mothering were certainly coloured by past events. However, the unusual expectations did not arise as much from her mothering experience with her older autistic sons as I had initially thought, but rather were influenced by a childhood dream and a very firm conviction that she would have three children who were very special. Infant–parent psychotherapy resulted in some change in Nadia's representational distortions and she was able to enjoy more pleasurable interactions with him. Even more importantly, the account illustrates the resilience of an infant in the face of adversity and his ability to make use of the therapeutic relationship to forge ahead with development, despite the deficiencies in some aspects of his relationship with his mother.

References

Baron-Cohen, S., Allen, J., & Gillberg, C. (1992). Can autism be detected at 18 months? The needle, the haystack, and the CHAT. *British Journal of Psychiatry, 161*: 839–843.

Baron-Cohen, S., Cox, A., Baird, G., Swettenham, J., Nightingale, N., Morgan, K., Drew, A., & Charman, T. (1996). Psychological markers in the detection of autism in infancy in a large population. *British Journal of Psychiatry, 168*: 158–163.

Brazelton, T. B. & Cramer, B. G. (1990). *The earliest relationship.* New York: Addison-Wesley.

Cramer, B. G. (1987). Objective and subjective aspects of parent–infant relations: An attempt at correlation between infant studies and clinical work. In: J. D. Osofsky (Ed.), *Handbook of Infant Development*, 2nd ed. New York: Wiley.

Fraiberg, S. (1987). Ghosts in the nursery. In: L. Fraiberg (Ed.) *Selected writings of Selma Fraiberg* (pp. 100–136). Columbus: Ohio State University Press.

Fraiberg, S. & Fraiberg, L. (Eds.) (1980). *Clinical studies in infant mental health. The first year of life.* New York: Basic Books.

Fraiberg, S., Shapiro, V., & Chemiss, D. S. (1980). Treatment Modalities. In: *Clinical studies in infant mental health. The first year of life.* London: Tavistock Publications.

Greenspan, S. I., Wieder, S., Lieberman, A. F., Nover, R., Lourie, R., & Robinson, M. (1987). *Infants in multirisk families.* Madison, CT: International Universities Press.

Paul, C. & Thomson-Salo, F. (1997). Infant-led innovations in a mother–baby therapy group. *Journal of Child Psychotherapy, 23*: 219–244.

Zeanah, C., Davis, S., & Silverman, M. (1988). The question of autism in an atypical infant. *American Journal of Psychotherapy, 42*: 135–151.

CHAPTER EIGHTEEN

The gift of connection: intervention with a two-year-old boy

Nicky Robson

Working with Michael challenged my beliefs and prior learnings about young children who present as if autistic. During this intervention Michael rather quickly, and without costly intensive intervention, began to engage with people and objects in a more appropriate manner. The work reaffirmed for me the importance of an infant mental health perspective in planning intervention for children with developmental difficulties. The therapeutic focus on Michael's "sense of self" and his "subjective self" (his sense of self as experienced with another) encouraged interaction and a shift to a more appropriate developmental path.

Michael's parents had been deeply concerned about his plateauing in development and their difficulties in communicating with him. He presented as very content to be "in his own world", which he did not try to share with his parents. However there was a "glimmer of hope" in that he would initiate eye contact. Despite this briefly engaging contact, he would not allow this gaze to be reciprocated or sustained. This fleeting willingness to peer out of his world became the focus of therapy. The therapy led to his engagement with "our world" and a markedly reduced need to live in his own. Despite having had a plateauing of development and the existence of autistic spectrum type characteristics for twelve months, Michael's development returned to a more appropriate pathway.

While this intervention cannot illumine the different pathways to an autistic spectrum disorder, and whether some are more fixed than others, it highlights the importance of looking for any glimmer of hope in very young children who present with autistic-like characteristics and initiating early intervention focusing on their emotional development, in particular facilitating the development of their sense of self and their capacity to relate to others.

Michael

Michael was the first of two sons born to the Jacobsen family who migrated to Australia during the final period of his mother's pregnancy with him. He was named after the paternal grandmother's father, born on the tenth anniversary of the maternal grandfather's death, an IVF conceived infant and the first-born son in a new country. He was considered a gift. Mr. Jacobsen's family was in Australia and as he spoke fluent English, he was able to continue his career here. Mrs. Jacobsen had found the move to Australia difficult. She left behind a valued career, friends, and her family. She said that she had initially felt down and had cried much of the time. That Michael had plateaued in development added to her anxious feelings that her life as she knew it was over, and a new one was still not fully tangible.

At the age of two-years-and-four months Michael was referred for an outpatient speech pathology evaluation following concerns by his parents and paediatrician about his eating, language, and social development. His parents were concerned that his skills in a number of areas had become static or even regressed over the previous twelve months.

Michael's diet was restricted to mashed food consistencies and bottle feeds, with no self-feeding skills. Mrs. Jacobsen would hold the bottle while he drank from it, his arms dangling beside him. His parents found his behaviour challenging with Michael screaming for up to three hours at a time, and they would be unsure of the cause. His father had not been as concerned initially with Michael's difficulties, feeling that he would grow out of it. As a child he was reported to have been fed until he was five years old.

Assessment

Michael seemed aware of his surroundings: he initially came to me and looked intently at my face, and eyes. He stroked my hair, and played with my nametag. I felt that a connection existed, despite being a fragile one. He presented with significantly delayed receptive and expressive language skills, and play skills. His pragmatic skills (the way that he used language to interact) were also delayed with him using vocalisations (cries) to protest, respond, or request, but not for other functions such as social forms, commenting, or description. He hummed to himself for his own enjoyment, rather than in a communicative way. He did not use gestures to enhance his communication. He accidentally knocked a toy saucepan over and the sudden clang made him startle and he began to cry. Michael could participate in limited interaction through eye contact. He could sustain it when he initiated it; however, it was limited to brief periods, and he did not allow any reciprocity to the interaction. His parents said that he enjoyed affection and contact with other children, and sought cuddles with his parents.

Michael's parents were understandably anxious about his development. However, I considered that his mother's anxieties had been heightened by events in her own life. In my countertransference her anxieties felt overwhelming, with little place for integration and thought. Further exploration of Michael's parents' history indicated that emotional or developmental conflicts may have been managed with food. Mrs. Jacobsen reported a period during her adolescence when she became "sort of anorexic" in response to her anger and grief over her father's death. She continued to be a slender woman, and ate without enjoying it.

The question of Michael having an Autism Spectrum Disorder/ Pervasive Developmental Disability was raised by his parents. Michael did not point and clearly demonstrated some autistic-like behaviours such as delays in his play, social, and communication skills.

Due to Michael's interest in affection and ability to sustain eye contact, I preferred to conceptualise Michael's difficulties as a Multisystem Developmental Disorder (ZERO TO THREE (2005)). The ZERO TO THREE (2005) Diagnostic classification of mental health and developmental disorders of infancy and early childhood noted that some clinicians may prefer to use this classification for infants and children rather than "Pervasive Developmental Disorders—not otherwise specified", that is, for those children who demonstrated autistic behaviours but revealed some potential for intimacy and closeness in relating. This conceptualisation suggested that these children's relationship difficulties were not a relatively fixed permanent deficit but may be open to change and growth (*DC:0–3R*, 2005, p. 39).

Greenspan and colleagues (1998) found a developmental relationship-based treatment approach to be of benefit for this group of children. A study of 200 children with Autism Spectrum Disorder who received developmental relationship–based treatment demonstrated that many children were capable of significant overall improvement. The fifty-eight per cent of children who demonstrated good to outstanding outcomes no longer demonstrated ritualistic behaviour and became spontaneous and creative in their communication and relationship patterns. However, they suggested that:

> Traditional treatment programs tend to be mechanical and structured rather than based on individual differences, relationships, affect and emotional cueing. Approaches that do not pull the child into spontaneous joyful relationship patterns may intensify rather than remediate the difficulty. (Greenspan et al., 1998, p. 8)

Their approach to treatment is relationship-based and guided by the development of functional emotional skills that are considered to provide the basis for intellect, sense of self, and skills such as turn taking, problem solving etc.

Before preverbal communication skills such as turn taking, use of gesture and imitation occur in a meaningful sense, there needs to be a consolidated ability to take an interest in the world, self regulate to manage and respond to the world and to engage in relationships with other people. Without these, any attempt to train preverbal skills will most likely mean that these skills are separated from emotional meaning and intent, and will not be owned or be an expression of self by the child. The early developmental work is therefore embedded in the therapeutic relationship rather than superimposed on an immature system.

Intervention

I referred Michael for a sensory processing assessment by an occupational therapist (due to his tendency to overly touch people and objects, and startle with sounds) and I offered regular weekly sessions lasting an hour. Michael's parents were highly committed to the therapy. Michael was seen weekly for six months. I focused on Michael with the eyes and mind of an infant mental health clinician in a therapy informed by the developmental relationship–based treatment approach (Greenspan et al., 1998).

Therapy aims

The initial aims of therapy were to assist Michael's development of his sense of self and the development of his subjective self; for us to be mindful of Michael as a subject; for his sense of agency to be strengthened and integrated, and for this "self" to be experienced with "another". Parental anxieties and frustrations needed to be contained, to create a space for hope and thinking about Michael and his needs, facilitating the interactions between Michael and his parents so that they were increasingly characterised by understanding.

Michael's world

Michael would enter the room anxiously and would not calm until the door was shut. His parents had reported his repetitive play in opening and shutting doors and focusing on the spaces between doorframes and the door. His play consisted of taking objects out of the containers and the doll's house and laying them on the floor. He treated all the toys as the same—as objects that he was careful to ensure did not touch, so that there were spaces between. He usually held a block in each hand, which limited his functional hand skills. His behaviour demonstrated a lack of appropriate play with objects, a lack of symbolic play and obsessional repetitive play. However, Winnicott (1941) suggested the use of these behaviours as an insight, a representational view of how Michael may experience the world. These behaviours may have indicated his need for containment, to have doors closed and for his hands to be filled to manage a feeling of impingement. He did not then need to use his hands in a functional sense; he did not need to grasp what was on offer. Did his play indicate his interest in whether he could allow something to enter "his space" or not, the spaces between objects and whether objects could come in and out? He appeared to tolerate the objects when there were spaces between them. I wondered whether his interest in taking objects out, doors that could shut things out or allow them in and the spaces between the objects and the door and its frame, demonstrated his working through of the development of his subjective self (Stern, 2000), of his self-with-another.

Michael's feeding behaviours also indicated his internal state. He appeared to be working through what he would take in from the environment and his relationship with his mother. It was as though he saw her as part of himself. He was hungry and she would feed him; his wish was met with no more active display of himself other than a cry. He did not participate in the feed by holding the bottle or even looking at her. It was as though he was maintaining the feeling of omnipotence that Winnicott (1988) suggested was part of the early feeding relationship, keeping his mother at a distance so that the feeding experience was just about his hunger being sated by a fantasy mother and not involving an interaction with a separate, independent mother.

His emotional development had become stuck and he was struggling to move from a position of omnipotence, anxiety, fragmentation, and impingement to a more integrated understanding of his self with respect to another, where his "true self" could survive and act as an agent in the external world (Winnicott, 1960). Issues that he appeared to be struggling with were, where did he end and others start, and what could he take in without losing himself?

The door opens

To develop Michael's "self" and "self with another", I worked directly with him, attempting to engage with him, wondering how he might be feeling or experiencing something, enjoying him, being mindful of his experience, playing alongside him, being there for him, receptive to any interactions he initiated. My attempts to engage him by sharing his focus of attention, initiating turn taking activities, and copying any movements or sounds that he made were initially met with dismissal. He would turn, look, or gesture me away.

I also tried to connect with Michael by sitting near him, following his lead and playing with the object he was attending to in another way. My aim was for him to sense the creativity, joy, and feeling of empowerment one could have in play. I used Michael's blocks (objects) as I wanted him to view people as friendly objects that could connect, be playful, creative, survive anger, or be left alone. I played with the blocks, putting two together building a small tower, breaking it apart, building another. I played calmly and sometimes I banged them loudly together musically.

Michael made many gains over the six months. His eye contact improved. Initially he would only allow one turn, that is he would look at the other and then the interaction was ceased. Gradually this increased to a turn each, before he looked away. He then allowed and enjoyed many turns each.

He sought his parents for cuddles intermittently throughout the session, and over time would entice them to play the games that he loved, the blowing game with his father and his mother gently tapping him on the sides of his face. He was initiating joyful interactions with his parents and participating in turn taking.

Over time his imitative skills developed. He enjoyed it when I copied him, no longer experiencing it as an impingement. Earlier he would ignore me or gesture me away. After some time, he looked pleased. I had connected with him; he would touch my forehead with his forehead. Later he smiled and laughed, or repeated the sound so that we could play a repetitive game, for example copying tiger roars. He appeared to be feeling less threatened in taking in what was being offered in the way of interaction.

As Michael began to allow interaction and to enjoy it his play with objects also changed. He began to put objects on the floor but did not mind if they touched; the action of taking them out became more important. The objects landed where they fell, the obsessive placing of the blocks had ceased. His own restrictions began to fall away. He allowed longer interactions: I would give him a toy, he threw it away, I would give it back to him, he would throw it away, looking at me, laughing, with a playful throwing of his arm.

Over time he began to put objects together. It was an exciting moment the day he allowed me to fold up a toy blanket, put it in a drawer and then put the drawer in the cupboard that he was holding. I felt that he was willing to experience and accept a part of me. Soon after, his play with objects became more appropriate. He put them back into their appropriate containers, stacked blocks, drew with textas, pushed buttons to make doors open, animals appear and toys spin around, moved a car along and took pretend sips from a tea cup.

Michael used to need to hold an object in each hand, perhaps for comfort, or to minimise the stimulation he received through his hands. He gradually began to put one down, freeing up a hand to explore other toys. He became less reliant on having his hands filled. Gradually he left the sessions with nothing in his hands. Free and willing to explore.

Michael's communication skills also developed. He wanted to share. Now he would request assistance, comment on a toy or an event and use social forms. He said "allo" when playing with a pretend phone, "igh, igh" waving goodbye. He began to copy words for example, "ess ou" for "bless you", and animal sounds, "u" for "woof" and a tiger roar.

Michael also made gains with his feeding, although the intervention did not focus on this directly. He took more solid foods, for example, sandwiches, chewing them, and he held his own bottle. He continued to require that his solid foods were fed to him in small pieces.

While Michael's development was still delayed, it was again moving along a more appropriate trajectory. He was enjoying his interactions with people, using his developing communication skills and exploring toys and relationships. He was now an active agent in the world.

Discussion

Containment of anxiety

The intervention focused on facilitating Michael's sense of self and his capacity to interact with the world, both people and objects. I considered the most important aspects of the work with this family to be the containment of anxiety, modelling a reflective stance of thinking about Michael's experience and the direct work with Michael. Bion's theory of containment was a guide in working to contain the parents' anxiety, and also Michael's (Shuttleworth, 1989). The thinking about the anxiety, talking about it and processing it contributed to making it more manageable, more contained. The parents' capacity to manage their anxieties by containing, thinking about them and surviving them might mobilise the child's anxieties and aggressions and allow an improvement in the child's capacity to symbolise (Hobson, 1990). Containment of anxiety also allowed Michael's defences to relax, and his parents' alarm and panic to reduce, creating a space for hope.

Parent–infant relationship

With the anxiety contained there were changes in the parent–infant relationship, with the parents being more receptive to Michael's communications and, with their frustrations and anxieties reduced, impinging less.

The quality of the parent–infant relationship influences pre-linguistic, means-end and symbolic development, that is, pre-communication skills. Bates (1979) reported that at eleven to twelve months of age the quality of the attachment relationship is associated with symbolic play, means-end and gestural communication. These findings were also supported by Barwick and colleagues (2004), who demonstrated that the quality of mother–infant play was associated with infants' pre-linguistic and social-affective communication abilities.

Acknowledging Michael's mind

The therapeutic reflective stance in considering Michael as subject was a vital part of the therapeutic process. This stance facilitated the thinking about Michael and his experience. Keeping Michael's mind and experience in mind while playing with him, talking to his parents or arranging the next appointment underlined his self as subject. He could no longer be considered an out-of-reach infant. He was here, now, in the present with us. This reflective thinking about Michael, how he felt, what he may have been expressing through his play, was recognised by him. He experienced it with my conjecturing to his parents about what he may be feeling and with my direct interactions with him. This seemed to have enlivened his mind, his capacity to integrate affective experiences and to think about them.

Engagement with Michael

My direct work with Michael focused on engaging him through attempts to share his experiences through affect attunement (shared affect) and joint attention (sharing interests). Stern (2000) described affect attunement as a feature of self-other subjective relatedness, a demonstration without words of how one person could experience and share another person's subjective experience, as "the performance of behaviours that express the quality of feeling of a shared affect state without imitating the exact behavioural expression of the inner state" (Stern, 2000, p. 142).

This affect attunement or right hemisphere to right hemisphere communication (Cozolino, 2002) seems likely to have stimulated the neural development of the right hemisphere, which is considered to be important with the broader aspects of communication, the emotional and non-verbal components of language; it has a sensitive period of development from eighteen to thirty-six months (Schore, 2004).

Using joint attention, I tried to share Michael's interests. Tomasello and Farrar (1986) demonstrated that joint attention led to greater language learning, rather than parent-directed attention. Joint attention is also considered the earliest indication of a rudimentary theory of mind at two to four months of age (Klin et al., 1991). This engagement with Michael facilitated the introduction of more traditional speech pathology work as he became interested in communicating and sharing experiences.

This direct work with Michael, sharing his experiences and affect, assisted in the integration of his "self", and in particular that the integrity of this "self" was maintained in his interactions with "another". The experience of having his subjective experience shared would have felt to him that he had been recognised, acknowledged and accepted, strengthening his sense of self. That this occurred with another gave him the security and trust that his self could interact with another and remain integrated. His capacity to develop a subjective self, his self with another and his sense of agency with others progressed. With this integration of his experiences and internal objects he reached the depressive position or Winnicott's stage of concern no longer fragmented, but able to tolerate ambivalence (Fairbairn, 1952). Over the six month period Michael began to demonstrate symbolic thinking reflected in his developing play and communication skills. He allowed connection with people and his toy objects. He developed confidence in his interactions with people and objects with an expanding curiosity and flexibility in these interactions.

He changed from being withdrawn, resistant to interaction from another and using objects rigidly defined with his own meaning, to a happier boy enjoying interaction with his parents and others, willing to explore new experiences and to learn about the world through a more appropriate use of objects.

Working with children like Michael presents as a treasured opportunity. With the recent research in the importance of the early years of development, in particular the role of the environment during critical and sensitive periods of brain development, there is an opportunity to look for any potential in a child and to work on this before difficulties become more fixed in the developing brain. I now approach my work with young children thinking: does this child have a strong sense of self, and a capacity to maintain this when relating with others? Facilitating these capacities would influence the developmental trajectory of the child.

References

Barwick, M. A., Cohen, N. J., Horodezky, N. B., & Lojkasek, M. (2004). Infant communication and the mother–infant relationship: the importance of level of risk and construct measurement, *Infant Mental Health Journal, 25*: 240–266.

Bates, E. (1979). *The Emergence of Symbols: Cognition and Communication in Infancy*. New York: Academic Press.

Cozolino, L. (2002). *The Neuroscience of Psychotherapy*. New York: W. W. Norton.

Fairbairn, W. R. D. (1952). Object-relationships and dynamic structure. In: *Psychoanalytic Studies of the personality* (pp. 137–151). London: Tavistock Publications.

Greenspan, S., Wieder, S., & Simons, R. (1998). *The Child with Special Needs, Encouraging Intellectual and Emotional Growth*. Massachusetts: Perseus Books.

Hobson, R. P. (1990). On psychoanalytic approaches in Autism. *American Journal of Orthopsychiatry, 60*: 324–336.

Klin, A., Volkmar, F. R., & Sparrow, S. S. (1991). Autistic Social Dysfunction: some limitations of the theory of mind hypothesis. *Journal of Child Psychology and Psychiatry, 33*: 861–876.

Schore, A. N. (2004). *Affect Dysregulation and Disorders of the Self*. New York: W. W. Norton.

Shuttleworth, J. (1989). Psychoanalytic theory and infant development. In: L. Miller, M. Rustin, M. Rustin & J. Shuttleworth (Eds.), *Closely Observed Infants*, (pp. 132–154). London: Duckworth Press.

Stern, D. N. (2000). *The Interpersonal World of the Infant: A View from Psychoanalysis and Developmental Psychology*. New York: Basic Books.

Tomasello, M., & Farrar, M. J. (1986). Joint attention and early language. *Child Development, 57*: 454–1463.

Winnicott, D. W. (1941). The observation of infants in a set situation. In: *Through Paediatrics to Psychoanalysis*, (pp. 53–69). London: Hogarth Press.

Winnicott, D. W. (1960). Ego distortions in terms of true and false self. In: *The Maturational Processes and the Facilitating Environment* (pp. 140–152). London: Hogarth Press & Institute of Psychoanalysis, 1965.

Winnicott, D. W. (1988). Establishment of relationship with external reality. In: *Human Nature* (pp. 107–115). London: Free Association Books.

ZERO TO THREE, (2005). *Diagnostic classification of mental health and developmental disorders of infancy and early childhood: Revised edition (DC:0–3R)*. Washington, DC: ZERO TO THREE Press.

CHAPTER NINETEEN

Attachment to one, two, or to group: an infant mental health intervention with an Indian family in transition

Sarah Jones and Sue Morse

Introduction

An Indian family was referred to the Hospital because their two and a half-year-old daughter was constantly screaming. Within months of being referred multiple separate paediatric, psychiatric, psychometric, and neurological assessments were attempted, all within the frame of Western medicine, resulting in conflicting opinions and conflicting treatments.

They were a family in transition, living between different cultures, an experience which offered little certainty, neither the old nor the new was comfortable. Through this work we kept facing the issue: how do the cultural differences between health professionals and the families they work with facilitate or obstruct therapeutic change?

We describe how we worked in the context of and at times in conflict with both ethnic culture and the dominant medical perspectives within a large paediatric hospital. The challenge was to learn about this infant and family through their culture, to create a space to think in the face of their puzzling child. The two therapists worked from an infant mental perspective, where the infant's experience of their world is central to the treatment. Our frameworks were drawn from psychoanalytic and family systems models with a developmental perspective. We also consider what can be learnt by questioning our reliance on assumed theoretical premises when we work with families from different cultures.

The referral and the arrival

Juhee, a two and a half-year-old girl, and her family had been referred to the Mental Health Service by their local maternal and child health nurse. Presenting problems in the referral letter included poor speech and increasingly disruptive behaviours of spinning, screaming, avoiding eye contact, and persistent undressing. The question of autism was raised in the letter.

Juhee, a large child in a beautiful satin and ribboned frock, arrived in our office with her mother, Laxmi, twenty-one years old, and her father, Ratna, thirty-two years old. Their other child, Juhee's one-year-old brother, dozed quietly in his pram. From the outset their Indian identity was displayed in their clothes, manner of speech, and the way they related to the therapists. Juhee's difficulties became quickly evident as she demonstrated loudly her frustration and rage. For a brief moment she played getting in and out of a toy wicker pram in our room. Her weight was too much for this thing, but no gestures were made by either parent to prevent a fall. She restlessly moved from toy to toy, slamming things down, tearing up papers, unable to settle or find comfort or containment. He parents talked to us throughout this turmoil of their daughter's distressing behaviour. When one of us tried to engage the girl she stopped her activity briefly then continued to throw a set of plastic skittles around one corner of the interviewing room. It was difficult to have any eye contact. The noise of her screams was piercingly loud. Despair could best describe the affect in the room.

The family story

Laxmi was born to Indian parents who emigrated to Australia when she was an infant. Laxmi was her parents' second child, an older brother now lived overseas and another brother lived in the maternal parents' home. As a child Laxmi travelled to India to stay with her grandmother. The first of these trips was when she was four for six months. At ten she returned again, this time for a year. At aged eighteen she was again in India, when the family of her husband-to-be made contact with her grandmother, enquiring about arranging a marriage to their son, Ratna.

A marriage was arranged for them by the two extended families. They met for the first time on their wedding day. Juhee was conceived almost immediately. The couple then returned to live with Laxmi's parents in Australia.

Laxmi was nineteen years old when Juhee was born. Laxmi had a warm engaging smile, which we learnt covered a lot of sadness and despair about her daughter. Both her culture and her youth was evident in the way she related to us, for example she never openly questioned or disagreed with anything that was said, and portrayed a family life beset by emotional stress and chaos, with forbearance.

Ratna, aged thirty-six, appeared more serious, more concerned about financial and long-term plans. He was the sixth male child in a family of ten children; his mother was the very central to the family, his father having died. He had followed the custom of leaving India to work to support the family and returning to them for an arranged marriage. He emphasised his long-term commitment to the welfare of his mother and siblings, and his extended family's expectations of his return to India with his family.

We heard a transgenerational story of immigration, change, and loss from the outset. Juhee was born full term, nine months after the wedding day. When she was two weeks old her father returned to India. At two months of age Juhee and her mother returned to meet the father's extended family, many of whom still lived with his mother.

The parents had been troubled by their daughter from birth. As a baby, Juhee was described as being very demanding, needing a "twenty-four hour roster system" of care. This care was provided in "shifts" by mother, her two parents, and mother's younger brother. Laxmi described her daughter as being very angry, difficult to feed, a poor sleeper and stated that, "Juhee did not want to know anyone else's problem." This tells us something of Laxmi's struggle in understanding the dependency of an infant and what was required from her as a mother. When Juhee was only fifteen months of age her younger brother was born. Laxmi appeared caring but defeated by her daughter. The parents' expectations of Juhee being a "good quiet daughter" were not fulfilled.

The couple's new relationship faced significant challenges. Indecision around which country to live in and the immediate pregnancy made it more difficult to establish their couple partnership in the context of caring for Juhee. At this time the family lived with the extended maternal family who were centrally involved with the care of the baby and domestic arrangements. Ratna took work in his father-in-law's business.

Developmental assessment

There was no family history of communication or developmental difficulties. Juhee was described as a very strong baby, being able to sit at four months. She walked at thirteen months and was described as an independent toddler who liked to do things for herself.

In the assessment, occurring over several sessions, Juhee had clear developmental delays in the areas of communication and social function, with marked behavioural symptoms. She also showed a positive propensity to change over this time and become more familiar with the situation.

She was restless, appeared not to listen and could be destructive. Her screaming appeared self-stimulatory; however over a session one could see that there was clear protest when activities changed or ended. Observation revealed that she could use simple gesture to request or ask. She was also described as affectionate, seeking cuddles from her parents; however her mother felt that she did not know who she was from other members of the family. Laxmi was upset that Juhee could not identify family members from photos. Her speech consisted of jargon that her parents could not decipher. It was neither Hindi nor English to them. Her comprehension was difficult to gauge and she was unable to attend to verbal instructions and was reluctant to interact. Her vocal skills were approximately at a twelve to fifteen month level. When attention was given by the therapists to Juhee's activities she could make eye contact, vocalise in acknowledgement and even offer a toy as if "showing". This was in contrast to her reaction to an activity or a toy that was presented to her. These she ignored or screamed at, erratically moving away. Juhee seemed extremely sensitive to impingement. She demonstrated no representative play, and would bang and knock things over. She did have pre-linguistic skills of object permanence, means-end relationship and cause-effect.

Over the first month her vocal imitation skills developed. She began imitating single words which were recognisable to her parents and had established new interactive routines with her family. For example, her father had proudly taught her an Indian folk song and she played "Round and round the garden". As part of our assessment we referred to our team's psychologist. The clinical psychology assessment did not suggest a diagnosis of autism but the one that was most consistent with Juhee's behaviour was Reactive Attachment Disorder, or *Diagnostic classification of mental health and developmental disorders of infancy and early childhood*: Axis II Relationship Classification: Anxious/Tense (ZERO TO THREE, 2005).

Diagnostic confusions

In the context of seeing other specialists within the hospital Laxmi and Ratna were given a number of possible explanations for Juhee's behaviour. Concurrent to our assessment the family had sought paediatric assistance. This lead to her being given a provisional diagnosis of Attention Hyperactivity Deficit Disorder with an immediate trial of Ritalin. The family reported that this had negative effects "turning her into a zombie", and consequently they abandoned the trial. This diagnosis was not confirmed. Further referrals were made to child neurology including MRI and electroencephalogram, and neurological explanations were slowly ruled out. Audiological assessment revealed normal hearing.

Whilst these investigations were taking place we continued our weekly sessions. When no medical diagnosis was offered they returned to the question of autism, despite her progress. The parents' request for a diagnosis could perhaps be heard as a reflection of their struggle to understand why or how their daughter had developmental difficulties. Was there something wrong with her brain? Was autism a helpful description of her difficulties? Our therapeutic tack was to avoid a foreclosure on a medical diagnostic label. Whilst acknowledging her constitutional vulnerabilities our therapy paid particular attention to her emotional regulation, language and learning how to be with people.

We made a referral to our Autism Assessment programme, at the parents' request. Whilst waiting for that service to see Juhee, the parents contacted a private autism assessment service. Again a referral to two services eventuated in Juhee being assessed by these services at approximately the same time. One made a diagnosis of anaclitic depression, emphasising the separation experiences of the infant and family, and the other Specific Language Disorder. These assessments were undertaken at about eighteen months after our work commenced.

Treatment

Following our initial assessment we embarked on a therapeutic intervention lasting approximately twenty months. Usually these sessions would be with Juhee, her brother, and her parents; sometimes they would include Juhee, her mother, and her grandmother. Separate weekly sessions were offered for Juhee for child therapy with a specific interaction and language focus.

We tried to encourage them to remain engaged in the pursuit of knowing and thinking more about their daughter and themselves. From the outset Juhee's developmental difficulties were apparent, screaming and "in your face". The parents seemed unaware of the high level of stimulation Juhee experienced with the constant changes in caregivers. This was probably highest when the family returned to India to show the father's family their new infant. For more than a month she was passed around the extended family for care.

In the initial session Juhee attempted to get her parent's attention with a tug or a look; however this communicative act was overlooked or seen but not recognised. This small observation, so hard to see amidst the confusion, seemed to present a window of possibility through which to view Juhee as not only a child who was distressed, delayed, and avoidant, but also as a child for whom there had been environmental failure where her efforts to relate had not been recognised. We worked with her momentary expressions of developmental possibilities. For example, finding and noticing her gestures, her intentions, and later in the work making a Juhee Life book, so that she had pictures and images of her own history to acknowledge the people and places in her life.

The parents acknowledged how difficult their early experiences of becoming parents to Juhee were, in the light of their son's more normal developmental path. They would often comment that he was able to feed well or sleep through the night, while they were still consumed with Juhee's difficulties. We came to understand the immense grief that both parents felt regarding acceptance of the disorder in Juhee. Ratna had not told his family of Juhee's developmental concerns. Maternal depression when Juhee was very young was continually alluded to by the parents as the slow painful process of remembering and mourning the early times of troubles with their first baby unfolded.

In the sessions we would work on the subtleties of her communication attempts, the parents' confusion in finding themselves as a very young couple faced with the demands of an unpredictably disruptive infant and the impact on their lives. We found ways to acknowledge Juhee's own nascent attempts to connect with them. One of us might play a game with her and discover her turn taking style was changing a little, or settle with her to draw and help her find some pleasure in doing it together. The other would work with the parents' despair or confusion in looking for help in a large hospital with such a large number of specialists' opinions.

There was the constant question of which country they would or should live in. India was the place the father yearned for, and continued to visit intermittently during our work with them. As the mother learned more about her daughter's needs, both from an emotional point of view and from a greater understanding of the importance of continuing professional interventions, she became more hesitant to return. Twelve months into the treatment Laxmi decided to travel overseas for a month. This caused a dilemma for the therapists, who needed to suspend their judgement of what was appropriate in the light of the emerging mother–infant relationship. After a gap of four weeks Laxmi described her elation when reunited with her daughter who responded to her mother with great recognition and pleasure. Paradoxically this absence, rather than compounding a problem, led to a reunion in which Laxmi felt recognised by her daughter for the first time.

Juhee and her family made significant progress. For example, initially as we approached the waiting room we would hear the noise and screams of Juhee. She began to respond with much greater recognition of what was going to happen when she saw us. We made a point of joining her play in the waiting room, commenting and interacting with her and not expecting her to renounce her activity on our arrival. Eventually she stopped demanding to stay in the waiting room and was able to leave the large plastic boxes she enjoyed, without protest. These signs were evidence of her being able to use us as a temporary secure base.

Slowly the parents could begin to see her behaviours as complex ways that she expressed herself and we found ways to talk with them about what she may be feeling or needing, or why she might be particularly distressed. They enrolled Juhee in a childcare centre when she was about three and a half and the staff there had a very affirming, supportive role with both Juhee and her mother. Laxmi would tell us how she liked to stay and talk with them when she arrived, and that they set limits on Juhee who seemed to react well to them. A visit was arranged for one of us to see her in that setting.

We were very aware of the real advantages for this girl and her parents of the extended family's support. Yet we needed to consider whether all these changes in the environment alongside the mother and father's struggle to appropriately respond to the needs of a dependent infant also somehow contributed to this child's sense of not belonging, not able to integrate the number of people and experiences leading to a disorganised attachment style. Not having a predictable safe base, especially in the first six to twelve months, both emotionally and physically may have affected Juhee's extreme behaviours and poor capacity for integration. In a constitutionally more robust child this may have been an enhancement to development. Our concerns were, however, that it may have, in this child, contributed to her diffuse, indiscriminate, disorganised, psychological response.

Termination of infant mental health therapy

We worked with this infant and family as a therapy pair for nearly two years, offering them combined family therapy work alongside speech and language therapy. Unfortunately the therapy was interrupted due to one of the clinician's prolonged ill health. During this time the parents chose not to continue treatment at the hospital but with their better understanding of Juhee's speech and language disorder moved to private speech pathology services. The conclusion of the work appeared to us as a similar reflection of the dilemma to which country would claim their loyalties. Which service would help the most? Whilst thinking the ending was premature we knew that they initially came in enormous distress with their daughter who had developed significantly, as they had themselves in caring for her. Their capacities to hold and contain and understand her were stronger and their decision to finish with us might have also reflected these changes.

Two year follow-up

Two years later we had a follow-up meeting. Juhee had made considerable developmental gains. She was half way through her first year at school, where she was reported to be doing adequately socially and coping with the learning demands. Juhee took her place in conversation being able to tell us about her experiences in school. Her speech reflected her ongoing limitations in language and social nuance. She seemed happy and her parents spoke with pride in their daughter.

Discussion

Infant–parent assessment and intervention

Zeanah and colleagues (1993) outlined an infant–parent assessment model which has its focus on the infant's interactions. He described a three part model where the clinician should focus primarily on the infant's relationships with "attachment figures rather than on the child's social behaviour in general" (Zeanah et al., 1993, p. 345). Second, the infant's history and direct observation of the infant with those attachment figures. Third, he suggested that for diagnosis a structured research method of assessing attachment should be used sparingly. What emerged early in our assessment were not only Juhee's vulnerabilities but also vulnerabilities within the parents' capacity to interpret and engage with their child. Zeanah proposed that for infants who do not seem attached to emotionally available, sensitive caregivers "the first effort of intervention should be provision of a stable and consistent caregiving adult who is or is likely to become emotionally invested in the infant" (ibid., p. 345). Juhee's problem was not an absence of possible attachment figures but too diffuse attachments for her vulnerabilities.

A secure base of therapy

Bowlby (1988) proposed the notion of therapy providing "a secure base". The therapist "provides the patient with a secure base from which he can explore the various unhappy painful aspects of his life, past and present many of which he finds it difficult or perhaps impossible to think about and reconsider without a trusted companion to provide support, encouragement, sympathy and on occasion, guidance" (Bowlby, 1988, p. 138). This best describes our therapeutic style, which at times we thought to be in jeopardy. The therapy with Juhee could have been challenged by all the other investigations taking place, but it appeared that the family remained engaged and found relief in our commitment to understanding their daughter.

Ambivalence

Laxmi's capacity for ambivalence, to both love and hate this child was a dynamic we worked with actively. How could this mother hold both these feelings, when this child was an intruder in many ways into her life, body and marriage at eighteen (Winnicott, 1949). How Juhee had interrupted her young teenage mother's life was being re-enacted by being given over to her mother's mother who was the "more capable mother". Some of the ways the mother spoke of her daughter, such as being "my bodyguard" and "not wanting to know anyone else" were ways the mother expressed her ambivalent feelings to her intrusive infant when she herself did not have a bodyguard, nor was able to be known by others.

Cultural challenges

It is clear that traditional child raising practices in Western and Eastern countries are different. Current Western attachment theory suggests that an infant's psychic health is determined by the quality of attachment with the primary care giver, usually the mother. What we learned from this family was the cultural normality of the organisation of family life around multiple mother figures, especially during the early months.

Both parents grew up within extended cultural systems of care and comfort being provided by a family group. Kurtz (1992) gave a detailed account of the problems in researching childrearing in other cultures from a traditional psychoanalytic model, and cautioned against those who arrive at pathogenic conclusions from their own observations. He described how the Indian child is shared by the women of an extended family, which emphasises group communion rather than primary attachment. Bharucha (2003) in her discussion of mothering in an Indian family described a shared attunement to the baby's needs in a group context.

Winnicott (1960) described the infant's capacity for "experiencing unintegrated states, as dependent on the continuation of reliable maternal care or the build up in the infant of memories of maternal care" (Winnicott, 1960, p. 44). The experience of continuous care, which is provided by significant and reliable attachment figures, is promoted by all cultures to different degrees. Traditional Eastern cultures provide this more often in a group context.

The notion of exclusivity of the mother/caregiver's preoccupation, holding and containment of the infant's emotional processes resulting in attuned care giving and understanding of the infant's signals and signs were not ones we could discern in the history of Juhee's first twelve months. Kurtz's work on the Hindu Indian culture explored the importance of group attachment and the capacities of both children and adults to attach to a small kinship group, where belonging, developing and exploring evolve along a continuum. Kurtz viewed the infant's attachment and identification with the whole group to be the necessary developmental pathway for maturation. This group identification process is said to occur earlier than the Western infant's identification with the group. Kurtz described how for the Eastern family cultural integration of the individual into the group is the primary and relatively early goal of childrearing. "Because psychoanalysts have sought to confirm in India merely the presence or absence of a Western development pattern, they have missed altogether the Hindu child's movement, by way of renunciation, away from the infantile attachments to the mother and toward a more mature participation in the group" (Kurtz, 1992, p. 61).

In this family there were a variety of people who greeted Juhee when she woke. The shared care meant that she may have been continually handed over when she was most distressed; to share her around might have been the only "solution" at hand. The lack of contingent care giving, that is where an adult is sufficiently attuned to an infant's cues so that there is a fit between the infant and the caregiver responses, was for Juhee more problematic. It was not, so much, the number of people caring for the baby but the failure of the system as a whole "to develop a sense of communal attunement" (Bharucha, 2003, p. 21). It was this notion that we came to value more significantly during the therapy, and was the basis of our intervention. Thus it was not the care system itself but the way "this child" with these difficulties responded to that care that was central to our work. How to speak of this with the family became one of our challenges.

Conclusion

With the possible opposing views of Eastern and Western models about the necessary conditions for infant mental health, it was important that neither one nor the other was considered right or wrong. The family was, like many families, in a cultural transition, which meant they too were straddling different cultural beliefs, loyalties and ties. The difficulties were how to translate our thoughts and suggestions whilst keeping an open mind and eye to the family's strengths and cultural values. The medical systems within the hospital could have, with the best intentions, offered a diagnosis which may have overlooked the enormous importance of Juhee's experiences of disruption in her early infancy and family developments. By focusing on these and their contribution to her difficulties we were able to offer a therapy that actively worked with these experiences and help towards resolving them.

Acknowledgements

The authors would like to thank the family, The Royal Children's Hospital infant mental health colleagues who helped with various versions of this paper and Ms. Jo Hall, Clinical Psychologist.

References

Bharucha, A. (2003). Multiple mothering in an Indian context. In: F. Thomson-Salo (Ed.), *Mothers and Infants: New Perspectives* (pp. 5–23). Melbourne: Stonnington Press.

Bowlby, J. (1988). Attachment, communication and the therapeutic process. In: *A Secure Base* (pp. 137–157). London. Tavistock/Routledge.

Kurtz, S. M. (1992). *All the Mothers are One*. New York: Columbia Press.

Winnicott, D. W. (1949). Hate in the Counter-Transference. International Journal of Psycho-Analysis, *30*: 69–74.

Winnicott, D. W. (1960). The theory of the parent–infant relationship. In: *The Maturational Processes and the Facilitating Environment* (pp. 37–55). London: Hogarth.

Zeanah, C. H., Mammen, O., & Lieberman, A. (1993). Disorders of attachment. In: C. H. Zeanah (Ed.) *Handbook of Infant Mental Health*, (pp. 332–349) New York: Guildford Press.

Zero to three (2005). *Diagnostic classification of mental health and developmental disorders of infancy and early childhood: Revised edition (DC:0–3R)*. Washington, DC: Zero to Three Press.

CHAPTER TWENTY

Feeding, the self, and working through the infant's pathological defences: the seriousness of playfulness

Campbell Paul

This is an account of work revolving around an older infant and his family whom we saw for about two years, from the time he was eighteen months old. Several modalities were used although I shall concentrate on my work with the infant. I would like to consider questions such as how the role of "direct" psychotherapy with the infant and the development of transference in an infant combined with parent psychotherapy around these issues may help understand and undo the destructive employment of psychological defences in the infant patient.

First meeting

Fourteen-month-old Tim was initially referred by a paediatrician because his parents remained extremely concerned about his eating and feeding behaviour. He would not allow himself to be fed. "He is aggressively anti it", said his distraught mother, "he gains weight OK but he won't let me feed him." He was being breastfed twice a day but *never* demanded the breast—he was never hungry. He had no solid food at that time, but breastfeeds were supplemented by cows' milk by bottle but *ONLY* in his mother's arms in the dark between 8.30–9.30 p.m.

She also said that he loved his milk. "It's like he decides certain things and that's it!" There were further associated somatic complaints: he had had "reflux" since birth, vomiting up feeds from his very first one—"he sicked it up", and tummy pains—"his belly was distended and full of gas". He was also a poor, fitful sleeper.

His family came from interstate in connection with Tim's father's work. The couple had been together many years and had had a miscarriage about ten months previously. The pregnancy with Tim had been complicated by mother having gestational diabetes. Paternal grandfather had suffered an unexpected heart attack and died during the last stage of the pregnancy and the parents were unable to return home for the funeral.

When Tim was delivered at thirty-six weeks, he was hypoglycaemic and had a dusky attack (apnoea) when first placed on his mother's breast and needed to be resuscitated. She was terrified by this, fearing his death. In hospital he cried a lot and the midwives were said to be happy to see him go. But he came home to fearful parents. Tim vomited up his feeds frequently and continued crying until his fourth month. He had a considerable number of investigations including an endoscopy and duodenal biopsy. After a period of frequent vomiting and positing at five months he refused solids altogether, except for an occasional banana. He would scream and push away solids. When his mother was advised to reduce breastfeeds to increase his hunger he only fed less and lost virtually no weight. His parent also reported him experiencing nightmares and that he played little with his peers at playgroup, instead collecting the toys to himself. Getting food into him was a life and death issue, whereas from the child's point of view refusal asserted some autonomy, whether in the area of gaze, eating or speech.

I saw him on two occasions initially and responded primarily to the issue of his feeding, suggesting that his parents allow him more space— to eat, to try foods at his own leisure, to take some of the intense heat and anxiety out of the situation. His parents tried this while on holiday, his eating improved somewhat and I did not see him for some months.

"Seeing" with video screening

When he was eighteen months old, they made contact again especially as his mother was very frightened because he was again refusing solids. We regularly use the one way screen for multidisciplinary infant mental health assessments, and Tim was seen in this context with both his parents. The team were able to reflect and make suggestions. For me this was a particularly powerful phenomenon. The interview itself seemed "ordinary", focused on the presenting symptom of food refusal, but I was shocked by what I had not seen in the session. What we saw on the videotape was an avoidant anxious boy, unable to engage in social play, with only sparse vocalisation, unable to engage in any sustained direct eye contact and with whom one had to work very hard to obtain any joint attention. In fact if one had used the CHAT, the Checklist for Autism in Toddlers (Baron-Cohen et al., 1992), Tim was clearly at high risk for the diagnosis of autism.

This was perturbing since it had not been my experience of him to consider autism in the session. This raises the role of countertransference in work with infants. Tim's play had been isolated and was not directed at others, seemingly devoid of any social meaning, and we were also struck by the quality of interaction with his parents. There was also Tim's severe gaze aversion. Even when I attempted to set up a game around his looking at and making the sound of the clock, "Ock ... ock" I could not get eye contact and he had difficulty being playful. An attempt at a hand game saw him gently but firmly repulse me.

Colleagues in reviewing the video also noted the complex interaction, especially an episode of "synchronous dysynchrony" (M. S. Moore, personal communication). As Tim looked towards his mother, her eyes closed and she looked away and down. Her arms were extended and stiff, not enfolding. The offer of the banana to eat was slowly refused, but in a non-personal way: Tim just turned his back on his mother, although he said "B". At that time the word "B" was a major currency in speech since banana was one of the few things he would sometimes eat.

I made some comments on this session: that it was as if Tim was "a person unto himself"—he would do things only on his own terms. This made his mother especially sad, reflective, and tearful as if I had unwittingly recognised what she saw as the real problem, that she and her husband could not reach him—he was distant. (Tim had recently gone into a pigeon house, wanting to be left alone and was quite content there for some time.)

With the aid of the collective conscious and unconscious of the team it became clear that this family was deeply troubled, and action was needed quickly. Frances Thomson-Salo joined me as a co-therapist and in a brief period of reassessment and attempts to free things up, we worked with the boy and his family together but soon moved to the different modality of seeing the boy for psychotherapy. I think that because of the subtle feelings in the interaction between Tim and myself, I felt that I could work with him in psychotherapy—and perhaps it needed to be alone. Frances Salo met with Tim's parents for therapy, which, while not described here, is gratefully acknowledged.

It was an unusual step to begin therapy with a twenty-one-month-old child alone, but to our amazement he took to it very readily and with weekly sessions of about forty-five minutes showed little anxiety about separation. Initially his parents were seen across the corridor with open doors but the doors were soon closed. As co-therapist, Frances Salo was able to hold anxieties for each of Tim, his parents and for me as we attempted to work with Tim out of sight of his parents. We had regular discussions which allowed our therapeutic goals to coalesce and to share the task with Tim's parents.

His parents reported further symptoms of concern—his need to be exceptionally tidy, always replacing one pencil before taking another and always keeping all his toys tidied away in their boxes and cupboards. He could not bear to look at or be with babies or children younger than himself. Usually when greeted he would hide his face behind his hands or turn away, even with someone whom he knew well. His extended family felt very concerned about him. Questions were asked as to whether he was delayed or damaged.

The therapy

It has been hard to characterise the exact nature of the therapy with this boy but it was guided mostly by Winnicott's (1971) ideas of play, and of transitional space and processes. There was a need to make real contact with Tim in a non-threatening, playful way. His defences excluded the other and we needed to find out why. There is room for speculation but perhaps he as a vulnerable infant became too much for his parents, lost and grieving themselves. They had both left their childhood homes, his father lost his own father so far away, just when he should have been rejoicing in his soon-to-be-born son. Tim also followed the grief of earlier miscarriages. We had little idea of Tim's parents' experience of themselves as children, but we did know that his mother's younger cousin to whom she was very close had severe eating problems as a child, which continues as an adult. She felt somehow also responsible for her care. Both Tim's parents seemed to have experienced some enduring sense of inner loss.

Perhaps the mutual turning away, the "synchronous dysynchrony" had developed as a mutually defensive process to avoid the pain of not being seen. Did Tim looking at his mother see her not "seeing" him? Maybe her view of Tim was blurred: she must also have seen her own grief about her cousin, miscarried babies and a complex relationship with her family. It has been hard to know but again it seemed that we had to work quickly even if in the dark. For all parents their baby means so many things to them … but maybe for Tim's parents all these pains interposed themselves in front of him.

In sessions with Tim I was guided by our work with younger infants and the idea that we had developed of "attuned play" in therapy. The play was quite simple. I found myself trying to pick up the subtext of Tim's cues. As in the video-ed session, his gaze was most important. (Then he had looked at the clock, an active process, and although he did not look at a person, there was an attempt to make it into a game. If not using gaze in a joint way, then we used sound—we each said "ock" or "clock" and repeated it. I tried to extend the game to include a small hand-touching game, much as one would with a young baby—but he, somehow, both ended the game—and continued it by repeatedly pushing my hand away. It was the beginning of a playful interaction between us.)

In a subsequent session he sat on my chair, which is sprung in order to recline, and I had the idea to make a rocking game. He enjoyed it—I gently tipped him back, he glanced at me, smiled and indicated he wanted more. He had to trust me in this game—at some stage he had also to look at me—when would I tip him next? In inviting me to rock him backwards in the chair he was able to allow himself to look at me with pleasurable anticipation and excitement. There was an element of the unexpected, the predictable unexpected. This game became known as Dr. Paul's game, somehow valued by his parents who dared not do it themselves with Tim, despite my enjoining them to do so. But when they did there was change—Tim in absolute delight tenaciously grabbed his father's gaze, who responded by providing the vocal "bump" with each movement of the chair.

Quickly his mother described Tim developing a strong relationship with me. This was evident between sessions by him saying my name, "Paul", or saying, "See Paul". It had begun to feel to us that his therapy was of an urgent nature: his parents, equally concerned, seemed still unable to engage and play readily with him. Yet I had found it difficult to fully recognise how quickly and strongly Tim became attached to me. It felt as though his parents handed him over to me in the therapy, silently acknowledging a real and therapeutic relationship, desperate for it to work for their son. However, as concerned and cautious parents they did seek further opinions and help from other clinicians.

Tim became increasingly adventurous, moving in and out of different play, sensory play forging the trust between us, solidifying the transference (and also the positive countertransference) and out of this play to other symbolic play. This development in his play occurred at home too. I worked with helping Tim explore happy, cross, and sad affects in a safe space, and this included the use of drawings of facial expressions. Cross could safely become rage and destruction and sad could become detachment and despair in this context. We adopted two toys, I became a tyrannosaurus rex, and Tim the turtle. These two creatures wrestled, tugged, bit, looked, fell, wrestled, bit, then snarled at each other for several minutes at the beginning of each session for some months.

Disorder became creatively enacted. He would tip the box of Lego on my head in absolute delight, then top it off by putting the box right over my head. I was then resurrected to play another role—to be crushed by the doll's house which he pushed on top of me. He climbed up high to become a "giant"—a small giant, no, a big giant (but NOT a monster). I could not name him a monster, so I suppose that I was encouraging the release of hostility (biting, kicking, and destructiveness) and providing along with this, names for these feelings as well as names for other aspects of the transference.

So we used gaze, his body (touch and proprioception) and sound via word games as one would work with a small baby and gradually built upon this a more symbolic playfulness. What was his basic anxiety? Winnicott's notions of psychotic anxieties, of not existing and of not being seen, developed by Bion (1962) as nameless dread, were helpful. Trevarthen and his colleagues (1981) extended his notion of intersubjectivity as an innate property of the infant, the capacity to both express and directly apprehend in others, rudimentary tensions and affects, from the very beginning, in stating that any innate intersubjectivity that is not matched by a sympathetic support from a company of other accessible subjects will not survive. This would be similar to a severe disturbance in the infant's experience of mutuality, as described by Winnicott.

Tim's defence had been to withdraw to avoid the pain of not being known as himself. Was this infant in the process of the development of an autistic disorder? Was his refusal to feed another component in his turning away from the other? We believe so. However, by the end of therapy one outcome was that feeding was not a concern.

He felt that I allowed him more space than he generally felt he was allowed. What of his language, speech and communication? I tried in my talking to help him experience his own subjectivity and sense of agency rather than subjecting him to language. I used language as communication around the toys rather than being anxious about the number of words he could say. There had been problems evident here too. Tim used little speech, initially a few uncommon single words, such as "B". "OK" was his response only when asked a precise question for which he could reply "Yes". "Yes" is like an active grabbing of what you want, "OK" an acceding to someone else's wish or idea. He confused pronouns—later if he wanted help he would say to others, "Help you!" He called his mother "Da", his early name for his father. We felt that a speech assessment was vital and so sought input from Sue Morse. In the psychoanalytically informed work that she did as a speech pathologist she helped Tim extend his use of language as communication, and this work is gratefully acknowledged.

Conclusion

In Winnicott's (1971) words, "If the mother's face is unresponsive, then a mirror is a thing to be looked at, but not to be looked into" (Winnicott, 1971, p. 113). But equally, if the baby's face is unresponsive, then it is something to be looked at—not into! I have adapted Winnicott in this second sentence, to highlight the possibility that a process begun before Tim's birth may have been continued afterwards—baby and parents locked into an experience of painful, defensive non-recognition and avoidance of each other.

We attempted a series of intervention with the hurried hot breath of lost time—which may be development lost!—breathing down our necks, to try to establish a real relationship with Tim. Work with his parents tried to enable them to put aside their own past to pick up on that relationship and carry it forward with him.

We felt that the technique of attuned play, adapting the process of parent–infant attunement to the therapist being attuned to the very early psyche-soma connections, to communicate with the infant patient with gaze, touch, and sound was a means to make contact with the infant's self to help him realise that there is an other and therefore a realisation that he does also exist.

In fourteen-month-old Tim we saw potentially extremely serious symptoms—possibly autism, masked by or presenting with the common symptom of feeding refusal. It was with the aid of a reflective team that we were able to see—to entertain the idea of Tim's severe avoidance of other and self. The video and the detached observer using their own transitional/observational space also allowed us to see features in the infant's own transference and our countertransference. His parents had somehow been aware of the problem and fostered their child's transference in therapy and slowly built upon it with him themselves. I emphasise that the parents' change was slow. We felt that we had to act urgently and could not wait for change to occur in the relationship with the parents before Tim could shift. With therapy he gained his own identity. He felt that there was space for his own desire and for his own words and thoughts, that these were no longer automatically frightening.

Acknowledgements

Thanks to the various families whose experiences have contributed to this chapter and who have allowed us to work alongside them in furthering our understanding of infants and very young children.

Sue Morse has been a creative and steady collaborator in the conceptual and clinical work with Tim, his family and with so many others.

Professor Bernard Golse, University of Paris, Dr. Dilys Daws, Tavistock Clinic, London and Dr. Mary Sue Moore, Boulder, Colorado, each contributed valuable comments to our thinking when this paper was presented at the Sixth World Association for Infant Mental Health World Congress in Tampere, Finland.

References

Baron-Cohen, S., Allen, J., & Gillberg, C. (1992). Can autism be detected at 18 months? The needle, the haystack, and the CHAT. *British Journal of Psychiatry, 161*: 839–843.

Bion, W. R. (1962). *Learning from Experience*. London: Heinemann.
Trevarthen, C. (1974). Psychobiology of speech development. In: E. Lenneberg (Ed.) Language and brain: developmental aspects. *Neurobiology Sciences Research Program Bulletin, 12*: 570–585.
Winnicott, D. W. (1971). *Playing and Reality*. London: Tavistock.

PART V

INTERVENTIONS WITH INFANTS EXPOSED TO FAMILY VIOLENCE

CHAPTER TWENTY-ONE

Infancy and domestic violence: an annotation

Brigid Jordan

This chapter highlights one possible impact of witnessing domestic violence on the health and development of an infant—the development of feeding difficulties and failure to gain weight. The aetiology of failure to thrive may be organic, psychological, or a mixture of the two.

Winnicott (1971) a British paediatrician and psychoanalyst, wrote that the first mirror that the baby looks into is her mother's face—as the baby looks into her mother's face she sees reflected back what the mother sees as she looks at the baby. Thus what the baby sees in her mother's face while drinking can have a powerful impact on the feeding interaction. If what is "dished up" with the milk is too frightening, or too intense, the baby might avert her gaze, be on and off the breast, clamp her mouth shut and completely refuse, or vomit what she does take in.

When violence occurred during breastfeeding, one can imagine that the baby could approach subsequent feeds in a hypervigilant state, and that for her and her mother feeding could evoke the memory of the trauma. The baby may accept the breast but not take much in. In the second six months of life (and particularly after teeth appear) feeding involves coming to terms with aggressive impulses and being confident that the mother can survive these. This can be a near impossible step for a baby whose mother is physically and emotionally bruised.

Attachment behaviours promote the infant's close proximity to parent and also evoke parental anxiety to keep the parent close to their infant. The infant is continually and simultaneously appraising potential danger or stress in the environment and the whereabouts and accessibility of their attachment figure. Bowlby (1959) described how attachment behaviour is complementary to exploration—when attachment behaviour is activated, for example, by fear, then exploration is shut down, and when attachment (proximity, security) is achieved, attachment behaviours shut down and exploration can occur. When the infant's attachment figure (and secure base) is under threat, the infant is not free to explore the environment. Thus an infant may be less likely to wean from the breast or accept solid food if their relationship with their mother is not secure, or if the environment is threatening and impinging.

There is a body of knowledge developing about infants who have witnessed violence—infants growing up in communities of violence as well as those living with family violence. Infants and toddlers exposed to overwhelming traumatic events experience similar symptoms to adults and older children with their symptoms having a developmentally determined expression.

Very young infants use primitive defences to cope with extreme anxiety and thus infants in situations which cause extreme anxiety have difficulty regulating effects. They may present as hypervigilant or extremely withdrawn. Withdrawal responses and avoidance, including avoidance of feeding, exploration and interpersonal interaction, may be evident (Drell et al., 1993).

In older infants post-traumatic response includes:

- Re-experiencing the traumatic event (traumatic play, re-enactment play, dissociative response, for example, dazed expression, stereotypical behaviour, extreme withdrawal, periodic unresponsiveness).
- Numbing of responsiveness (emotionally subdued, socially withdrawn, restricted play).
- Hyperarousal (irritability, emotional lability, temper tantrums, hypervigilance or signs of fear and aggression, for example, headbanging, scratching own face) (Zeanah & Scheeringa, 1996).

Factors that are considered to lead to severe responses include:

- Intensity of traumatic event.
- Child's proximity.
- Witnessing versus hearing about the event.
- Familiarity/identification with perpetrator, victim or both (Osofsky, 1996).

In domestic violence all of the factors that increase the severity of the post-traumatic response apply. Usually in traumatic circumstances the immediate support and emotional availability of caregivers mitigates adverse effects. However, the obverse may happen when the trauma is perpetrated in the family—the presence of the violent parent is a cause for alarm for the child. The parents' capacity to deal with the trauma themselves is an important influence in how successfully they can provide their child with the emotional resources to deal with trauma. Parents exposed to violence are likely to have difficulty being emotionally available, sensitive and responsive to their children (they are in survival mode, they may be dissociating or suffering from other Post-Traumatic Stress Disorder (PTSD) symptoms themselves, that is, they may be traumatised by their own exposure to violence (Osofsky, 2000)).

The literature emphasises that the reinstitution of a safe, stable and nurturing environment is crucial for recovery from trauma. The intervention for an infant hospitalised with failure to thrive in response to family violence may include

- A referral to statutory protective services to ensure safety for the mother and infant. This may include seeking a court order with conditions that support the mother–infant relationship as the primary nurturing relationship.
- Allocation of a primary nurse as an adjunct attachment figure and a primary nursing team if the infant was an inpatient.
- A structured programme that enhanced the infant's autonomy and pleasure in feeding, provided developmentally appropriate play therapy and interaction experiences, and minimised impingement and anxiety for the infant.
- Mother—psychotherapy to be available to hear the story of the infant and her carers.

References

Bowlby, J. (1959). The nature of the child's tie to the mother. *International Journal of Psychoanalysis, 39*: 350–373.

Chatoor, I. (1997). Feeding disorders of infants and toddlers. In: S. Greenspan, S. Wieder, & J. Osofsky (Eds.) *Handbook of Child and Adolescent Psychiatry: Infants and Preschoolers; development and syndromes, 1*: 367–385.

Drell, M., Siegel, C. & Gaensbauer, T. (1993). Post Traumatic Stress Disorder. In: C. H. Zeanah (Ed.), *Handbook of Infant Mental Health*, (pp. 291–304). New York: Guilford Press.

Osofsky, J. (1996). Introduction: Assessing and treating young victims of violence. *Zero to Three 15*: 5–8.

Osofsky, J. (2000). Infants and Violence: Prevention, intervention, and treatment. In: J. Osofsky & H. E. Fitzgerald (Eds.), *WAIMH Handbook of Infant Mental Health, 4*: 161–196. New York: John Wiley.

Winnicott, D. W. (1971). The mirror role of the mother and family in child development, *Playing and Reality*. London: Tavistock.

Zeanah, C. H. & Scheeringa, M. D. (1996). Evaluation of post-traumatic symptomatology in infants and young children exposed to violence. *Bulletin of Zero to Three, 16*: 9–14.

CHAPTER TWENTY-TWO

Working with a sick baby born of a rape

Campbell Paul

W hile no expert on the tragedy of rape I offer some of my thoughts from a clinical perspective. As it is one hundred and fifty years since Sigmund Freud was born, it is timely to reflect on the question of where we have come to in our understanding of human sexuality and related issues since then.

Sexual violence is an issue both overwhelming in its enormity and yet in many ways hidden. The World Health Organisation (Krug, 2002) special publication on violence details that women in a range of countries, from ten per cent in Brazil to forty-six per cent in Peru, report incidents (often repeated) of attempted or completed forced sex by intimate partners during their lifetime. (Other examples are twenty-three per cent in UK, fifteen per cent in Canada.) Up to fifty per cent of women have therefore experienced something like rape or a similar assault within their own intimate relationships. As infant mental health workers, I suspect it is an issue we rarely ask about. What does it mean that so many women, presumably so many mothers of the infants referred to us, have been so violated? Do they make a complete disjunction between these assaults and the acts of sexual union that led to the conception of their babies? Or do they make a range of accommodations?

Rape occurs in a range of settings—what meaning does it have for the woman? What effect does it have upon the human integrity of the man? I shall, however, leave aside this question, one that is riven with controversy, to concentrate on mothers and infants. The consequences for women are many: gynaecological trauma, infections, STDs, HIV/AIDS, as well as a range of psychiatric and psychological disturbances (depression, post-traumatic stress disorder, suicidal ideation)—and of course the likelihood of an unwanted pregnancy. Other social consequences can be profound: women may be blamed, shamed, and excluded from their own families, indeed in some communities expelled from the entire community. (In Kenya, women raped by soldiers were, on joining the settlement, rejected by their husbands and set up their own community with their children.) Women may be blamed for bringing shame upon their families or partners, and justice seems so often a totally remote concept. Rape is at least to some extent a product of social mores, rules, and behaviour, whether these are acknowledged or not. In some communities the woman and the baby are seen as the evil, guilty partners and are sometimes killed. Rape has for centuries been used as a weapon of war as part of a more conscious, systematic process but can also occur in the midst of severe social chaos or poverty where law has broken down, This was recently the case in Liberia where at least forty per cent of women had been raped and feared that this would happen to their daughters, and the president, Ellen Johnson Sirleaf, in leading a fightback courageously declared her experience of attempted rape when previously in prison.

Even in the twentieth and twenty-first centuries, in the former Yugoslavia and Rwanda, women were held captive for the purpose of demoralising and destroying a community—a form of genocide—through alienating and shaming women, their husbands, their sons, their fathers as well as the children themselves. The trauma of the capture and sexual assault itself is then perpetuated on a daily basis as the family is faced with the offspring of their tormentors in their midst. How these infants themselves fared in this context is not clear—we can only imagine how disruptive it must be.

In statements that victims of rape made to the Medical Foundation for the Care of Victims of Torture in the UK, many women said that they did not blame the child, whom they saw as an "innocent victim of war" (Papineni, 2003, p. 362). While it is not known how many infants have been abandoned, clearly many still live with their mothers, who may identify with the child and also fear the infant being described as "filth" by the whole community. In Rwanda, such children are often known as "les enfants de mauvais souvenir" (children of bad memories) or "children of hate" (Papineni, 2003, p. 825).

How difficult it must be to seek help in such circumstances: the mother is doubly aware of her shame in that she knows that she was forced to gratify her oppressor's desire and she knows that everyone in her community knows this as well. What does she believe her infant will know? What does she glean from his eyes to her?

Correspondents Report (Australian Broadcasting Corporation 10.2.06) addressed some of these questions in a programme in which two Bosnian women discussed their dilemmas. Safeda wondered when to tell her adopted son that his Muslim mother was raped by a Serbian soldier. Safeda was ill and about to die and was in great conflict about whether to tell her son about his conception. His biological mother had abandoned him so that he had not been breastfed; he was adopted by a Muslim couple. One question was whether he should try to find his mother—"Not really, he has parents, there's love from the adoptive parents, his mother especially". Another question was whether to tell him that he was Muslim—"He is more Muslim than Christian ... We will see this happen again. ... Their children live with us." The second woman, who was single, was raped by soldiers and became pregnant. She poignantly said of her son, "He's my whole life. When I go, he'll be all on his own. But my son will be a good man." Even though her son had a very divergent parenthood and traumatic conception, his mother was able to detach him from the wrongdoing done to her by his father. Can she talk of his father? Can she even think of his father? As clinicians we see some mothers whose babies present with problems, who say, "His father is not around" or "I don't know who her father is". Should we explore this with mothers or leave things unsaid?

Also of interest was the process of making the television documentary, of daring to talk about a topic of which so many were ashamed. For these mothers, despite the inevitable traumatic memories experienced by the mother or adoptive mother, the child was a person in his own right—detached, as it were, from the "father", if I can use that term. Somehow they made this dissociation possible.

For families whom I see at The Royal Children's Hospital, Melbourne, this disjunction is not always possible, as with Helen, twenty-eight years old, and her five-month-old daughter, Sarah. (Names have been changed to protect confidentiality.) Helen had been sexually assaulted and anally penetrated by a stranger when she was alone in the street one night. She has suffered considerable anxiety symptoms and severe gynaecological and bowel symptoms with intermittent pain and rectal bleeding. She subsequently became pregnant to her husband, unrelated to the sexual assault. She found the whole process of intercourse, pregnancy, and childbirth very traumatising, but managed it in a private, self-contained way. Her daughter, Sarah, had become embroiled in Helen's sexual trauma as she reminded her of the assailant of some years before. The baby presented with distress and feeding difficulties, refusing bottles and Helen had "lost all confidence in her". For Helen, as it unfolded in therapy, it was hard to provide any sense of containing limits for her. She felt guilty for connecting her daughter to the violence done to her. But as she became aware of this unconscious connection: men—violence—rape—her memory—sexuality—her daughter, there seemed to be some degree of freeing that enabled her to provide more appropriate limits and containment and to help her regain better self-regulation and homeostasis.

Helen and Sarah were doing well but there remained tensions and lacunae in the relationship between Sarah's father and mother—many things had never been said between them. They recently commenced marital counselling which Helen seemed to find confronting and helpful, but there was some freeing of Sarah from this sexual trauma.

What of those babies conceived in communities which are not in the grip of war or equivalent chaos? There are many babies conceived in rape in our communities whom we do not know about. In a three-year longitudinal telephone survey in the United States of America (USA) about trauma and health, four thousand women were followed up three times a year and six per cent reported rape-related pregnancies (Holmes et al., 1996). The context is that in USA an estimated six hundred and eighty thousand women of more than eighteen years old are assaulted each year but sixty per cent of all rape cases are females of less than eighteen years old, so that the figure may be much higher. Only fifteen report the crime to the police. The researchers asked about non-consensual assault, with force or threat of force (with some sexual penetration of vagina/rectum/mouth). Eight per cent agreed to interview. The results suggested a 13.6 per cent lifetime prevalence rate of rape. In USA there are estimated to be about thirty-two thousand rape-related pregnancies per year. For many this means having to experience the difficulties of being a very young teen mother. These figures are in the context of an estimated three million unintended pregnancies in USA per year. Often the offender was known—even well known—to the baby's mother, which suggests links to ongoing family violence. There is a high prevalence (more than forty-five per cent) of multiple assaults. Many were never disclosed to law enforcement or health workers. (There are different contexts: date rape, marital rape, incest, and random sexual assault.) Were they disclosed to the child? It is a complex problem: thirty per cent for example did not discover they were pregnant until the second trimester, so that termination of the pregnancy becomes problematic. Thirty per cent opted to keep their baby, fifty per cent had an abortion, six per cent placed the child for adoption and twelve per cent had a spontaneous termination.

Chantelle

Here I shall describe Chantelle, who was born early—too early in many ways. Her mother, Kerry had a complicated pregnancy, with high blood pressure and pre-eclampsia leading to a semi-urgent Caesarean section at thirty-four weeks. Chantelle had severe respiratory distress syndrome and needed five days of ventilation; she also had a mass in her abdomen and possible pre-birth brain damage, so that her start was very problematic. Kerry, aged thirty-five, had also had a very traumatic life, with many presentations to mental health facilities and multiple diagnoses, mainly of Borderline Personality disorder but including bipolar disorder. She had certainly been very sad and anxious about Chantelle's birth, fearful that she might not be able to bond with her or able to care for her. She feared losing her baby, but was nonetheless very honest about this experience and her feelings. She talked of her concerns that she had poor control of her own anger. "I sometimes think of hitting her—but I would never do it." She had found herself losing most of her relationships over the course of her early adulthood, including those of her long-term foster parents who felt that they could no longer bear the hurtful disappointments that resulted from their attempts to keep in touch with Kerry. She was unpredictable—one minute she was sad and needing their love, at other times angry, distancing, and rejecting, and on rare occasions violently threatening.

Kerry revealed that she had been a child born of rape. She never knew her father—her birth mother found it impossible to talk about it, only that Kerry was conceived by force, by a man whom she had never known. Kerry found this out in her early teens. There remained big gaps in her memory which seemed to make things worse for her— she was a person who could never know herself. She had begun self-harming at fourteen years but was, however, able to sustain her studies and get a job.

Her partner relationships had been many, complicated, and disrupted, but in recent years she had settled with Sam, her current partner; there had been consistency, albeit with dependency. She hated him—he had raped her. She had refused sexual relations with him, but he insisted and forced her—she felt violated and dirty. Chantelle was a result of this intra-marital rape. It was as if Kerry existed without any sense of self and boundary, just as she fantasised it had happened to her mother—a repetition. Chantelle had medical problems: she had small brain haemorrhages and she looked "odd" but no specific diagnosis was made. Kerry said how hard it was to care for her baby—she wanted so desperately to do this but felt incompetent and unable; she felt that she needed help with basic aspects of child care. Indeed the ward nursing staff were very concerned at the way Kerry bathed Chantelle, whom she let slip into the water. Chantelle was very stiff and mechanical and it was a joyless and unsmiling procedure. Kerry seemed very detached from Chantelle who herself had persistent avoidance of direct gaze with her mother as well as others. It was as if Kerry, although a bright woman, had no idea about her baby's body, no idea how to hold, mould, contain it.

She said that Chantelle being sick made her very confused and she wondered whether Chantelle's illness was a punishment for Kerry's problems or whether Chantelle was being punished. For what? For being "her" daughter? Kerry said that when she looked into her daughter's face she saw herself—but as a shell of a person, as somehow "bad, damaged goods". Her past was projected into her daughter—or was it her daughter herself, she found it difficult to distinguish. She thought that maybe Chantelle was really just her husband's daughter and there was none of herself in her daughter at all. Somehow there was a mockery of herself. Projections seemed to fly about like missiles and in the midst of this Kerry saw herself reflected in her daughter's face as bad, unwanted, abandoned, and somehow evil. With the huge gaps in her personal narrative she fitted the fantasy of her own father violating her mother and herself into her self concept, that she must be bad and unlovable, like him. She also fitted this into her view of her daughter.

Donald Winnicott (1971) wrote about the importance of the mirror role of the mother (and it could be the father), whose task is to enliven the baby through face-to-face engagement (and holding of the baby). In this context, the baby, looking at the mother sees herself reflected in the mother's face. For Kerry, as she looks into her baby's face, she sees a shameful, damaged image of herself reflected and this is the image of emptiness that Chantelle may then see reflected back to her through what she sees in her mother's face; she then avoids the gaze of her mother and others.

Kerry was admitted to a mother–baby psychiatric unit with Chantelle for a couple of weeks, but still felt unsafe to look after Chantelle, despite improved self regulation, feeding, sleeping and containment of her medical problems. Chantelle went home with her parents, but Kerry was not allowed to be alone with her on a Protective Services' order, as she was unable to say that she felt completely safe caring for her daughter. Chantelle remains an infant of concern, although developing a relationship with the family support worker who visits regularly and has a vital role with Chantelle and her mother.

Chantelle was able to play, but usually began an interaction with a tense, hypervigilant gaze, her eyes reaching to the back of the eyes of whoever met her, so that there was a shift in the way she related to people. Her penetrating gaze seemed to be one of self defence. As Chantelle and her parents have moved out of The Royal Children's Hospital geographical area we are not directly involved in her ongoing treatment. Her parents are her primary carers, she is now one-year-old and her physical and social development seem satisfactory. We remain concerned about her emotional development. Will she be able to be helped out of this chain of intergenerational traumatic projections? Kerry has been honest about her baby, in a protective way, even though the risk is high that she may harm her. The workers have strong feelings about Chantelle and have been able to work with them. Kerry was welcoming of our interventions (the mental health service), as well as those of her own therapist, the infant-focused family worker and Protective Services. So there is some cautious optimism.

To summarise, when pregnancy results from rape, the family, the community, everyone has views about the woman—if they know—and about the potential baby. But what does the mother feel about

herself and her baby, who is often seen as a "bastard" infant, as evil
and a punishment? Can she love her baby? I think that a critical role
for health professionals is to gently engage with parents and the baby
in an attempt to identify the powerful projections that lodge on the
baby, and hopefully attempt to detach some of these. In the two cases
here, the mothers volunteered their history of sexual assault. What of
the many women whose babies have symptoms of a range of common
infant mental health paediatric problems but who are unable to tell us
about their assault? How can we establish trust in such women in a way
that is facilitating? So much depends on the context. These two women
presented their babies through a non-stigmatising child health system,
which may have made it easier for them to trust. For others it may be
that a longer term relationship-based home visiting early intervention
programme (Zeanah, 2006; Lyons-Ruth, 2006) can provide the necessary sense of safe containment to share feelings of shame and anger.
Agencies such as sexual assault units can play a vital role in supporting
communities if they provide a safe, supportive setting in which terrible
events can be disclosed to someone who will sensitively listen. Perhaps
through these means we can help the mother see that her baby's own
story must develop, separate from the narrative of the rape that resulted
in the conception—that her baby becomes an independent person.

For clinicians seeing mothers before they have made disclosure of
sexual abuse, when we ask a mother if her pregnancy was "planned",
we are asking a lot. It is not an easy question. For a woman who has been
sexually assaulted, especially within her partner relationship, it can be a
crucial question. She would be wise to assess us well before answering
this question—if she does divulge the fact of rape leading to conception
and the baby about whom she is consulting us. She needs to know that
we—and the system in which we work—can support her in a containing, non-judgemental way. But if she feels safe to tell us, I believe that
there is a remarkable opportunity to help enliven the baby. By speaking
of it, the mother may be able to begin to consciously disconnect any
poisonous projections which there may be onto her baby. She may feel
better able to see her son, her daughter—as a separate person.

The baby whose very existence means violence can be seen by his
mother as always a reminder of the violence—the baby is the embodiment, literally, of the perpetrator and at the same time the embodiment
of herself as a victim. To look at the baby can be painfully distressing.
But WE can look—we can meet and greet the baby as a new person, we

can engage him or her, and help the mother more by possibly seeing the baby NOT as a representative of hate but as one of hope. It seems a unique opportunity since it may prove impossible for a mother to talk of this again until in the midst of the intensity of her baby's adolescence, it having been a dark secret for so many years. If the mother can talk of it, this can prevent some of the build up of sadness, self-loathing, hatred, and detachment that can occur. At other times a shallow defence of denial of the rape and its impact can lead to parents avoiding an intimate relationship with their child. So I believe that it is important to be receptive to such stories and secrets—the time of the new baby's life is one of great change, flux, and of promise. I hope that we are all able in our different contexts to help babies and their parents find—lose—and find again—each other, be sad—and then happy all over again. The baby can become a person.

References

Australian Broadcasting Corporation. (10.2.06). *Correspondents Report.*

Holmes, M. M., Resnick, H. S., Kilpatrick, D. G. & Best, C. L. (1996). Rape-related pregnancy: estimates and descriptive characteristics from a national sample of women. *American Journal of Obstetrics & Gynecology. 175*: 320–324.

Krug, E. G. (2002). *World Report on violence and health.* World Health Organization.

Lyons-Ruth, K. (2006). Contributions of the mother–infant relationship to dissociative, borderline and conduct symptoms in young adulthood, paper presented at the Tenth World Congress of the World Association of Infant Mental Health, Paris, 2006.

Papineni, P. (2003). Children of bad memories. *The Lancet. 362*: 825–826.

Winnicott, D. W. (1971). The mirror role of the mother and family in child development. In: *Playing and Reality.* London: Tavistock.

Zeanah, C. H. (2006). Attachment disorders in family and social context, paper presented at the Tenth World Congress of the World Association for Infant Mental Health, Paris, 2006.

CHAPTER TWENTY-THREE

Sara: psychotherapy with a mother–infant dyad with a background of violence

Dimitra Bekos

I shall focus on the first three months of infant–parent psychotherapy with fifteen-month-old Sara, and her mother. Through selected clinical vignettes, I will explore Sara's experience of early trauma from the premature disruption of her attachment to her mother, and physical abuse by her father. I hope to also demonstrate the powerful dynamics of infant–parent psychotherapy and particularly my experience of one infant's extraordinary capacity to understand and communicate the complexity of her feelings and experiences, without the use of words and how active a participant an infant can be in their own therapy.

Sara's history

Sara was conceived as a result of what her mother alleged to have been a rape by her husband. Her mother reported that she did not know she was pregnant with Sara until four months into the pregnancy. At this time her mother said that she had little awareness of herself and her surroundings and claimed that she was "just trying to stay alive" and survive the violent abuse that was being inflicted upon her by her husband.

In the midst of this turmoil, however, she recalled having some sense of her body changing, namely that she perceived it to be "getting sick" and "breaking down", but she had little space to think about it. Sara's mother also said that when she realised that she was pregnant, she felt enormously distressed because she did not want this baby. Throughout the pregnancy, her relationship with her husband continued to be volatile. She made several unsuccessful attempts to leave him.

From the age of six and a half weeks till six months of age, Sara was left in the family home with the maid, and with the father on occasion, while her mother worked full time and late into the night. She only had contact with Sara late at night (to give her a night feed) and on Sundays. On several occasions Sara was left behind with her father, while her mother took her eldest daughter, leaving the family home for days, to escape her husband's violence. Sara had been physically hit, thrown to the floor and kicked by her father while in his care.

The first session

During this, her mother told me how baby Sara was unresponsive and withdrawn, not an interactive little girl. She said that she felt that Sara responded to her least, not accepting bottle feeds from her and rejecting her attempts to provide physical holding, especially when Sara hurt herself, which frequently occurred or when she became distressed. She said Sara often separated herself, and played quietly in a corner, and her mother told me that she had a lot of difficulty looking at Sara, as she looked so much like her father. Her mother seemed convinced at this stage that Sara's personality was identical to her father's.

The following vignette is from my first contact with Sara and her mother and it shows acutely their struggle and the helplessness and despair that both were living with.

> On entering the room, Sara's mother placed Sara on the floor. Sara walked towards the cupboard and began to quietly explore the different toys on top of it. She had her back to her mother and me, making very little eye contact with us. Her mother said, "See, she doesn't like to interact much, she just plays by herself like nothing is bothering her". At this point I attempted to engage Sara in play. In response to this, she would look at me briefly before tentatively approaching me and trying to shove a plastic piece of food in my

mouth, before retreating to the corner of the room. I felt confused and frustrated having this plastic food forced into my mouth, and overcome by a feeling of flatness and helplessness in my attempt to create a more alive interaction between myself and Sara. This play continued for some time while her mother began to cry and tell me of her despair and wish to die.

During this, I looked over to Sara and noticed she had her thumb jammed in the cupboard door. She sat silently, in shock. I immediately released her thumb. After a few seconds she began to cry out loud, still sitting with her back to us. Her mother remained in her chair just looking over at Sara. In response to this I gently lifted Sara on to her mother's lap and talked to her directly about how she had been hurt, and her mother and I had not been watching. I noticed the unease in the mother and Sara's embrace, a rigidity in her mother's arms and a restlessness and agitation in Sara. Her mother quickly distracted Sara making no reference to her pain and hurt and I noticed a sudden shift in Sara's emotional response. She stopped crying and quickly wriggled out of her mother's arms and moved over to the corner of the room again, while her mother continued to tell me of her own distress.

It became clear from the initial session that major difficulties existed in Sara and her mother's relationship, and that these began from the moment of conception. Her mother's early projection of breeding a monstrous baby who would be like her abuser, angry and terrorising, coupled with the belief that this baby was causing internal damage, affected her capacity to hold and soothe Sara on both a physical and emotional level. It became clear that her mother had little, if no capacity, to respond to her baby's distress and intuit her needs and tolerate and moderate her baby's anxiety, without becoming immersed and persecuted by her own experience of trauma. For Sara, who conjured up in her mother's mind what was felt to be unbearable, it appeared that any attempt at settling or soothing from her mother left her feeling highly anxious, agitated, and distressed, resulting in her own attempt to try to hold herself together. In retrospect, I probably would not have lifted Sara onto her mother's lap, as at this stage it was difficult for her mother to hold her, physically or emotionally. I think that this possibly replicated Sara's past experience with her mother and gave her yet another experience of not being held.

Sara's mother's emotional state, her depression and suicidality seemed to further complicate her relationship with Sara. In subsequent sessions it seemed that the flatness I experienced in my contact with Sara was an indication of her mother's traumatised and dissociative states, suggesting that there had been little room for an alive and loving interaction between them. The physical hurt that Sara experienced in the room early on in her therapy seemed to also be significant when considering her early relationship with her mother. In the initial sessions there were several moments where Sara would physically get hurt in the room and continue on without any apparent recognition of her own pain. In addition to reflecting the physical abuse Sara experienced, the survival mechanisms that she employed as a result of her experience, and the hurt she felt internally, it also seemed to convey her mother's unconscious wish to hurt her. I emphasise this to be an unconscious wish, as I believe that her mother's awareness of such a possibility would have been very distressing to her.

Given the circumstances, it seemed important to help unhook her mother's projection of Sara as being like her father and begin to help her see Sara differently and become more aware of her as a separate person with her own feelings and experiences. Although painful at times, it seemed imperative to create a space for the mother's powerful projections and to begin to accept the hostility and hate that she felt towards her baby. Thomson-Salo and Paul (2001) stated that "the work is to create a gap between mother and infant ... In that space the therapist can work with the parent's projection to try to make them more reality-oriented ... As the hate is accepted by the therapist this allows some hope for loving and being loved and valued" (Thomson-Salo & Paul, 2001, p. 18).

Moving into therapy

Over the next month Sara and her mother continued to attend weekly therapy. In this time feelings of rejection and hostility emerged, as did the helplessness and despair that both her mother and Sara experienced in their tenuous relationship. There appeared to be a growing anger in Sara and an emphasis on her rejection of her mother's milk and food, which her mother at times experienced as Sara's rejection of her. This was illustrated in the following vignette taken from a session approximately one month into their therapy.

Sara wanted to taste all the plastic foods, banana, tomatoes, chips and hamburgers. She ate voraciously and then handed the food to me to hold. She found a plastic piece of meat and again attempted to shove it in my mouth. I said to Sara that she needed me to know something about this food and how it needed to be forced in my mouth. In response to this, her mother began to tell me that when she had left Sara on her own in the early months of her life she thought that she had been force fed by the maid. She continued to tell me that Sara no longer wanted to be fed by her and that she threw away the food that her mother gave to her, particularly the milk. As her mother talked, Sara began to take the food from me, put it in her mouth and then throw it on the floor. She seemed frustrated and angry and I felt that she was showing me an experience of having something unpalatable forced into her that could not be digested. Sara's mother continued to talk about Sara being left on her own and how much she was probably unaware of Sara's early experiences. She seemed to express helplessness and regret. In response to Sara's expression of frustration and anger, I commented on the mixed feelings Sara had towards her mummy for not being there while things were happening to her, and that maybe she felt so hurt and cross with this. Her mother responded by saying, "Yes, she would feel angry with me, a lot maybe has happened to her when I wasn't there".

It felt crucial here to offer both Sara and her mother a space to communicate their story to me, and to each other. Morgan, in her thoughts on infant–parent psychotherapy commented on allowing "the mother to come forward and allowing her narrative to be heard while at the same time still acknowledging and still connecting to the infant while the narrative is being spoken" (Morgan, 2013, this volume). In this vignette Sara communicated so powerfully in her own way to her mother and me how she could not drink in her mother's milk, which I believe represented her mother's fear, depression, and hate, arising from her unresolved trauma. In addition I thought that Sara conveyed her anger about the rupture in her attachment to her mother, and the loss of a containing mind, which could hold and process her fears and anxieties and feed them back to her in a way that she could understand and digest.

In the second month of therapy, as Sara and her mother began to have an experience in which both their stories were being heard, and

Sara particularly found a way to communicate her experiences without words, I noticed a slight shift in her mother's projection of Sara as the terrorising, abusive husband. This shift in seeing Sara as separate and different to her father allowed her mother to attempt to see and respond to Sara's pain and distress and even anger, with greater sensitivity and tolerance. In the following vignette Sara seemed to use the therapy to help me convey her anger, pain, and distress to her mother.

> Sara began to throw around a ball of hard clay. Once retrieving it she would place it in her mouth, which created some anxiety for her mother and myself. Sara seemed frustrated and angry. In my attempt to take this from Sara, I recalled feeling unsafe and having to find a way to protect myself as I did not want to get hurt. In response to my countertransference I wondered aloud if maybe Sara was showing me and her mother that she was left unprotected, unsafe, and exposed to things that hurt her. Sara was crouched on the floor looking for the ball but also facing me, listening to what I was saying. At this moment she stood up and bumped her head against the doll's house. She began to cry—clearly in a lot of pain. Sara ran towards the door. I picked her up and passed her over to her mother. There was a change in her mother's response. She cradled Sara and caressed her, kissing her head. Sara continued to cry, all the while pointing to the door. Her mother then said, "She is like me when I get frightened or hurt, I want to run away". I saw this as an opportunity to comment on her mother's understanding and how she could now see herself in Sara, and that there were things that Sara had that were similar to her and she was not all like her father. Sara looked at her mother and me. I made an interpretation around how unsafe and unprotected she felt when alone, how scary it was when her mother was not able to be there to protect her.
>
> In response to this, her mother became teary acknowledging her baby's distress and her experiences. After a few moments Sara held on to her mother's face with both hands, bringing it close to her own face, trying to press it up against hers. I commented on how Sara wanted to hold her mother close to her and never let go and wanted her mother not to leave her. Sara then began to pull at her mother's hair as though she were attacking her. Her mother withdrew and placed Sara on the floor, and I acknowledged the mother's pain, and hurt and her difficulty in bearing Sara's rage.

I then commented on the hurt and cross feelings that were there when Sara remembered "missing mummy" feelings, to help convey to the mother Sara's experience of abandonment. Sara stood there crying as her mother tied her hair back, which I think was her own attempt to hold back or control her own feelings. Sara became even more distressed, standing there watching her mother, and sobbing aloud. As her mother had struggled to respond to Sara emotionally, I commented on how it just felt too long to wait and how Sara just wanted to be in her mother's arms now. Her mother acknowledged this and picked up Sara and rocked her and kissed her several times. I then talked to Sara and her mother and commented on how hard it was to have cross feelings with someone whom you love. Sara fell asleep in her mother's arms.

I think that Sara falling asleep in her mother's arms, which she could barely do in the beginning of her therapy, was an indication of the relief she experienced from having her feelings received and understood by her mother, which is so central in providing a sense of containment. The interpretation of the love and hate or anger coexisting, and the words given to Sara's experience of abandonment, probably contributed to freeing up her mother, allowing her to provide a "holding" to Sara and her feelings.

In the following sessions there was greater interaction between Sara and her mother, in which there seemed to be a sense of enjoyment and increased attunement to Sara's feelings. Her mother began to express her sadness and remorse in relation to Sara's experiences and the impact that this had had on their relationship. She said that she felt that she had missed a lot of Sara's early days and months and felt that even when she fled her husband's violence, she continued to miss seeing Sara's needs. Her mother reflected on her depressed and dissociated states as a result of her own trauma and how she perhaps left Sara crying and hurt several times without noticing. She also expressed her sense of loss in the relationship with Sara particularly when reflecting on Sara's independence, such as wanting to do things on her own like feed herself, and put herself to sleep when she felt tired. There appeared to be developing in her mother a more reflective and receptive mind, which could think about her infant's struggles and needs. Similarly Sara seemed to be developing a greater capacity and sense of security in expressing the complexity of her feelings towards her mother, and trust that these feelings would be received, resulting in some attempt by her to establish a safe and loving bond with her mother.

The following vignette taken from a session approximately two and a half months into their therapy demonstrated this capacity in Sara further.

> Sara had been unsettled throughout the session. She repeatedly picked up the dinosaurs and roared out aloud, then handed them to her mother who flinched and appeared frightened. Sara was showing us how frightened she was of the dinosaurs, who I think represented her experience of a frightened and frightening mother. After some time Sara picked up the little doll's blanket and held it close to her chest. She placed her thumb and finger in her mouth and curled into a ball on the floor in front of her mother's feet and leaning gently against my knees (as I was sitting on the floor). Sara closed her eyes and sucked on her thumb and forefinger. I gave her arm a gentle stroke and commented how hard it was to have all these loving and cross feelings inside and how she felt she was left alone to settle herself. Sara glanced at me and then turned away, indicating by trying to push my hand away that she did not want any soothing. I encouraged her mother to hold her as she was too little to be settling herself and it was important for Sara to know that her mother was now available to settle her. She attempted to hold Sara. Sara wriggled out of her mother's arms saying "No" and then crawled under her mother's chair, in between her mother's legs, with the blanket. Her mother gently placed her hand on Sara's shoulder.

I think Sara was telling her mother and me about her struggle to find an available, non frightening mother who could comfort and soothe her. I saw her determination in finding a "holding" from her mother, when she curled up into a foetal position, in between her mother's legs under the chair. I think this may have been Sara's way of expressing her desire to get close to her mother and perhaps even some communication of her as a baby wanting to get close or back inside her mother's womb. Her mother's capacity to meet Sara here emotionally can also be seen.

As Sara began to experience her mother as more available and containing of her emotional states, particularly her rage, and a reliable and safer bond was forming between them, she began to show me what it was like to live with a mother who was depressed and weighed down by her trauma. This was highlighted in the following vignette at the beginning of the third month of therapy:

> Sara was handed a female doll by her mother. She began to bite and chew its head aggressively before throwing it to the floor. I commented on her need to show me and her mother the cross feelings she was experiencing. Sara then insisted on putting her mother's bag over her shoulder which was clearly too big and too heavy for her to carry. She struggled and shrieked at any attempt I made to remove the bag from her. This was distressing to see, as Sara hung the bag around her neck, with the straps pressed tightly against her throat and the weight of the bag hanging down her back. She then began to scribble frantically on a piece of paper. I decided to draw an angry face to try to communicate an understanding of her feelings, but she pushed my hand out of the way and scribbled over my drawing. I said to her that there was something that she needed to show us, some very big cross, upset, hurting feelings which needed a lot of room, that these feelings were big heavy ones that she was carrying around with her. Sara became increasingly distressed. I said to her how she could not carry this bag alone any more, that it was too heavy for a little child to manage. I removed the bag from her. There was no protest from Sara.

Remembering?

I thought that Sara was letting me know of her carrying her mother's depression and unresolved feelings, and the pain and distress that she was feeling as a result of this. Throughout the third month of the therapy when Sara's experience of the impact of her mother's trauma was recognised and sensitively and empathically received by her mother and myself, she began to tell us through her play of her own experience of being abused by her father.

> Sara lifted up the baby doll struggling to hold it. I commented on how she was a little baby herself trying to hold the baby, baby Sara. Sara then forcefully threw the doll in its cradle. I said that I thought that Sara was showing us how she had been thrown in her cot

and hurt. Sara seemed frightened and moved towards her mother holding onto the doll's blanket indicating that she wanted to be held. Her mother cradled Sara kissing her as Sara sucked on her thumb. I decided to pick up the baby doll and hold it in my arms, while saying to Sara that she was letting me and her mother know how she had been hurt so much and how awful it was and how scared she felt. I then placed the baby doll gently in the cradle, covering it with a blanket and stroking its head gently, as Sara watched intently. Sara wriggled out of her mother's arms and repeated my actions with the baby doll, placing it gently in the cradle before crawling back onto her mother's lap.

After some time Sara picked up the doll and faced her mother. She began to drop the doll and scream in distress. She repeated this several times. I said that she really needed her mother to know how she was dropped and hurt. Sara then crawled back onto her mother's lap. Her mother attempted to soothe Sara and handed Sara her blanket. Sara settled and placed her thumb and forefinger in her mouth. She looked frightened and in need of soothing. I talked to Sara about how her daddy did some scary and hurtful things like throwing her in her cot and that some scary feelings had come up in the room today. I handed her the toy cup (which represented the therapy milk) as a way of expressing the safety of the therapy. Sara removed her thumb from her mouth and replaced it with the cup, gazing directly into my eyes, all the time cradled in her mother's arms.

When I spoke to Sara directly, I could see that she knew that I was talking to her about her experience, and that there was an understanding. Morgan said that, "we all speak to the baby ... so that there is some talking and the baby knows this. The baby listens, looks, the baby connects, the baby connects to the voice. The baby connects to the expression on our faces" (Morgan, 2013, this volume).

Working through

As her mother's awareness of Sara's feelings developed and Sara communicated her experiences of trauma to her mother, there appeared to be some noticeable shifts in their relationship. Her mother demonstrated an increased capacity to respond to, contain, and acknowledge and give words to Sara's experiences, and Sara seemed to experience her mother as a more reliable and available attachment figure. This was a marked contrast from the initial presentation. The final vignette highlights these changes.

> Sara's mother was watching Sara playing with the doll's house. She said to me that she thought that in the beginning she could not hold Sara because all she could see was Sara's father. She was tearful explaining to me that in the beginning she had not wanted or loved Sara. She said that she felt she was only now beginning to have a relationship with her. She also said that she felt she could now look at Sara and that only sometimes struggled when Sara was angry, because it reminded her of her husband's anger. At this stage Sara walked up to her mother and looked up at her. Her mother said, "What is it darling, what is it you want to say?" I decided to kneel beside Sara and speak for her. "Mummy, I just want you to know that I am not all my daddy but I am also a bit like you, but I am mostly Sara and my angry feelings are mine and not the same as my daddy's". Her mother nodded her head and picked up Sara and held her. Towards the end of the session Sara had fallen and cut her lip. As Sara cried mother held her, gently wiping her lip and kissing her on her cheek. Her mother talked to Sara about her fall and her hurt lip. She reached into her bag and offered Sara her bottle of water. Sara rested comfortably in her mother's arms drinking. Her mother had also told me that Sara was now taking the milk bottle from her having both morning and night feeds.

Thomson-Salo and Paul (2001) suggested that, "the ghosts from the parents past include unresolved traumatic experiences with internal and external objects. The infant may remind the parents of someone hateful and abusive … she may remind the parents of a part of their own self which is hated and disavowed … She then collects these projections and the cycle begins of hating the baby for what she represents. In 'being with' the baby, several aspects of parental hate are addressed when the therapist does not accept the parent's wiping out of the infant and … can tolerate the parent's hate. This gives the parent hope that the baby who has been hated may be able to be understood and has not been damaged" (Thomson-Salo & Paul, 2001, p. 17).

For Sara some of the ghosts from her mother's past seemed to have been laid to rest through this work, and both Sara and her mother were freer in their loving interaction with one another, which was a significant shift in their relationship. The therapy continued for a further two and a half years and there were times where some of these difficulties re-emerged. The complexity of the mother's trauma and ongoing struggle at times made it harder for her to hold onto her thinking in relation to Sara's anger and therefore Sara being separate from her father. Although the latter part of the therapy primarily focused on supporting the mother, it was also an opportunity to continue to help her disentangle these projections, leaving her more open and available to Sara and her emotional world. As Sara's language developed she was able to communicate her own feelings to her mother as we see in the final vignette.

When Sara was two-and-three-quarters years old, her mother had told me that sometimes it was hard to manage Sara's aggression as it reminded her of Sara's father and she felt frightened. In the process of reminding Sara's mother of her daughter's aggression being developmentally appropriate and that it was different to the violence that she had experienced from Sara's father, Sara stopped playing and said to her mother, "No, no mamma, no dadda, (pointing towards herself) Sara."

References

Morgan, A. (2013). What I am trying to do when I see in infant with his or her parents. In: F. Thomson-Salo & & C. Paul (Eds.), *The Baby as subject: Infant–parent psychotherapy from The Royal Children's Hospital, Melbourne.* This volume.

Thomson-Salo, F. & Paul, C. (2001). Some principles of Infant–parent psychotherapy: Ann Morgan's contribution. *The Signal*, Nos 1–2, WAIMH.

PART VI

REFERENCE PAPERS

CHAPTER TWENTY-FOUR

Some principles of infant–parent psychotherapy

Frances Thomson-Salo and Campbell Paul

W e describe a way of working therapeutically with infants which was developed at The Royal Children's Hospital by Dr. Ann Morgan over twenty years ago. It continues to inform the clinical work there and is an important part of the teaching of the University of Melbourne Masters in infant and parent mental health which developed out of that work. We audiotaped six interviews with Morgan and quote from them.

Introduction

Morgan shares Winnicott's compassion and wisdom in believing that love and hate are inextricably intertwined in all relationships. Her approach to infant–parent psychotherapy is that when there is a problem between the mother and the infant the therapist works with both the mother and the infant, and that means not just having the infant present in sessions but actively working with the infant. This is different from most parent–infant psychotherapy in which the parents' projections are contained and worked with but the therapist does not engage directly in therapeutic work with the infant. Morgan emphasised that a link must be made between the therapist and the baby as a subject in his own right which allows a gap to be created between mother and baby, a space which allows growth.

Despite current knowledge about infant capacities and needs Morgan thinks that it is still hard for therapists to see the baby independently of the mother's account and that when they do not "see" the baby they have colluded with the parents in "killing" off the baby. If the therapist does not work with the baby then something that is not faced in the mother is not faced in the baby. It gets repeated in the baby and this leads to the intergenerational transmission of difficulty.

Where an infant is referred for an infant mental health consultation in hospital the work is shaped by different time constraints than work in an outpatient setting. But the principles outlined here will be equally relevant.

Morgan's clinical background

Morgan worked as a paediatrician for thirty-five years at The Royal Children's Hospital. Nearly two decades ago she became the first co-ordinator of the multidisciplinary Infancy Group, whose members are drawn from the fields of psychiatry, psychoanalysis, psychology, social work, nursing, and speech pathology.

It may help to give some case material. About twenty years ago Morgan was consulted about a seven-week-old gaze avoidant girl, Alana, whose parents thought she was blind, deaf, and autistic. The mother had previously worked with autistic infants. The father thought that his daughter had some response to him although he was losing hope because of her withdrawal. Morgan said,

> When I first saw the infant, her hands lying very passively on the blanket, her eyes closed and sucking on the dummy, very unresponsive with all of us standing around the cot, the first thing I did was to talk to her very quietly, barely above a whisper and she stopped sucking immediately. Then I held onto her hand and stroked it a bit while I was talking to her. Unbelievably, she began to stroke my finger and then her own finger and it was as if she could feel both fingers, and she kept stroking her own finger and stroking my finger. All the time I was talking to her I was certain she heard me, that she was aware of the other but also was making the other aware of her. I think it meant a great deal to the mother when we talked about the

fact that her daughter could hear perfectly well, that she was very aware of me and was, I think, thinking about it.

The father understood immediately when she said that the baby could hear and see Morgan, and the mother was able to take in what had happened even if she did not initially fully understand its significance in relation to her ambivalence.

We think that it would have been difficult to have worked only with the parents' representations when their difficulties were already having such an effect on their interaction with their daughter. With evidence that the baby had not been irrevocably damaged, the parents were able to let Morgan see their painful struggle with ambivalence: they gave the staff a video which the father had made of his daughter having a bath. Alana, who had always been unable to look at her mother, had rolled over so that she was looking at the camera. The water was lapping over her face, which her parents were totally unaware of and she was not struggling. What Morgan did in connecting with the infant was to lessen the power of the parents' representations that were already having such an effect on their daughter, so that the mother could see her daughter more realistically.

Morgan's contribution to infant–parent psychotherapy

Morgan's statement on behalf of the baby is unequivocal:

> It's important to work with the baby because if you don't you can get caught up with working with the infant in the mother and you can lose the baby. So right from the start there is a statement that you have to work with the baby.

The situation is urgent for the infant

Longitudinal studies (Murray, 1997; Sroufe, 2000) as well as the neurobiological evidence (Nelson & Bosquet, 2000; Schore, 2000) bear out Morgan's point about the situation being urgent for the infant and that therefore as much help as possible should be offered to her. The longer that negative experiences remain unmodified the greater the likelihood that there will be changes in the brain which may mean that therapeutic work cannot ameliorate the early deprivation. Morgan reflects Winnicott's view that the mother will recover from her illness but the baby may not.

> The baby will be set in his development, either severely disturbed or psychotic but also hated because he has become so difficult. It may mean that even very early we can miss the boat. Often what has gone wrong for the baby girl is not picked up until she herself becomes pregnant.

Apart from Winnicott (1941), Lebovici (cited in Cramer, 1995), Ferholt and Provence (1976) and Greenspan (1992), the predominant paradigm in infancy work has been not to work directly with the infant but to work with the parents. Working with the parents is seen to affirm them as parents and not to exacerbate guilt or envy. But we think that most parents, if they present with a distressed infant, want help for their infant and welcome the therapist's direct intervention.

Morgan has always worked with the parents and the infant. Other clinicians have recently begun to move in that direction. Norman (2001) described direct work with a six-month-old girl, giving a fuller theoretical justification from a psychoanalytic point of view for this work.

Mother–baby issues require mother and baby to be seen together

Morgan emphasises that it is very significant what happens to the baby in the room and how alert the therapist must be to that. The work with the infant frees the mother to start thinking in a wider way.

> You can help the mother a great deal without the baby being there but you're not working with the baby. If you don't have the baby in the room, you can help the mother so that she can begin to think, but what you're doing is working with her anxiety, with what's going on between her and you.

Working with mother and infant together mobilises the health in the dyad. In the following example the mother puts this into words. In one session she put her baby in the pram so expertly that she did it without looking at him and then fed him with his face covered with a cloth, obliterating his face. The next time Morgan talked to the baby and he was eager to come out of the pram. Morgan asked if the mother thought it made a difference when Morgan talked to the baby. The mother replied, "Yes, because I feel that things change; if he's not in the room then I'm stuck just repeating a story whereas I can see him differently if you are talking to him."

> Nearly all mothers can shift from looking at things totally from their own neediness and wanting you to mother them more, so that if you include the baby they feel more adult and that the need is in the baby. Then they can begin to think about that rather than only being in touch with their own needs. The mother can then hold more onto the thought that she is going to be able to parent and is an adult, even though she does not altogether want to be one.

What are the specific differences that arise from having the infant present in infant–parent psychotherapy? Parents seem to find it therapeutic that the therapist is trying to understand the experience from inside the infant's world rather than looking from outside as if it were inexplicable. They see that, whatever the infant's difficulties, the therapist responds to a live person and the infant's response communicates to them in an important way that there is an undamaged part of the child. When the therapist does something relieving with the infant the mother in turn feels mothered and a good internal object can be experienced again. But Morgan acknowledges that Lebovici's (cited in Cramer, 1995) view of infants as subjects in their own right (with complex representations that may be influenced directly by a therapist) is difficult for therapists not to lose sight of, and they frequently do not see their interaction with infants as significant.

The therapeutic intervention

It is well known amongst clinicians how quick the results in this work often are. Sometimes, even when infants who look as though they have given up are referred, a single session with an infant therapist is enough to reverse the cycle of despair. How do we understand what happens?

Infant–parent psychotherapy is usually seen as the therapist aiming to make conscious for the parent(s) the links with the past, whereas in the way of working described here, this does not necessarily have to take place. The aim of the therapeutic contact is that there is an experience in which consciously or unconsciously the difficult feelings are shared and the therapist's thinking about them is in some way communicated to the parent and infant. It is often verbal but need not be, and can be communicated through interaction or play.

The core principle is to "be with the baby"

For Morgan, the core principle in infant–parent psychotherapy is to "be with the baby", as well as with the mother or parents. She elaborates the core principle:

- The therapist relates to the infant as subject.
- The therapist and the infant begin an exploration of not-knowing.
- The therapist aims to make a link or connection with the infant.
- The therapist offers the infant an experience (rather than the promise of a relationship).

The infant as subject

Morgan sees the infant not as the object of investigation but as the subject. She works actively at making a connection with the infant.

> I use my bracelet a lot and I hold it out so that the baby can hold it and then I gently pull back so that there is some pulling even with a very young baby. The baby then has an awareness of the other, of someone who recognises the baby's agency, and as a result he can begin to sense his own agency.

Winnicott thought that unless infants have a sense of agency in what they do, the world is experienced only as an impingement. Infants use gaze and touch to explore their mother and the world around them, including the therapist. In offering ourselves to be related to, we give infants the possibility to be active in their knowing of the world. We are acknowledging the infant as a subject with her own sense of agency, which is extremely significant.

> The baby makes a contact with me and is fascinated because I am fascinated with him. I am with another human being as with an adult and that is as powerful a recognition as possible and the infant recognises that in me. In the intersubjectivity between the child and

myself, I know that the infant understands that I understand, and he knows that what he is getting is communication.

An exploration of not knowing

Morgan describes as very important the point that you look at an infant with "already knowing eyes" while knowing absolutely nothing about the infant in front of you, suspending all your experience in order to meet the family afresh.

> You bring all your experience to bear yet you hold it in abeyance so that you can look at the baby with absolutely not-knowing eyes, like being "without memory or desire" (Bion, 1965, p. 1970). I have a lot of knowledge about babies, I've been looking at them for a lifetime so I am more likely to see something about the baby. Yet it seems to me very important that when I'm with the baby, my look-ing at the baby is no different in some ways from the baby look-ing at me—there's an exploration of not knowing in both of us. That may be what you can offer the mother, an exploration of this unknown baby, by using your experience. But I think the signifi-cance of the infant is constantly being denied, as though somehow you can understand what is going on in the baby just by listening to the mother. I think the essential element is to make a link with the baby and the rest follows because you can't really make a comment about the baby without thinking about the baby and the mother knows that.

The link

The purpose of the link is to allow a gap, a transitional space so that something can happen in that space.

> It's important for me to know what the baby sees in me as well as what I see in the baby and it's that link between us that really holds us together and that can quite often hold the baby. I can feel the link with the baby, that the baby has cottoned on to me and I have cottoned on to the baby, even if it's transient, and then I can begin to talk to the baby. How the baby responds to me is where I start from, I make a link with the baby so that somehow the baby

recognises that I recognise the baby, and also that I'm available for him to make a connection with me.

I think that often with a baby who's continually on the breast, the link between mother and baby has broken down so that the baby *has* to be on the breast, the link is actual, concrete, and there's no gap. Then the baby's eye contact with you means that there is a gap beginning and what I think is important about helping the mother see this link, is that it allows a space in which something else can appear: in the mother's mind a thought or in the baby a beginning of a preconception.

Where, for example, a mother thinks that her sick child is going to die there may be no gap to let another in, no gap in which the mother might think that it might be better if the child died. There is therefore no gap in which the child can think their own thoughts.

What is important is that by the second or third session, some experience is repeated which the baby recognises, and the baby has a feeling that she is there in her own right. The baby has a contact that is separate from and not through her mother, which in turn helps the mother realise that there is some separation. There is a look of relief on the baby's face and on the mother's, and you can see this as early as four months. I think that you can do the linking with the voice, even just with gaze, although if the baby is crying she needs the voice. And you can do it with a baby even meeting as infrequently as once a week. But what I think is terribly important is to have that link with the baby in the room with the mother. Because if you don't you are colluding with the mother in all kinds of ways, including with the rivalry with the infant in her, and if you *have* that link it somehow can break that nexus and you really can work with both.

Offering an experience

Morgan emphatically disagreed that it could be damaging to relate to the baby and then drop out of the baby's life, if for example the contact was during a brief hospital admission.

Every link the infant makes opens up a world for him; it's not a relationship but an experience of connecting. I think that what one hopes if one is doing an intervention, even with a baby in hospital, is that the mother's response will be different and that in itself hopefully would alter the baby's relationship with the mother.

Babies can have a sense of the rhythm of the work, as they do in infant observation when the observer comes and goes.

> What you could say to an older infant to help him understand would be that, "It's important to see you and then there'll be some time when I don't see you and then I'll see you again". You could say, "How hard it is, you want to be with someone and then you're not with them." I think that's important to put into words.

The fullest therapeutic experience comes when the therapist can make a space for the negative feelings to be explored without condemnation while at the same time conveying to the parents that the baby will be kept safe. There is acceptance of the verbal exploration of the hate at the same time that it is totally unacceptable to act on it.

> I think that even very ill parents know that the child is at risk and that something terrible is happening, and if no one is protecting the child this makes the situation worse for the parent. I was very keen on the double message when I started the Infancy Clinic, that the mother was given the message that she could be sick or anxious but that at the same time we would see that the baby was safe. And that not only the mother got the message but that the baby got the message. When therapists don't get the message through to the baby you can see that the baby gets flatter. He isn't being pulled into the message that "I know what's going on, and I know that you know that I know". That's the language that I find so important to convey to people who are not used to working with babies.

The firmness of Morgan's position about working with the infant is part of her offering a strong coupling with the mother as the father ideally does. She thinks that rather than the couple being the mother with her own mother, it is in the infant's best interests that the couple is the mother and the father.

> The infant, the mother's mind and the couple all need to survive and it's an enormous struggle in the three of them as to which

couple is going to survive, which one of the three is going to be excluded.

Love and hate

Can we think of infant–parent psychotherapy as working with the intergenerational management of ambivalence and hate?

> Awareness of the parents' ambivalence fractures the idealising of mothers and motherhood. To say that the baby is loved is to say that the baby is also hated. I think that "love" includes hate whereas "being in love" does not include hate and we haven't got one word for love-and-hate. To me, love is in the depressive position, you've gone through the paranoid schizoid stage where you have to have the split and an acute getting rid of hate. In the work we're dealing with primary feelings and relationships which are not only primary in so far as they are early but they are feelings that we struggle with for the rest of our lives.

However wanted a baby is, their survival cannot be taken for granted. Having a baby faces the new parents with profound emotional issues. Pre-conceptive ambivalence needs to be worked through. A strong couple, a mother united with the father, is the best guarantee of the infant's survival. The baby's arrival stirs up the mother's fear of loss of her sense of self, with the infant sometimes experienced as a parasite. Morgan emphasises that the father's envy and hatred of the infant is triggered by the pressure the child exerts on the adult sexual couple in pulling the mother away from her relationship with the father. A strong relationship between the couple holds the father's feelings in check.

> The hate really stems from the feeling of "my life or yours" and the only way to separate psychically is to be able to tolerate the ambivalence. I think that that sense of losing our life if we allow an infant to grow is a developmental stage we all go through. As Graham Greene says, the chains are around you after that. I think that, with good reason, that's part of the terror of losing your mind.

Where the triad may be most under attack is when the hate is hidden, for example in the mother's mind attacking the internal good object, as in postnatal depression.

Some mothers find it hard to just be with their babies, some find it unbearable facing the ambivalence. They either have to give constantly to the baby or may be busy with things that have to be done, and the baby often doesn't settle, leaving the mother with not-knowing her baby.

How does this link with a psychosomatic symptom in a baby? The issues that a mother faces with the arrival of her baby are sometimes literally and psychologically life-or-death issues, and the mother's mind frames the baby's world. As the psychosomatic language is the first language of the baby, psychosomatic symptoms give voice to the baby's emotional pain or a shared pain. The ghosts from the parents' past include unresolved traumatic experiences with internal and external objects. A baby may remind the parents of someone hateful and abusive, or an unmourned baby. The baby may remind the parents of a part of their own self which is hated and disavowed such as the needy, vulnerable part, or may have been born ill or disabled which complicates the parents' ambivalence. The infant then collects these projections and the cycle begins of hating the baby for what the baby represents and defending against the guilt of awareness of hate.

In being with the baby, several aspects of parental hate are addressed. When the infant is seen as a subject the therapist does not accept the parents' wiping out of the baby and implicit in this is that the therapist can tolerate the parents' hate. The exploration by infant and therapist of the mind of the other gives the parents hope that the baby who has been hated may be able to be understood and has not been damaged.

An additional reason for working with the infant as well as the parents is that it is important not to work prematurely with the mother's hatred. With work with the infant the parents can see more easily that their fantasies of having totally damaged or killed off the infant are not reality. Alana's father understood immediately when Morgan said that the baby could hear and see her, and the mother was able to take in at some level what had happened.

Countertransference

Infant–parent psychotherapy is often short-term yet the projections in the transference and countertransference can be very powerful. Knowing that second by second the infant is influenced, and their personality shaped by the environment exerts a pressure on the therapist. While including the infant in the work may be thought of as substituting too active an intervention in the place of thinking, or being driven by the need to relieve our anxiety or to act out a rescue fantasy that we could succeed where the parents have failed, we do not think that these are the motivations for direct work.

Many infant therapists think that the therapist has to bear a greater burden of pain when the infant is in the room and they can see that the infant's cues are being missed rather than when they only hear the absent infant being talked about. It can be difficult to get the balance right between attuning to the despair of the parents and of the infant, and intervening appropriately. The tightrope which therapists walk is that with some very ill parents, if the therapists are experienced as taking the baby's side too quickly, they may risk losing the parents.

Conversely, the demands of the work may make therapists more vulnerable to collusion. Where there is no gap between mother and baby it is possible for the therapist to feel as immobilised as the baby does and to go along with what the family presents.

> If you have an urgent demand from the mother and I've been caught up in it somehow, you then realise that the baby has been excluded.

Not seeing the infant

We all miss the baby and have to keep working on it. It may be disturbing to have this pointed out. In many assessments the clinicians would say the mother was lovely and had a very nice interaction and I'd say, "It's easy to love a baby, the baby's only got to smile and we smile". What have they done with the other side, there's no way that the mother can feel sentimental like that all the time? They have absolutely blocked it out.

When therapists work only with the mother and do not see that the baby's problems are being missed, then the baby disappears because the mother has killed off the baby so that she has the therapist and doesn't recognise the baby's need. But it is a killing off which the therapists don't have to face. I come from a different point of view. What I am consumed with is to keep the baby alive and to keep the baby in the world so that the baby isn't dropped.

That's why I think it's always important that the mother knows she can only work with me if she knows I'm going to work with the baby too.

While understanding many of the reasons why some therapists do not work with the baby, Morgan commented,

> Clearly there is the universal fear and dread of the infant, and one response is sentimentally to see the baby as perfect and therefore one still doesn't "see" the baby. It is a very difficult thing to put the child as the subject of investigation. Once you start using yourself in that, it's risky. I think it is really this fear that you are becoming emotionally involved with the infant.

Limitations in infant–parent psychotherapy

Where either parent is very sick, I think infant psychotherapy is not going to do very much as a brief intervention but you can protect the infant and every day that you protect the infant helps. Even, however, with active psychotherapy for the infant which would help him in his own right, if the parents' illnesses are not also treated then that has repercussions.

Summary of the therapeutic action

When early in the infant's life the projections from the parents have hardened there has been a fixed identification of the infant with some internal object in the parents' mind rather than an empathic relationship with the infant. The work is then to create a gap between mother and infant, a transitional space which may never have existed before. In this space the therapist can work with the parents' projections to try to make them more reality-oriented, and also with the infant so that the parents see their infant differently. As the therapist becomes a container for the hate and the toxic projections for which the infant was previously the receptacle, what is reflected back to the mother is something saner. As the hate is accepted by the therapist, this allows some hope of loving, and being loved and valued. For the infant's part, being related to as a subject and without the parental projections is enormously relieving and hopeful. Just as child patients brought for psychotherapy often have a sense in the first meeting of how different the therapist is from what they have experienced before, it is the same with infants. The smile or laughter that frequently appears indicates the infant's relief.

References

Bion, W. R. (1970). *Attention and Interpretation*. London: Tavistock.

Cramer, B. (1995). Infant Creativity. *Infant Mental Health Journal, 16*: 21–27.

Ferholt, M. D. & Provence, S. (1976). Diagnosis and treatment of an infant with psychophysiological vomiting. *Psychoanalytic Study of the Child, 31*: 439–459.

Greenspan, S. I. (1992). *Infancy and Early Childhood: The Practice of Clinical Assessment and Intervention with Emotional and Developmental Challenges*. Madison, CT: International Universities Press.

Murray, L. (1997). The early mother–infant relationship and child development: a research perspective. *Infant Observation, 1*: 80–92.

Nelson, C. & Bosquet, M. (2000). Neurobiology of fetal and infant development: implications for infant mental health. In: C. H. Zeanah (Ed.), *Handbook of Infant Mental Health*, 2nd edition. New York & London: Guilford Press.

Norman, J. (2001). The Psychoanalyst and the baby: a new look at work with infants. *International Journal of Psychoanalysis, 82*: 83–100.

Schore, A. N. (2000). Effects of a secure attachment relationship on right brain development, affect regulation, and infant mental health. *Infant Mental Health Journal, 22*: 7–66.

Sroufe, L. A. (2000). Early relationships and the development of children. *Infant Mental Health Journal, 21*: 67–74.

Winnicott, D. W. (1941). The observation of infants in a set situation. In: *Collected Papers: Through Paediatrics to Psycho-Analysis*. London: Tavistock Publications, 1958.

CHAPTER TWENTY-FIVE

The infant who looks but does not see

Campbell Paul

The word "infancy" comes from the Latin "incapable of speech"—but things do happen before speech. It could be said that speech and language constrict experience by squeezing the pre-verbal into a straitjacket. Language facilitates the false dichotomy of body and mind which is so frequently the problem facing the child presenting with psychosomatic symptoms. The infant mental health clinician then must strive to understand and communicate the pre-verbal world of the baby in the context of his family.

This chapter addresses a hypothesis that problems in the earliest mother–infant interaction are related to the unconscious anxieties, conflicts, and powerful projections of the mother. Second, such problems can lead to potentially dangerous defensive responses in the infant, and third, they can result in serious developmental disturbances.

We are now developing more systematic ways of observing the baby and her interpersonal and self-regulatory skills. This field opens up huge areas for enquiry into human development and dysfunction. Here I shall confine myself to the consideration of the role of "looking" and "seeing" for the infant–mother couple, but the broader ramifications are wide-ranging. I leave aside the role of the father in the task of emergence from early infancy.

The clinical problem which prompted these ideas was that of two very young babies referred to the Department of Child and Family Psychiatry because their parents were terrified by the belief that the babies could look but would not see. They did not believe that they were blind. For both families this presented a profound crisis.

Looking and seeing are amongst the earliest of the skills that the human being utilises. To see: "to perceive by the sense seated in the eye" (Chambers 20th Century Dictionary); "to have or exercise the power of discerning objects with the eyes" (Concise Oxford Dictionary). Contrast with "to look: to direct the sight with attention" (Chambers 20th Century Dictionary); "to use one's sight" (Concise Oxford Dictionary).

"To see" implies the automatic sensory perception of an image whereas "to look" implies the active utilisation of the perceptual ability—the notion of volition is assumed. The young baby is not a helpless being at all, and the use of her eyes is a supremely powerful tool. The issue is whether the infant is captured by stimuli, or like the adult, she captures the stimuli.

To be able to hold and fix the gaze of another confers great power; instance the "staring out" games of childhood, the magical power of the eyes in myths and children's stories and of the eye in folk medicine. The eyes are an open window into the mind, providing access to its darkest depths of love, sexuality, and hate. The feeding couple are similar to the courting couple in their use of vision—only in these two settings is there such intense direct eye contact; for seventy per cent of the feeding time the mother and infant also drink in each other through mutual gaze. There are quite strong cultural and social rules that otherwise govern gaze. It is rare for direct silent gaze to exceed several seconds other than between mother and baby (unless the couple is about to make love or fight). The average mother spends seventy per cent of her play time with her infant in direct gaze, with average episodes of twenty seconds (Stern, 1980).

Andrew

Andrew was conceived as an "accident", his parents having failed on a fertility programme and being reconciled to having only one child. His mother had retrained for a return to work, and was shocked by the discovery of her pregnancy. Despite the intense desire for another child earlier, she thought hard about the pregnancy continuing. She had just got ready to resume her "own life" and she felt she had to abandon it. Amniocentesis was performed at seventeen weeks and was normal.

During the pregnancy, which brought with it nausea and some mild hypertension, she had recurrent vivid and perturbing fantasies of giving birth to a child who was blind or severely retarded. Things did not feel right. Whilst carrying her first child, her daughter, she feared the birth of a child with an arm missing, an event which later happened to her friend. "I felt that I wished it upon her." She had been a volunteer in a centre for autistic children as a young adult and feared that Andrew would be autistic.

Andrew was born at thirty-seven-weeks by Caesarian section, and he looked very well despite mild neonatal jaundice. He cried little and details from this period were difficult for his mother to recall. Feeding, however, was very problematic. His mother had great difficulty establishing him on the breast. She felt that he was a "lazy feeder" and she had to force his face into the depth of her breast for him to be able to attach to the nipple. He could not see her while feeding but eventually breastfeeding was established until he was weaned at fourteen weeks of age on admission to hospital.

At four weeks his parents were convinced he had once smiled but then ceased both smiling and direct eye contact and his mother continued to be concerned about him. He persistently turned his head and eyes to his right since the age of three weeks and had demonstrated minimal responses to sound. Audiology assessment concluded that he had ability to hear but that there was little responsiveness to sound. Otherwise his development appeared normal. He had good neck and head control, and when prone was able to move his head around.

His parents believed that he deliberately avoided looking at them and his mother became increasingly persecuted. They would sneak into the room, hoping to catch him looking meaningfully but felt he was too quick for them. "He hates me!" his mother confided. He would not easily be held and would arch his back. She felt he was in a retreat "in his own world and only pops his head out occasionally, like a turtle". Life became intolerable at home and they brought him to the Emergency Department insisting that he be admitted. They would not take him home until they knew the cause! Both parents became very tearful as they envisioned him a "vegetable", psychotic and retarded at thirty years old, lying immobile in a large bed, institutionalised. His mother feared she would "crack up"; she was sleepless, agitated, unable to go home from hospital. She talked about her fears that as with her friend's child she may have "wished" this upon Andrew, that it could be her fault. Her husband impressed as a man with fewer talents than his wife had; he had been in special school for slow children overseas. His parents simply reassured the anxious couple, saying that Andrew's father was the same as a baby and he "grew out of it". Mrs. A., despite her distress, treated her husband with benevolent indulgence. Her life was one of many compromises, second best to her sister in all except the ability to bear children. She was however, characteristically philosophical about the problems prior to the catastrophe of Andrew. Perhaps this was her usual defence.

Examination of Andrew in hospital confirmed his parents' observations. He did not hold eye contact nor fix or follow objects before him. The ophalmologist believed he could see since he clearly rapidly averted his gaze when confronted by him. When surrounded by several people, Andrew appeared to look to a space between them, usually to his right. A multitude of tests proved negative and the diagnosis of severe atypical developmental delay was made.

Six days after admission, however, he was clearly smiling in response to people, including his mother, although still difficult to engage visually. He played with his own hand on one occasion. He sucked his finger and looked at me, then at his hand and smiled. His mother, who was present, expressed great relief. The pattern of increasing eye contact continued over the following week and after an eleven day admission the parents were able to then take him home, puzzled and confused. Had they made it all up? We have seen Andrew regularly over the subsequent months and his development moved apace. In stark contrast, he engaged visually with tenacity. At twelve months he stood and vocalised and his parents saw him as very cuddly.

Jane

Jane presented to the hospital at seven weeks when her distraught mother complained that Jane avoided eye contact, did not smile and had problems feeding. She was convinced her infant was autistic. Jane was the only child to her father, an administrator, and her mother, a health professional, both American emigrants. They were in Australia with no other family and had been enjoying a hedonistic lifestyle. Too many cocktails one night led to the lapse in contraception and Jane's conception. Mrs. B. had always felt that she never wanted children; her husband was very keen for a family of several children. They had never discussed Mrs. B's reluctance to be a mother until after Jane's hospital admissions. She had never really liked babies, they only cried. To the paediatrician she confided that she always feared having an autistic child. The pregnancy went very smoothly and she was able to work until three weeks before delivery. People did not notice her being pregnant until after twenty-eight weeks and there was no change in their lifestyle. Although Jane was active in utero from twenty weeks, she intruded little into her mother's conscious thoughts.

The birth went equally well; a small episiotomy was the only complication to a spontaneous vaginal delivery at forty-one weeks after a brief labour. The plan had been to breastfeed but there was no help or advice. Being a health professional, Jane's mother got the "best treatment" and was left alone in a single room. Her breasts became very engorged and the pain was intense. Her nipples cracked and Jane only exacerbated her mother's pain, unable to take the milk when let down. Breastfeeding was aborted with large doses of pethidine on the third day but Jane proceeded to use the bottle. She was difficult to settle, needing constantly to be picked up when awake yet unable to mould into or cuddle her parents. She would only be held at arm's length or with her head above her parent's left shoulder. Back arching was a distressing response to attempts by the parents to cuddle her.

On the second day, her mother was convinced that Jane was reluctant to engage or even look at her face. She had previously worked with severely autistic children and feared Jane was autistic. This fear grew as no eye contact developed. Before discharge from the maternity hospital, Jane's parents went out for dinner together. There was no outward sign of her mother's recent state and she described a vague elation as she thought she could simply walk away from the hospital as if she had never been pregnant and had no daughter. This story was related as Jane was held against her mother's chest and over her shoulder, staring blankly into the corner of my room. She planned to return to full-time work when Jane reached ten weeks and employ a full-time nanny to care for her.

Mother and baby left hospital on the fourth day, returning home as Mr. B. had taken two weeks leave to help. He seemed to have greater facility comforting Jane, but the concern about her not looking at them increased. Her mother became more and more agitated. She found herself crying, sleepless, lying awake at night dwelling upon the fate of her autistic retarded child in the next room, petrified of her waking since she would have to go to her, again to be denied recognition. There was no evidence of a smile prior to Jane's hospitalisation. Episodes of screaming and irritability especially at feed times, seemed to increase although Jane continued to thrive. Her mother could stand it no longer and after one midnight visit to the Emergency Department, she insisted on the child being admitted.

Babies and fertility were important issues in both parents' families. Jane's mother and her sister were both adopted, although Mrs. B said that she never thought about it, not until the end of the pregnancy when she had a brief realisation that she was adopted and wondered about her biological mother. She said she gave it not another thought. Mr. B's parents lost their first son when Mr. B was young and they proceeded to adopt children subsequently. Again, the couple never discussed these issues together or with their families of origin.

It had been difficult to appreciate the real nature of the symptom Jane's parents described since with her five-day hospital admission at seven weeks, there was significant improvement almost overnight. Jane began to fix gaze with her parents and others. On admission, however, the hospital staff, including an ophthalmologist and neurologist, confirmed the lack of fixation of gaze upon faces, although Jane did follow and fix upon some inanimate objects. Other aspects of her development appeared normal.

I had the opportunity at a later date to view a home video taken of Jane at two and a half weeks old. During the hour-long tape, shot in a number of settings over several days, there was not one instance of direct eye contact with her mother and attempts by her mother to engage her were clearly strained and agonising for her. It was a painful experience for me to watch this video. In a long sequence of Jane being bathed, she had her head turned to the right and away from her mother, to the point that her eye was occasionally dipped into the bath water. Although one might not expect sustained meaningful mutual facial gaze at this stage, the limited attempts by her mother to engage her and Jane's apparent drive to avoid even face contact, were extremely marked.

As with Andrew, the hospitalisation saw a turning point in the development of responsiveness to people and for her parents. Since discharge she was seen regularly and at seven months was developing normally. There remained, however, a real but difficult-to-describe distance between Mrs. B and her daughter. She felt that she had to accept the fact that she was not fully available to Jane as a baby and that she would have to catch up with her later when she would start to talk. Delving any further into any ambivalence she may have felt towards Jane and her own past was seen as too threatening.

Kay

I will also briefly mention the problem presented by a mother and baby from the country. The eight-week-old baby had major feeding problems and was being fed twenty times a day with a child's feeding cup containing her mother's expressed breast milk. She did however, have one feed at the breast but only before dawn. The mother and baby had to be in total darkness for her to suckle. The period from conception onwards had been a constant disaster for this previously competent mother. She had four and a half-year-old twin boys and experienced three miscarriages which occurred closely spaced in between the twins and her baby girl. Her husband refused to acknowledge this last pregnancy until she went into the labour ward; he could not cope with another loss.

After the birth, her breasts were painfully engorged, needing large doses of analgesia. So abundant was her milk that she felt the baby could not feed. That the baby would not feed was her experience, rejected by her baby at the outset. The baby would not feed when she could see the mother. She was otherwise progressing well but had attributed to her, great will and determination. The sight of preparations for breastfeeding led the baby to become very agitated, flap her arms, arch her back and cry. The baby would not tolerate the sight of the breast. Her mother saw this as anger and rejection.

Through the course of two sessions, she began to acknowledge her fear of the child and of her terrifying power. With tears running down her face, she volunteered a denial of feeling that she might have had thoughts to harm her baby, the baby who had ruthlessly controlled her life for so long, the baby carrying the legacy of those whom she had miscarried.

One of the problems here lay in the infant's inability to look at the mother while feeding. We can but speculate about the way the mother looked at her new baby refusing to feed, but the mother felt that her child knew too much and this she knew through the baby's behaviour, especially her refusal to feed from her and to look at her.

Discussion

The two main areas that I will focus on are the development and meaning of gaze behaviour in infancy and the role that the parents' projections and ambivalence play in the infant's development, emotional, social, and neurobiological.

Gaze behaviour

The marriage of developmental psychology and psychoanalytic thinking has led to a revolution in the understanding of infancy. At around six weeks there is a dramatic change when the infant's gaze becomes more clearly eye-to-eye with the mother. This coincides with the watershed in development—the establishment of the social smile. However, even at three days of age, the infant can imitate complex components of facial expressions of sadness, joy, and surprise.

Much of the earlier experimental material is based on the techniques that attempt to avoid the concept of "emotionality" in the infant and consider a cognitive biological process alone. It raises the whole question of the fundamental origins of affect and emotion.

Bradley (1989), writing about the role of "negativity" in normal infant development, stressed the dangers of idealising the infant as an experimental subject. The relative absence from the developmental psychology of the study of negative, painful aspects of the infant is a defence which obscures the understanding of the emotional life of the infant. He maintained that negativity plays a necessary and productive role in development from infancy on through adulthood and that its presence can be used to demonstrate the infant's innate capacity for intersubjectivity (Trevarthen et al., 1981).

Infants can be shown to exhibit the rudiments of individual consciousness and intentionality, that is, subjectivity and they can adapt or fit this subjective control to the subjectivity of others, that is, intersubjectivity. This intersubjectivity is demonstrable by observing the infant's visual functions—focusing gaze, direction handling, and exploring objects, facial expressions etc. Intersubjectivity can be further defined as a complex form of mutual understanding present from at least two months of age with innovation of meaning by the infant as well as by the mother.

Bradley concluded that early negativity results from the frustration of the infant's will. His experience with filming normal mother–infant couples in set play demonstrated clearly that negativity is a naturally occurring phenomenon, largely evident in the babies' active and passive gaze aversion behaviour. Other examples of such behaviour were postural hunching, factional glances, active resistance to mothers, protesting vocalisations, facial expressions, biting and differential response to others present. These behaviours were not simple reflexive ones and were specific to particular circumstances or related to the quality of stimulation. "Negative" behaviours then would in a good-enough set-up provoke active attempts by mother to understand her child and facilitate the fulfillment of his purposes. What meaning can be given to gaze avoidance as described in the babies referred to earlier?

Massie (1984) studying the early home videos and movies of children later diagnosed as autistic described the avoidance of gaze as one of a series of defensive behaviours. He noted such gaze aversion in these videos of babies as young as only one-week-old.

Gaze aversion itself involves several stages:

i. the object of vision is moved out of the foveal to the peripheral field
ii. the object is moved out of the visual field
iii. the eyes are turned
iv. the head is turned
v. there is also the enigma of the blank gaze and its associated facial features—the process of "looking through someone".

All these behaviours imply some act of agency by the infant, and have the potential, then, to be perceived by the parent as attacking or persecutory. Mutual gaze is a two-way process.

Stern (1985) put forward a model to bridge the gap between the observed behaviour of the infant and his presumed mental life. Stern believed that the infant begins to experience a sense of an "emergent self" from birth, and that the "core", "subjective" and "verbal selves" are built upon this foundation. The infant can experience the process of his own "emerging organisation" from within. Stern proposed that within the child's mind are formed series of modules "Representations of Interactions that have been Generalized (RIGs)". An example of this might be the ten-month-old infant's ability to condense perceptually a series of faces into one face which is fully representative of the features of all those seen, yet that particular face had never been shown.

RIGs are one of many processes by which the sense of self develops. The four main phases are:

1. The "emergent self". The baby actively forms a sense of an emergent self, a sense of his own internal organisation imitating and creating. This is especially noticeable in the state of alert inactivity. The day-old baby has sufficient organisation to be able to distinguish and discriminate the smell of milk of his own mother from that of others.
2. The "core self" (two to three months onwards). There exists a sense of self plus other, and he develops self-agency, self-coherence, self-effectivity, and a sense of self-history.
3. The "subjective self" (seven to nine months onwards). During the commencement of this phase the baby discovers that he and others have separate minds: the I-you experience. The domain of inter-subjective relatedness becomes more evident along with the process of affect attunement.
4. The "verbal self" (twelve to fifteen months onwards). This ushers in the consolidation of symbolic play and formal language.

Each of these "domains" of development is ongoing and built upon each other—they are not simply stations along a linear pathway. They are also very much interactive.

The mind of the infant then resides somewhere between her self and the mind of the mother—in some space between and within both. Winnicott (1964, p. 88) made his famous assertion: "There is no such thing as a baby ... the unit is the environment-individual setting. I see the 'environment' as including the *mental life* of the parents, especially the mother acting also as the focusing lens for the wider society." Winnicott in describing the "mirror-role" of the mother, wrote that the baby looking at the mother's face sees in the mother what the mother sees in her baby (1971). He stated that "if the baby looks and does not see himself, there are consequences; his creative capacity begins to atrophy and he may look elsewhere in his environment for input" (Winnicott, 1971, p. 112).

The blind infant generally succeeds by the use of other sensory modalities. We are reminded, that gaze behaviour has a cultural determination, for example, cultures where the baby is always carried on the mother's back and unable to see her face, and of Japanese children, for whom it is disrespectful to look directly into the eyes of their parents.

Stern (1985) described the infinite minor subtle differences which are reflected back to the infant and allow the infant to distinguish self from other by a long continuous process. Winnicott put it elegantly by saying that "If the mother's face is unresponsive, then a mirror is something to be looked at—not to be looked into" (Winnicott, 1971, p. 112). There is then no shift from perception to apperception.

What happens if the mother's unconscious projections interfere with this process, if gaze becomes a persecution, if the mother cannot hold her own hate and confusion back from the infant and the reflective process? In these clinical examples, the hypothesis is that somehow the ambivalence, the denial of the existence of Jane and Andrew, left them each without a "mind". Jane's mother was able to experience the total absence of her daughter, just days after her birth. In addition, she felt rejected and not needed by her infant—she would not feed at her breast. She had almost totally repressed the significance of her own adoption; her own mother was useless yet loved (good only for eating cream cakes). She felt she could not really get to know Jane—that was left to a large degree to her husband and the nanny.

Massie (1984) proposed a risk-vulnerability model to account for the development of some of the early childhood psychosis. With sufficient vulnerability and what he terms "traumatic parenting" (an interference with bonding, traumatic stimulation or depression), the child is at risk of developing a psychotic illness or partial expression of one. With our cases, the question is whether the fear of a psychotic, autistic or blind child can represent enough of a state of "traumatic parenting" to account for a cut-off state in the infant via his overuse of defensive mechanisms? The fear of a severely damaged child may be a function of the wish for such a non-demanding child, or the death of an unborn child. Both babies here were perceived by their mothers to be persecutory and attacking—"s/he hates me". This intense intrusive process in such an instance would be experience of accusation from the condemned innocent. Gaze must be therefore avoided, yet sought after for reassurance about the mother's goodness and virtue. The intervention within the hospital seemed to break this cycle.

How can one explain the remarkable changes observed in the two infants who did not look? I believe the symptoms as presented were real and genuine, that the babies did not look. The improvement was, however, rapid and sustained. Something must have happened between the babies and those around them, but how? Cramer and Stern (1988) described how parents might transmit their unconscious mental themes to their child, and how altering the parents' mental representation led to symptom removal in the child. They videotaped a series of brief psychodynamically oriented psychotherapy sessions with a mother and her ten-month-old son who had many symptoms, including sleeplessness, agitation, regurgitation, and perceived aggressiveness. Systematically they identified the mother's "interacted themes". The infant's symptoms are viewed as arising via the enactment by the mother of her own core conflictual memories and expectations with her child. Cramer and Stern attempted to deduce these themes from observed behaviour of mother and boy, such as the mother's fears that her child was aggressive and her fear that he would harm her. The boy's behaviour was to bang his head on his mother's chest, and poke his fingers in her mouth and eyes. She said that he wanted to hurt her. In the therapy, she connected this behaviour to his birth, which traumatised her, and her own life-long fears of bodily damage. Another concern was her belief that he did not want to be held; this was linked to her own fears of physical and sexual intimacy. The observers were able to document changes in the amount of time the child sought physical contact with his mother. As the process of her projecting her fears on to him was worked through with the therapist, simultaneous changes in the mother's behaviour could also be documented.

Successful intervention must be seen in a systemic way—that depending upon the needs of the family and the severity of the problem, the intervention must include at least the mother and baby, but also the father and other family and relevant professionals. I believe that the baby must be included since only in doing so can we acknowledge that the baby does have a mind, which must be the basis of action for the mother's care of her infant. The mother talks as though she believes the baby experiences will, self-agency, a sense of self. This mind, I believe, lies somewhat within each, and in the space between mother and infant. Stern (1985) asserted that the infant discovers an awareness of her own mind and that others have separate minds at around the age of nine months. What happens before this time? He believed that the newborn is already capable of experiencing a sense of emergent self-organisation. This is reflected in the infant's demonstrable experience of the world in a transmodal or amodal manner. We can demonstrate that the baby experiences phenomena in many perceptual modalities at once. For example, one-month-old babies could correctly discriminate visually which of two dummies of different shape they had previously never seen, but explored tactilely within the mouth. The tactile image was also experienced as an internal visual image. They can discriminate the smell of their mother's own milk at three days of age.

The infant's body and somatic sensations and perceptions make the reference point for this process of experience of organisation. The mother and other caretakers function to modify these bodily experiences initially and through the process of attunement facilitate the infant developing her own sense of a core self and a subjective and verbal self.

There are parallels, then, to Winnicott's ideas developed before the explosion of experimental data about early infancy, of his notion of "psyche-soma" as an indivisible unity but able to be viewed from the two different perspectives. We are left to speculate about the role played by the mother's unconscious in the development of the infant's mind—his psyche-soma—and whether without intervention these babies may have followed the path of defensive behaviour becoming established as more organised primitive defences and later serious symptoms.

Winnicott (1971, p. 114) puts the dilemma more optimistically:

> "When I look I am seen, so I exist,
> I can now afford to look and see."

References

Bradley, B. S. (1989). *Visions of infancy*. Cambridge, England: Polity Press.

Cramer, B. & Stern, D. N. (1988). Evaluation of changes in mother–infant brief psychotherapy: A single case study. *Infant Mental Health Journal, 9*: 20–45.

Massie, H. N. & Rosenthal, J. (1984). *Childhood Psychosis in the First Four Years of Life*. New York: McGraw Hill.

Stern, D. N. (1985). *The Interpersonal World of the Infant: A Viewpoint from Psychoanalysis and Developmental Philosophy*. New York: Basic Books.

Trevarthen, C. B., Hubley, P., & Murray, L. (1981). Psychology of infants. In: *Scientific Foundations of Paediatrics*. London: Heinemann.

Winnicott, D. W. (1964). *The child, the family and the outside world*. London: Penguin Books.

Winnicott, D. W. (1967). Mirror-role of mother and family and child development. In *Playing and Reality*. London: Tavistock, 1971.
Winnicott, D. W. (1971). *Playing and Reality*. London: Tavistock.
Winnicott, D. W. (1975). *Collected Papers: Through Paediatrics to Psychoanalysis*. London: Hogarth.

The spare room: a father confronts his fatherhood

Joanna Murray Smith

Stephen. Forty. Well dressed. Confident. Very intelligent.

Let me just say this as a preface. There are a lot of things I like about my life, and the thing that gives me the most satisfaction, in an incidental way, is the spare room. A good man deserves a spare room. A mark of success is having a place where useless and obsolescent objects can be stored. The kinds of things you only think about when you're staring at them, you never miss. They are the transitory relics of a human being's inability to focus or commit. And that's fine. I'm man enough to know it. The spare room eliminates guilt and depression caused by awareness of money wasting and intellectual dilettantism. You chuck everything in the spare room and you close the door. It doesn't seem like much, but believe me, it is. It's everything.

[BEAT]

My wife is Fran. She has big eyes and long legs and she drives with one foot on the accelerator and the other foot on the brake. At the same time. She's proud of this. Until recent events overtook it, this one act of marital treason was the thing that brought me closest to the edge of insanity. Apart from this, the big difference between us is that she thinks things only exist if they're spoken. Whereas I'm suspicious of things that are spoken and trust the existence of something much more if it's silent. She bangs on about everything. We're watching the news and she starts on about the starving masses and that's fine. But I care about the starving masses without trivialising them with words that can never be adequate to the horror. Somehow, she thinks I am only my spoken self. I can't persuade her, or maybe I don't want to, that the better part of me doesn't have a voice.

And that's how it was from the start. I'm not kidding, she'd wake me up at three a.m screaming: BERTIE or STEPHANIE or AURORA or SEBASTIAN. At one point she was considering Mandela. Mandela McPherson. Almost certainly the only one at kinder. At that point I think I did ask why stop there? Why not … Butrous Butrous McPherson … Some nights she'd take my hand and lay it on her belly and say: Just think, we made it, it's in there, real. Isn't nature incredible, isn't a woman's body a brilliant mysterious thing, doesn't love deepen with the act of creation, you know the stuff. All well and good. All true. Just … what? Overstated. I had the distinct impression that there was only one appropriate response to fatherhood, and that was Misty Eyed. What she wanted was a misty eyed handy man. The sort of fellow who would cry tears of joy at the spiritual dimension of procreation whilst niftily assembling an Ikea change table, cot, and nursery wall unit.

Okay, look, I've got tertiary qualifications. I've read every Thomas Hardy and all the Russians, I can even make pasta, I'm not an idiot. But I'm not a handyman. I have a visual/spatial problem which rules out all diagrams and if they'd only call it something, name it, Spatially Challenged Affliction or whatever, people would start feeling tender towards me instead of holding me in contempt.

Well, well, excuse me, but no. I'm thinking, predominantly, that I'm standing on the dock and my life is on the ocean liner and we're connected by one, blue crepe streamer and it's stretching, stretching and then … the realisation that I'm never, ever, ever going to leave the dock. There is no leaving. There is no future point of embarkation on HMAS The Good Life. I've jettisoned my ticket for one very brief moment of ordinary hanky panky and there … Gosh … there on the upper deck is every single man I've ever known and disliked. Yes … Bradley Kershaw from the rowing team and Two Boots Maltravers from first year law … whose head was so far up the Dean's arse, you could only see the soles of his boots ... and every surly waiter I've ever endured, the various bureaucratic arseholes, customs officials, aggressive roof plumbers, the guy at the Thai takeaway who always leaves one dish out of the order necessitating a return to the shop, my cousin Ted the walking Cornflake and Harry who made a pass at Fran in our living room while I was in the study writing him a fucking reference ... all of them ... off they go ... ready for the banquet of life, the strange and interesting sexual positions, the whimsical trips to the Seychelles or Tibet, the self-indulgent spending on, you know, phones that transform into irrigation systems, whatever ... there they go, so blasé ... so expectant that of course life is just a pleasurable cruise. And here I am on the dock. Holding a Target bag full of nipple shields.

Okay, I'm selfish. I never asked to have a baby. It just came. I used to see Fran's body as this gorgeous soft, firm, luxurious, sweet-smelling ... thing. This gorgeous, inviting, impractical refuge and I'd sink into her and smell her neck and taste her skin and feel hungry for her and the appetite was completely connected to the sense that she was not necessary, not something that worked for you, that had some kind of technological imperative, some orderly managerial role in your life, but something extra and highly impractical. And then ... who would believe it ... that luxurious human day-spa that was Fran's body, that invitation to indulge, turned out to be hiding an extraordinary Meccano set of functioning parts. And there it was. A few tiny pieces of not immediately tantalising machinery in Fran's body came together with perfect synchronicity and a human life started. Kaboom. There it is. And you can bang on as much as you like about pro-choice and God knows I'm all for it, but nobody's telling me human life doesn't start in an instantaneous breeze, a breath of air that eddies and flows and dips over you right about the time ... you feel like a cigarette.

In moments, there's a heart-beat. And forty weeks later, your ship, the ship you've always believed had a very very nice cabin waiting for you, sets sail. And you're on the dock with a streamer blowing kisses to Two Boots Maltravers.

At the hospital ... We'd taken in a full kit of stuff, all the books had aromatherapy oils and photos of sunset in the Himalayas and a couple of camellias from the garden, because apparently women like this stuff when they're experiencing interminable diabolical pain. It's amazing how a few drops of lavender essence can make all the difference. And then ... what?

Fourteen hours later, there she was. Pale blue and wrinkled like one of those weird puppies. I saw her and nothing happened. I mean, nothing is an overstatement. I felt confused. I felt ... as if I had a small anonymous role in a major event. Like the guy who, say, who suggested a convertible for JFK's ride through Dallas ... or the NASA scientist who designed moon-boots.

It couldn't have happened without me, but who was to know. Really. There was Fran and My God, she was beautiful. She always looked good exerted. Hiking at Kosciusko, when I proposed. Rushing down the city street towards me waiting outside the cinema, flushed, hair loose. I like her raw. And here she was, smooth, hot skin, unbelievably fantastic breasts and a smile that said: Hello, I've just been to Pluto and it was a blast and now I'm home and I've brought something back with me and she's ours, and she's moving in to the spare room, so you'll have to move the golf clubs and she's never, ever, ever, moving out.

And then ... how was it? We started visiting and being visited. You know, showing her off. And friends said those things, the right things and aren't you thrilled? Aren't you thrilled? Isn't she incredible? Isn't it the most incredible? And I'm thinking most of the time ... how disappointed everyone would be to know that mostly I'm tired. I'm tired in a way I've never been tired before, so deep in my bones and what I want to do is crawl into bed, alone, and just stay there, nurse myself, be left there, with nothing calling for me, no Fran, no baby and then I'd think: I'm the father! I'm the strong one! She's breastfeeding, left at home with the baby all day, in shock, never sees the real world, depressed about her body, cracked nipples and I'm the one who's complaining. Me. Who still gets to go out for a café latte at eleven and talk to adults about political events or popular culture while she's at home nursing a human hand grenade in a bomb site? What a fucking selfish prick. No wonder women went berserk in the seventies with men like me walking around. No wonder they said all men were rapists! I'm a disgusting insensitive spoilt middle-class Yuppie male who is completely out of touch with what is important and real and true. I'm the reason Andrea Dworkin exists.

And I wanted to fall, to tumble, to tip headlong into love. Believe me, I wanted to. But I couldn't trip. I didn't fall. I felt ... like a witness to somebody else's story. Like I was in a movie. And Fran and the baby were up there, in some beautifully rendered story of love and pain and transition, and I was in my seat, eating popcorn, simultaneously wanting to be in the story and relieved that I wasn't.

And then ... when was it? Maybe around four months ... I couldn't sleep. There was an electrical storm and the lightening kept flashing into our bedroom and the rain was pouring down and I got up. It was that spring when there was wild flooding and some months before, there was a story in the newspaper about new parents who had woken up and went to check the baby and floodwaters were lapping the edge of the cot. A half hour longer and the baby would have drowned. This was in my head and I went to check the kid.

There were no flood waters. But she was awake. I looked into the cot and there she was, her huge eyes looking up at me. She didn't cry. She seemed perfectly happy just lying there, enjoying the lightning flashes. And our eyes locked. I had thought, foolishly, during those forty weeks, that the baby was ... somehow just another bit of me. That suddenly, there was just this extra accessory made available, an extension of an already familiar apparatus that was myself. But when I looked at her, lying there half in shadow, this bundle of life, I had this sudden sense of ... what? Her intactness and differentness. That, really, regardless of the process of getting here ... she was weirdly unto herself and quite possibly would not love liquorice and rugby. She had her own little momentum, an energy that was ... distinct. Something ... shifted. I can't say that I fell, nothing so perfect as that. But I had a sudden sense of ... the impossibility of keeping her ... safe. And the moment the idea of it hit me, I realised how huge it was and how much of me had been filled up with the thought ... That life stretched ahead, not so much a calendar of lost opportunities for me, but of hazards and obstacles to her wellbeing. Forks in toasters, Eloise Worledge intruders, cars in driveways, peanut allergies, sadistic teachers, pederastic priests, unexplained lumps, unsafe balconies, plane crashes, suicide bombers ... . I mean the Twin Towers were full of somebodies babies ... babies grown into stockbrokers or janitors ... and what could I do?

What could a thirty-eight-year-old graphic designer from Templestowe do to stand in the way of her vulnerability? This little one looking up at me, as if to say: Well, well, you're the caretaker, caretake.

And I thought well, it's just not possible. It's just not feasible. A year or two, perhaps, if I'm vigilant, I'll keep her safe. I'll watch the driveways, never leave her in a locked car, feed her organic everything and even try, try to take an interest in the world at large, the rainforests and the ozone layer and women's health issues ... try to make it better for her. But to be honest ... a few years would be it. And even then, even then, a glance in the wrong direction, a sudden distraction, a quirk of fate, engine trouble in the plane, a suicidal train driver, a gas leak ... meteors ... the chances of her actually making it were ... slim. Slim.

Baby. My baby.

Okay, Fran and I had shared most things. I had told her about my one homosexual experience as a nineteen-year-old. She had told me about the anorexia. I confessed my fetish about women applying lipstick. Once we talked about hiring a ... a woman ... so that she could watch me making love to someone else which was a fantasy of hers. I mean, there really wasn't much we couldn't say. But now ... now ... the baby had walled us in ... Not together, but into two separate spaces. There wasn't a way to share it. And now, it seemed as if I was inside my own, ghastly bubble. There was nothing I could say to her ... that would not ruin us. She was keeping her end up.

She was battling ... for all I knew, other demons, not letting on, somehow getting through the vast, impenetrable strangeness. And if I said these things (beginning to break :) ... that the ... mmm ... the ... love was ... not absent but ... (breaking :) strangely not absent, but ... too intense ... too present ... too huge ... then, then ... my sense was, that all three of us would collapse, would fold into the chasm and never get out. Sometimes the pretence at normalcy is actually what delivers it.

And for three days I wept. I left the house, as if I was going to work, but didn't go and wept in the car. The day went like this: happy, kisses, leaving, in the car, driving down the Peninsula, weeping, eating a chicken sandwich, weeping, walking on the pier, weeping, drinking a milkshake, weeping, driving home, happy, kisses. And this was what I thought. That no matter if we got through this, no matter if I did ... fall ... did collapse into the baby ... did begin to feel like a ... father ... Even if I did and the weeping stopped and I didn't feel strange anymore and my life felt like my own and suddenly the change-tables and baby clothes and play-gyms all began to resemble my life and everything went back to normal and we got takeaway and had dinner with friends and saw movies and changed jobs and planted gardenias, even if all that happened, it would still never be like it was.

It will never be Fran and me.

It will never be simple.

Love arrived in a new form and it was terrible in its size and it would never, ever go.

And you could leave your wife, you could change girl-friends, you could fly away from complicated relationships, but you couldn't do anything about this kind of love, because nothing ... neutralised it.

And the sadness ... the sadness was ... The simple recognition that loving is an act of suffering ... And the knowledge was eating me up from the inside, spreading throughout me, stretching into my corners, agitating at me, knocking at my heart, whining, wheedling, insisting its way into me and I was fighting and I was fighting but I couldn't win. I couldn't turn away and I couldn't win. Just like the spare room, she'd moved into me and she was never moving out.

INDEX